Christ Exalted Sermons

of

JONATHAN EDWARDS

Christ Exalted Sermons
— of —
JONATHAN EDWARDS

HENDRICKSON
PUBLISHERS

Christ Exalted Sermons of Jonathan Edwards

P. O. Box 3473
Peabody, Massachusetts 01961-3473
www.hendrickson.com

ISBN 978-1-61970-968-3

Originally published by Hendrickson Publishers in *Sermons of Jonathan Edwards*.

Printed in the United States of America

Second Printing — June 2017

Contents

Preface

Jonathan Edwards (1703–1758)

The kind of religion that God requires, and will accept, does not consist in weak, dull, and lifeless "wouldings"—those weak inclinations that lack convictions—that raise us but a little above indifference. God, in his word, greatly insists that we be in good earnest, fervent in spirit, and that our hearts be engaged vigorously in our religion: "Be fervent in spirit, serving the Lord" (Romans 12:11).

Jonathan Edwards, *A Treatise Concerning Religious Affections* (1746)

For most twenty-first century Americans, Jonathan Edwards is a murky figure from the distant past. Most will recognize that he was a preacher, a few might remember his connections with colonial New England. And some might even associate him with the Great Awakening, the first spiritual revival in North America.

In fact, Jonathan Edwards is considered one of this country's greatest theologians, a thinker and philosopher who had a prophetic grasp of the impact that Enlightenment thinking and scientific endeavor would have on Christian thought and experience.

His Times

Edwards was born just eighty-three years after the Mayflower found safe haven in Plymouth Harbor on the western side of Cape Cod Bay in Massachusetts. Fewer than half of the 102 passengers on that famous voyage were English Separatists—those who sought to purify the established Church of England, and for their efforts were persecuted and forced out of England. Known as Puritans, it was their faith and values that were codified in the Mayflower Compact, and ultimately became the foundation of New England civil code and the very fabric of society and life in New England.

For a moment, imagine the times. When Jonathan Edwards lived, the colonies in America were not united. In fact, they were separated by religion and politics and countries of origin. Each colony had its own distinct values and laws, its own immigrant populations, its own industry and commerce. New England was just that: New *England*. They were English people intent on creating a godly commonwealth in a new land—the sort of government and society unavailable to them in England.

When Edwards lived, the colonies were tethered to Europe, England mostly, and those ties were tested repeatedly. Sometimes those ties were tightly reined in by English troops and governors intent on maintaining control of the colonies and garnering as much revenue for the Crown as possible. In other periods, the colonies seemed to be left to their own devices, to set up their own government and make their own decisions.

In 1700, the European population in all the American colonies was two hundred and fifty thousand; ninety-one thousand of whom lived in New England. By 1775, the population of the colonies had increased to two and a half million. During Edwards' lifetime, the colonies experienced considerable growth with all its attendant pressures and difficulties, particularly in New England, where everything—its values, its laws, its very society—was defined and designed in the light of Puritan Christianity.

There it is again—that word *Puritan*. It is a distorted word today, having come to refer largely to sexual mores that should more honestly be credited to Victorians. Puritan values were about strong families, ethical and moral behavior, and a strong work ethic—and their laws codified the behaviors that were expected of a godly people. While the law can, at least for a time, influence behavior, it cannot guarantee that the hearts of the citizens are righteous. It was no different in New England.

The Massachusetts colony assumed that all settlers were or should be Christian. In fact, it insisted, prohibiting immigrants who were Roman

Catholic or otherwise outside the fold. At the beginning in particular, a good portion of the early settlers came to escape religious persecution. Their faith was vital and personal. After all, nominal faith is unimaginable in a persecuted church. But within the first one hundred years of the colony—by the time Edwards was ready to begin his ministry—the Puritans were no longer the persecuted church; instead they had become the established church, with all its attendant benefits, including power and the tax revenues collected to support the church. And in an established church, nominal faith becomes the norm.

Edwards faced a generation plump and happy with their flourishing businesses and relatively peaceful lives. It was a generation filled with spiritual apathy, materialism, and worldliness, whose spiritual life was far from the vibrant faith of the settlers who had sailed from England just two generations before. Confronting this spiritual apathy would become Edwards' life work.

His Early Life

Jonathan Edwards was born in East Windsor, Connecticut, the fifth of eleven children and the only son—the son and grandson of Congregational pastors. He was a great student, fluent in Hebrew, Greek and Latin by the age of thirteen. He was also gifted in natural science and scientific methodology, and in philosophy. He entered the Collegiate School of Connecticut (later Yale) in 1716 to continue his formal education, and graduated at the head of his class in 1720, then immediately began his divinity studies. He served for a short time as pastor of a Presbyterian church in New York City, then returned to Yale in 1724 to become a senior tutor.

In 1726, Edwards accepted a call from the Congregational church in Northampton, Massachusetts, to serve as assistant pastor to his grandfather, Solomon Stoddard. Stoddard was a highly regarded cleric, a man beloved by his congregants and respected by the Native Americans. Edwards would serve in this church for twenty-three years, long after the death of his grandfather in 1729.

His Family Life

In 1727, Jonathan Edwards married Sarah Pierrepont, a young woman he had met while he was a divinity student at Yale. Their marriage was remarkable by the standards of any age. Jonathan adored his wife Sarah, whom he called "my dear companion." Together, they created a loving home and thriving family, a safe haven where Edwards was able to study and work. Sarah complemented Jonathan; she was practical and socially adept, while he was distracted and intellectual. Theirs was a marriage filled with companionship, lively conversation, and joy. Edwards and Sarah were attentive and available to one another; they nourished one another, enjoyed one another, and valued one another.

Like everything he did, Edwards was intentional about his family life. Jonathan and Sarah had eleven children, who all lived to adulthood. Edwards made his family a priority, routinely spending the hour before dinner each night with the children. When he traveled out of town, Edwards would take one child with him. Often in the afternoon, Edwards and Sarah would set out on horseback where chores and responsibilities would not interrupt their conversation. They each recognized that their family and their relationship were worthy of the same attention given to study or work.

His Ministry

Jonathan Edwards is inseparably linked with the spiritual revival called Great Awakening, for it was under his preaching in Northampton, Massachusetts, that the Awakening came in 1734. Edwards had followed his grandfather Solomon Stoddard as pastor of the Congregational church in Northampton. Stoddard himself was a great revivalist, preaching five successive revivals, but by the time Jonathan took the pulpit in 1729, he discovered the people "very insensible of the things of religion"—their faith was dry and stale and impotent.

There is an irony of sorts in this story. One of the reasons for Stoddard's great popularity is he relaxed church membership requirements: rather than proof of conversion, he opened the sacraments to everyone except those living openly scandalous lives. This "open admission" effectively removed the necessity for an individual personal spiritual experience with Jesus Christ. This policy, although it could be argued as necessary for a society that defined itself only in Christian terms, ultimately served to lead people away from faith, not towards it.

Edwards, on the other hand, had an intimate understanding, both from personal experience and from his studies, that God was knowable, and that it was only in a personal relationship that true "religion" would be found. He began preaching, and while it took several years, by 1733 he began to see change. In 1734, he preached a series on justification by faith, and by the end of that year, the spark had been lit in Northampton.

Revival had been occurring already in New Jersey, through the work of Theodore Frelinghuysen and Gilbert Tennent, encouraging people out of their spiritual lethargy. The message of revival was this: "Outward morality is not enough for salvation. An inward change is necessary." This message is very familiar to the American Protestant ear today, but it was a fresh word to people who had depended on their morality, their outwards actions, their conformation to "Christian" behavior, to secure their place in God's Kingdom.

Revival grew in Northampton, rippling throughout the area and even into neighboring Connecticut. Edwards continued his preaching and God continued blessing. In 1740, the Awakening exploded through the work of Anglican George Whitefield, who arrived in Boston for his second visit to the colonies, this time a six-week evangelistic tour of New England. Edwards was at the center still, but Whitefield became the instrument of expansion, bringing about the most widespread revival that the colonies had ever experienced.

By 1750, the Awakening had receded from public prominence, but it was in this year that Edwards' position with the Northampton church was severed after twenty-three years. The reason? He wanted to change the policy of "open admission" to the sacraments, begun by his grandfather. Edwards' insistence that "only persons who had made a profession of faith could be admitted to the Lord's Supper" enraged his parishioners, and he was asked to leave.

After a few lean months of unemployment, Edwards found a remarkable new work, that of pastor to settlers and missionary to Indians in Stockbridge, a work begun by David Brainerd in the western frontier of Massachusetts. In 1757, he was chosen president of the College of New Jersey (Princeton), and subsequently relocated in order to begin his work, leaving Sarah behind to finish the packing in Stockbridge. A few months after arriving in his new post, a smallpox epidemic broke out, and Edwards chose to receive the new (and risky) inoculation against the disease. Shortly after, he died from complications from that vaccination, on March 22, 1758. His final words in a message to his beloved Sarah were:

> *Give my kindest love to my dear wife, and tell her that the uncommon union which has so long subsisted between us has been of such a nature as I trust is spiritual and therefore will continue forever.*

His Legacy

Though largely associated with the Great Awakening, Edwards leaves a legacy far outside the reach of this remarkable work of God's grace in America. It was Jonathan Edwards who wrestled with the new issues of scientific discovery, the Enlightenment, and the Age of Reason in light of Christian teaching and experience. It was Edwards who faced the emerging climate of humanistic rationalism over the teaching of a personal and loving God. It was Edwards who developed the uniquely American themes of a redeemer nation and a covenant people, a theme that echoes still today in the American mind. It was Edwards who tackled the problem of spiritual deadness by recognizing the necessity of a personal religious experience and by embracing the supernatural work of the Holy Spirit to awaken and illuminate the heart.

Edwards left a remarkable body of work. He recorded his observations of the Great Awakening in several works, including *A Faithful Narrative of the Surprising Work of God* (1736), in *Distinguishing Marks of a Work of the Spirit of God* (1741) and in *Some Thoughts Concerning the Present Revival of Religion in New England* (1742).

In 1746, he wrote his most famous book, *A Treatise Concerning Religious Affections*. In it he examines the importance of religious "affections" or those "passions that move the will to act," arguing persuasively that true religion resides in the heart, the home of affections, emotions, and inclinations. While in Stockbridge, Edwards completed *Freedom of the Will, and Nature of True Virtue*, and began his massive *History of the Work of Redemption*, which he never completed.

And, of course, Edwards left his sermons. "Sinners in the Hands of an Angry God" (included in *Revival Sermons of Jonathan Edwards*) is very likely his best remembered sermon, often used as an example of the Puritan obsession with eternal damnation and a wrathful God. True, it is a call to repentance, one made to an audience who harbored none of this century's distaste and doubts concerning the reality of God's final judgment. However, in fact, this sermon is atypical of Edwards' preaching. He spoke more often of God's love and the joys of the Christian life than of the fires of Hell.

Edwards' preaching reflected two of his core beliefs: first, God is the central focus of all religious experience—not humankind or reason or morality. As one writer observes, "Edwards' universe, like his theology, is relentlessly God-centered." And second: knowing God is not merely a rational knowledge—mental assent to particular beliefs—but also a sensible knowledge—experienced, sensed. As the taste of sweetness is distinct from the understanding of sweetness, so a Christian not only believes God is glorious, a Christian also senses the glory of God in his heart.

This collection is a fine sampling of Edwards' sermons during his time in Northampton and Stockbridge. Some are revival sermons, calling for repentance and amendment of life; some are pastoral, some instructional, and others written for specific occasions. But each one is a brilliant and personal invitation to know God both through our intellect and through our affections. These are sermons that challenge our minds, but also, and perhaps more importantly, compel us to open our hearts to the sweet love and joy available to us in our life in Christ.

> *I am bold in saying this, but I believe that no one is ever changed, either by doctrine, by hearing the Word, or by the preaching or teaching of another, unless the affections are moved by these things. No one ever seeks salvation, no one ever cries for wisdom, no one ever wrestles with God, no one ever kneels in prayer or flees from sin, with a heart that remains unaffected. In a word, there is never any great achievement by the things of religion without a heart deeply affected by those things.*
>
> —Jonathan Edwards, *A Treatise Concerning Religious Affections* (1746)

Safety, Fullness, and Sweet Refreshment in Christ

Originally published between summer 1728 and winter 1729. Re-preached in 1752.

"And a man shall be as a hiding-place from the wind,
and a covert from the tempest; as rivers of water in a dry place,
as the shadow of a great rock in a weary land."—Isaiah 32:2

In these words we may observe:

- *The person who is here prophesied of and commended, [that is,] the Lord Jesus Christ, the King spoken of in the preceding verse, who shall reign in righteousness.* This King is abundantly prophesied of in the Old Testament, and especially in this prophecy of Isaiah. Glorious predictions were from time to time uttered by the prophets concerning that great King who was to come: there is no subject which is spoken of in so magnificent and exalted a style by the prophets of the Old Testament, as the Messiah. They saw his day and rejoiced, and searched diligently, together with the angels, into those things. 1 Peter 1:11, 12:

  > Searching what, or what manner of time, the Spirit of Christ which was in them did signify, when it testified beforehand the sufferings of Christ,

> and the glory that should follow. Unto whom it was revealed, that not unto themselves, but unto us, they did minister the things, which are now reported unto you by them that have preached the gospel unto you with the Holy Ghost sent down from heaven; which things the angels desire to look into.

We are told here that "a man shall be a hiding-place from the wind," etc. There is an emphasis in the words, that "a man" should be this. If these things had been said of God, it would not be strange under the Old Testament; for God is frequently called a hiding-place for his people, a refuge in time of trouble, a strong rock, and a high tower. But what is so remarkable is, that they are said of "a man." But this is a prophecy of the Son of God incarnate.

- *The things here foretold of him, and the commendations given him.* "He shall be a hiding-place from the wind, and a covert from the tempest:" that is, he shall be the safety and defense of his people, to which they shall flee for protection in the time of their danger and trouble. To him they shall flee, as one who is abroad, and sees a terrible storm arising, makes haste to some shelter to secure himself; so that however furious is the tempest, yet he is safe within, and the wind and rain, though they beat never so impetuously upon the roof and walls, are no annoyance unto him.

He shall be as "rivers of water in a dry place." This is an allusion to the deserts of Arabia, which was an exceedingly hot and dry country. One may travel there many days, and see no sign of a river, brook, or spring, nothing but a dry and parched wilderness; so that travelers are ready to be consumed with thirst, as the children of Israel were when they were in this wilderness, when they were faint because there was no water. Now when a man finds Jesus Christ, he is like one that has been traveling in those deserts till he is almost consumed with thirst, and who as last finds a river of cool and clear water. And Christ was typified by the river of water that issued out of the rock for the children of Israel in this desert: he is compared to a river, because there is such a plenty and fullness in him.

He is the "shadow of a great rock in a weary land." Allusion is still made to the desert of Arabia. It is not said, as the shadow of a tree, because in some places of that country, there is nothing but dry sand and rocks for a vast space together, not a tree to be seen; and the sun beats exceedingly hot upon the sands, and all the shade to be found there, where travelers can rest and shelter themselves from the scorching sun, is under some great rock. They who come to Christ find such rest and refreshment as the weary traveler in that hot and desolate country finds under the shadow of a great rock.

We propose to speak to three propositions that are explicatory of the several parts of the text.

I. There is in Christ Jesus an abundant foundation of peace and safety for those who are in fear and danger. "A man shall be a hiding-place from the wind, a covert from the tempest."

II. There is in Christ provision for the satisfaction, and full contentment, of the needy and thirsty soul. He shall be "as rivers of water in a dry place."

III. There are quiet rest and sweet refreshment in Christ Jesus for him who is weary. He shall be "as the shadow of a great rock in a weary land."

I. There is in Christ Jesus abundant foundation of peace and safety for those who are in fear and danger.

The fears and dangers to which men are subject, are of two kinds; temporal and eternal. Men are frequently in distress from fear of temporal evils. We live in an evil world, where we are liable to an abundance of sorrows and calamities. A great part of our lives is spent in sorrowing for present or past evils, and in fearing those which are future. What poor, distressed creatures are we, when God is pleased to send his judgments among us! If he visits a place with mortal and prevailing sickness, what terror seizes our hearts! If any person is taken sick, and trembles for his life, or if our near friends are at the point of death, or in many other dangers, how fearful is our condition! Now there is sufficient foundation for peace and safety to those exercised with such fears, and brought into such dangers. But Christ is a refuge in all trouble; there is a foundation for rational support and peace in him, whatever threatens us. He, whose heart is fixed, trusting in Christ, need not be afraid of any evil tidings. "As the mountains are round about Jerusalem, so Christ is round about them that fear him."

But it is the other kind of fear and danger to which we have a principal respect; the fear and danger of God's wrath. The fears of a terrified conscience, the fearful expectation of the dire fruits of sin, and the resentment of an angry God, these are infinitely the most dreadful. If men are in danger of those things, and are not asleep, they will be more terrified than with the fears of any outward evil. Men are in a most deplorable condition, as they are by nature exposed to God's wrath; and if they are sensible how dismal their case is, will be in dreadful fears and dismal expectations.

God is pleased to make some sensible of their true condition. He lets them see the storm that threatens them, how black the clouds are, and how impregnated with thunder; that it is a burning tempest, that they are in danger of being speedily overtaken by it, that they have nothing to shelter themselves from it, and that they are in danger of being taken away by the fierceness of his anger.

It is a fearful condition when one is smitten with a sense of the dreadfulness of God's wrath, when he has his heart impressed with the conviction that the great God is not reconciled to him, that he holds him guilty of these and those sins, and that he is angry enough with him to condemn him for ever. It is dreadful to lie down and rise up, it is dreadful to eat and drink, and to walk about, in God's anger from day to day. One, in such a case, is ready to be afraid of everything; he is afraid of meeting God's wrath wherever he goes. He has no peace in his mind, but there is a dreadful sound in his ears; his mind is afflicted and tossed with tempest, and not comforted, and courage is ready to fail, and the spirit ready to sink with fear; for how can a poor worm bear the wrath of the great God, and what would not he give for peace of conscience—what would not he give if he could find safety! When such fears exist to a great degree, or are continued a long time, they greatly enfeeble the heart, and bring it to a trembling posture and disposition.

Now for such as these there is abundant foundation for peace and safety in Jesus Christ, and this will appear from the following things:

1. Christ has undertaken to save all such from what they fear, if they come to him. It is his professional business; the work in which he engaged before the foundation of the world. It is what he always had in his thoughts and intentions; he undertook from everlasting to be the refuge of those that are afraid of God's wrath. His wisdom is such, that he would never undertake a work for which he is not sufficient. If there were some in so dreadful a case that he was not able to defend them, or so guilty that it was not fit that he should save them, then he never would have undertaken for them. Those who are in trouble and distressing fear, if they come to Jesus Christ, have this to ease them of their fears, that Christ has promised them that he will protect them; that they come upon his invitation; that Christ has plighted his faith for their security if they will close with him; and that he is engaged by covenant to God the Father that he will save those afflicted and distressed souls that come to him.

Christ, by his own free act, has made himself the surety of such, he has voluntarily put himself in their stead; and if justice has anything against them, he has undertaken to answer for them. By his own act, he has engaged to be responsible for them; so that if they have exposed themselves to God's wrath, and to the stroke of justice, it is not their concern, but his, how to answer or satisfy for what they have done. Let there be never so much wrath that they have deserved, they are as safe as if they never had deserved any; because he has undertaken to stand for them, let it be more or less. If they are in Christ Jesus, the storm does of course [therefore] light on him, and not on them; as when we are under a good shelter, the storm, that would otherwise come upon our heads, lights upon the shelter.

2. *He is chosen and appointed of the Father to this work.* There needs to be no fear nor jealousy, whether the Father will approve of this undertaking of Christ Jesus, whether he will accept of him as a surety, or whether he will be willing that his wrath should be poured upon his own dear Son, instead of us miserable sinners. For there was an agreement with him concerning it before the world was; it was a thing much upon God's heart, that his Son Jesus Christ should undertake this work, and it was the Father that sent him into the world. It is as much the act of God the Father as it is of the Son. Therefore, when Christ was near the time of his death, he tells the Father that he had finished the work which he [God] gave him to do. Christ is often called God's elect, or his chosen, because he was chosen by the Father for his work; and God's anointed, for the words Messiah and Christ signify anointed, because he is by God appointed and fitted for this work.

3. *If we are in Christ Jesus, justice and the law have its course with respect to our sins, without our hurt.* The foundation of the sinner's fear and distress is the justice and the law of God; they are against him, and they are unalterable, they must have their course. Every jot and tittle of the law must be fulfilled, heaven and earth shall be destroyed, rather than justice should not take place; there is no possibility of sin's escaping justice.

But yet if the distressed trembling soul who is afraid of justice, would fly to Christ, he [Christ] would be a safe hiding-place. Justice and the threatening of the law will have their course as fully, while he is safe and untouched, as if he were to be eternally destroyed. Christ bears the stroke of justice, and the curse of the law falls fully upon him; Christ bears all that vengeance that belongs to the sin that has been committed by him, and there is no need of its being borne twice over. His temporal sufferings, by reason of the infinite dignity of his person, are fully equivalent to the eternal sufferings of a mere creature. And then his sufferings answer for him who flees to him as well as if they were his own, for indeed they are his own by virtue of the union between Christ and him. Christ has made himself one with them; he is the head, and they are the members. Therefore, if Christ suffers for the believer, there is no need of his [the believer's] suffering; and what needs he to be afraid? His safety is not only consistent with absolute justice, but it is consistent with the tenor of the law. The law leaves fair room for such a thing as the answering of a surety. If the end of punishment in maintaining the authority of the law and the majesty of the government is fully secured by the sufferings of Christ as his surety, then the law of God, according to the true and fair interpretation of it, has its course as much in the sufferings of Christ, as it would have in his own sufferings. The threatening, "thou shalt surely die," is properly fulfilled in the death of Christ, as it is fairly to be understood. Therefore, if those who are afraid will go to Jesus Christ, they need to fear nothing from the threatening of the law. The threatening of the law has nothing to do with them.

4. *Those who come to Christ, need not be afraid of God's wrath for their sins; for God's honor will not suffer by their escaping punishment and being made happy.* The wounded soul is sensible that he has affronted the majesty of God, and looks upon God as a vindicator of his honor; as a jealous God that will not be mocked, an infinitely great God that will not bear to be affronted, that will not suffer his authority and majesty to be trampled on, that will not bear that his kindness should be abused. A view of God in this light terrifies awakened souls. They think how exceedingly they have sinned, how they have sinned against light, against frequent and long-continued calls and warnings; and how they have slighted mercy, and been guilty of turning the grace of God into lasciviousness, taking encouragement from God's mercy to go on in sin against him; and they fear that God is so affronted at the contempt and slight which they have cast upon him, that he, being careful of his honor, will never forgive them, but will punish them. But if they go to Christ, the honor of God's majesty and authority will not be in the least hurt by their being freed and made happy. For what Christ has done has repaired God's honor to the full. It is a greater honor to God's authority and majesty, that, rather than it should be wronged, so glorious a person would suffer what the law required. It is surely a wonderful display of the honor of God's majesty, to see an infinite and eternal person

dying for its being wronged. And then Christ by his obedience, by that obedience which he undertook for our sakes, has honored God abundantly more than the sins of any of us have dishonored him, how many soever, and how great soever. How great an honor is it to God's law that so great a person is willing to submit to it, and to obey it! God hates our sins, but not more than he delights in Christ's obedience which he performed on account. This is a sweet savor to him, a savor of rest. God is abundantly compensated, he desires no more; Christ's righteousness is of infinite worthiness and merit.

5. *Christ is a person so dear to the Father, that those who are in Christ need not be at all jealous of being accepted upon his account.* If Christ is accepted they must of consequence be accepted, for they are in Christ, as members, as parts, as the same. They are the body of Christ, his flesh and his bones. They that are in Christ Jesus, are one spirit; and therefore, if God loves Christ Jesus, he must of necessity accept of those that are in him, and that are of him. But Christ is a person exceedingly dear to the Father: the Father's love to the Son is really infinite. God necessarily loves the Son; God could as soon cease to be, as cease to love the Son. He is God's elect, in whom his soul delighteth; he is his beloved Son, in whom he is well pleased; he loved him before the foundation of the world, and had infinite delight in him from all eternity.

A terrified conscience, therefore, may have rest here, and abundant satisfaction that he is safe in Christ, and that there is not the least danger but that he shall be accepted, and that God will be at peace with him in Christ.

6. *God has given an open testimony that Christ has done and suffered enough, and that he is satisfied with it, by his raising him from the dead.* Christ, when he was in his passion, was in the hands of justice, he was God's prisoner for believers, and it pleased God to bruise him, and put him to grief, and to bring him into a low state; and when he raised him from the dead, he set him at liberty, whereby he declared that it was enough. If God was not satisfied, why did he set Christ at liberty so soon? He was in the hands of justice, why did not God pour out more wrath upon him, and hold him in the chains of darkness longer? God raised him up and opened the prison doors to him, because he desired no more. And now surely there is free admittance for all sinners into God's favor through this risen Savior, there is enough done, and God is satisfied; as he has declared and sealed to it by the resurrection of Christ, who is alive, and lives for evermore, and is making intercession for poor, distressed souls that come unto him.

7. *Christ has the dispensation of safety and deliverance in his own hands, so that we need not fear but that, if we are united to him, we may be safe.* God has given him all power in heaven and in earth, to give eternal life to whomsoever comes to him. He is made head over all things to the church, and the work of salvation is left with himself, he may save whom he pleases, and defend those that are in him by his own power. What greater ground of confidence could God have given us than that the Mediator, who died for us, and intercedes for us, should have committed to him the dispensation of the very thing which he died to purchase and for which he intercedes?

8. *Christ's love, and compassion, and gracious disposition, are such that we may be sure he is inclined to receive all who come to him.* If he should not do it, he would fail of his own undertaking, and also of his promise to the Father, and to us; and his wisdom and faithfulness will not allow of that. But he is so full of love and kindness that he is disposed to nothing but to receive and defend us, if we come to him. Christ is exceedingly ready to pity us, his arms are open to receive us, he delights to receive distressed souls that come to him, and to protect them; he would gather them as a hen gathereth her chickens under her wings; it is a work that he exceedingly rejoices in, because he delights in acts of love, and pity, and mercy.

I shall take occasion from what now has been said, to invite those who are afraid of God's wrath, to come to Christ Jesus. You are indeed in a dreadful condition. It is dismal to have God's wrath impending over our heads, and not to know how soon it will fall upon us. And you are in some measure sensible that it is a dreadful condition, you are full of fear and trouble, and you know not where to flee for help; your mind is, as it were, tossed with a tempest. But how lamentable is it, that you should spend your life in such a condition, when Christ would shelter you, as a hen shelters her chickens under her wings, if you were but willing; and that you should live such a fearful, distressed life, when there is so much provision made for your safety in Christ Jesus!

How happy would you be if your hearts were but persuaded to close with Jesus Christ! Then you would be out of all danger: whatever storms and tempests were without, you might rest securely within; you might hear the rushing of the wind, and the thunder roar abroad, while you are safe in this hiding-place. O be persuaded to hide yourself in Christ Jesus! What greater assurance of safety can you desire? He has undertaken to defend and save you, if you will come to him: he looks upon it as his work; he engaged in it before the world was, and he has given his faithful promise which he will not break; and if you will but make your flight there, his life shall be for yours; he will answer for you, you shall have nothing to do but rest quietly in him; you may stand still and see what the Lord will do for you. If there be anything to suffer, the suffering is Christ's, you will have nothing to suffer; if there be anything to be done, the doing of it is Christ's, you will have nothing to do but to stand still and behold it.

You will certainly be accepted of the Father if your soul lays hold of Jesus Christ. Christ is chosen and anointed of the Father, and sent forth for this very end, to save those that are in danger and fear; and he is greatly beloved of God, even infinitely, and he will accept of those that are in him. Justice and the law will not be against you, if you are in Christ; that threatening, "in the day that thou eatest, thou shalt die," in the proper sense of it, will not touch you. The majesty and honor of God are not against you. You need not be afraid but that you shall be justified, if you come to him; there is an act of justification already past and declared for all who come to Christ by the resurrection of Christ, and as soon as ever you come, you are by that declared free. If you come to Christ it will be a sure sign that Christ loved you from all eternity, and that he died for you; and you may be sure if he died for you, he will not lose the end of his death, for the dispensation of life is committed unto him.

You need not, therefore, continue in so dangerous a condition; there is help for you. You need not stand out in the storm so long, as there is so good a shelter near you, whose doors are open to receive you. O make haste, therefore, unto that man who is a hiding-place from the wind, and a covert from the tempest!

Let this truth also cause believers more to prize the Lord Jesus Christ. Consider that it is he, and he only, who defends you from wrath, and that he is a safe defense; your defense is a high tower; your city of refuge is impregnable. There is no rock like your rock. There is none like Christ,

> the God of Jeshurun, who rideth upon the heaven in thy help, and in his excellency on the sky; the eternal God is thy refuge, and underneath are everlasting arms.

He in whom you trust is a buckler to all that trust in him. O prize that Savior, who keeps your soul in safety, while thousands of others are carried away by the fury of God's anger, and are tossed with raging and burning tempests in Hell! O, how much better is your case than theirs! and to whom is it owing but to the Lord Jesus Christ? Remember what was once your case, and what it is now, and prize Jesus Christ.

And let those Christians who are in doubts and fears concerning their condition, renewedly fly to Jesus Christ, who is a hiding-place from the wind, and a covert from the tempest. Most Christians are at times afraid whether they shall not miscarry at last. Such doubtings are always through some want of the exercise of faith, and the best remedy for them is a renewed resort of the soul to this hiding-place; the same act which at first gave comfort and peace, will give peace again. They that clearly see the sufficiency of Christ, and the safety of committing themselves to him to save them from what they fear, will rest in it that Christ will defend them; be directed therefore at such times to do as the psalmist. Psalm 56:3, 4:

> What time I am afraid, I will trust in thee. In God I will praise his word; in God I have put my trust: I will not fear what flesh can do unto me.

II. There is provision in Christ for the satisfaction and full contentment of the needy and thirsty soul.

This is the sense of those words in the text, "as rivers of water in a dry place," in a dry and parched wilderness, where there is a great want of water, and where travelers are ready to be destroyed with thirst, such as was that wilderness in which the children of Israel wandered. This comparison is used elsewhere in the Scriptures. Psalm 63:1. "O God, thou art my God; early will I seek thee: my soul thirsteth for thee, my flesh longeth for thee in a dry and thirsty land, where no water is." Psalm 143:6. "I stretch forth my hands unto thee; my soul thirsteth after thee, as a thirsty land." Those who travel in such a land, who wander in such a wilderness, are in extreme need of water; they are ready to perish for the want of it; and thus they have a great thirst and longing for it.

It is said that Christ is a river of water, because there is such a fullness in him, so plentiful a provision for the satisfaction of the needy and longing soul. When one is extremely thirsty, though it is not a small draught of water will satisfy him, yet when he comes to a river, he finds a fullness, there he may drink full draughts. Christ is like a river, in that he has a sufficiency not only for one thirsty soul, but by supplying him the fountain is not lessened; there is not the less afforded to those who come afterwards. A thirsty man does not sensibly lessen a river by quenching his thirst.

Christ is like a river in another respect. A river is continually flowing, there are fresh supplies of water coming from the fountain-head continually, so that a man may live by it, and be supplied with water all his life. So Christ is an ever-flowing fountain; he is continually supplying his people, and the fountain is not spent. They who live upon Christ, may have fresh supplies from him to all eternity; they may have an increase of blessedness that is new, and new still, and which never will come to an end.

In illustrating this second proposition, I shall inquire:

1. *What it is that the soul of every man naturally and necessarily craves?*

First, the soul of every man necessarily craves happiness. This is an universal appetite of human nature, that is alike in the good and the bad; it is as universal as the very essence of the soul, because it necessarily and immediately flows from that essence. It is not only natural to all mankind, but to the angels; it is universal among all reasonable, intelligent beings, in heaven, earth, or Hell, because it flows necessarily from an intelligent nature. There is no rational being, nor can there be any, without a love and desire of happiness. It is impossible that there should be any creature made that should love misery, or not love happiness, since it implies a manifest contradiction; for the very notion of misery is to be in a state that nature abhors, and the notion of happiness, is to be in such a state as is most agreeable to nature.

Therefore, this craving of happiness must be insuperable, and what [is something that] never can be changed; it never can be overcome, or in any way abated. Young and old love happiness alike, and good and bad, wise and unwise; though there is a great variety as to men's ideas of happiness. Some think it is to be found in one thing, and some in another; yet, as to the desire of happiness in general, there is no variety. There are particular appetites that may be restrained, and kept under, and conquered, but this general appetite for happiness never can be.

Secondly, the soul of every man craves a happiness that is equal to the capacity of his nature. The soul of man is like a vessel; the capacity of the soul is as the largeness or contents of the vessel. And therefore, if man has much pleasure and happiness, yet if the vessel is not full, the craving will not cease. Every creature is restless till it enjoys what is equal to the capacity of its nature. Thus we may observe in the brutes; when they have that which is suitable to their nature, and proportional to their capacity, they are contented. Man is of such a nature, that he is capable of an exceedingly great degree of happiness; he is made of a vastly higher nature than the brutes, and therefore he must have vastly higher happiness to satisfy. The pleasures of the outward senses which content the beasts, will not content man. He has other faculties of a higher nature that stand in need of something to fill them; if the sense be satiated, yet if the faculties of the soul are not filled, man will be in a craving restless state.

It is more especially by reason of the faculty of understanding that the soul is capable of so great a happiness, and desires so much. The understanding is an exceedingly extensive faculty; it extends itself beyond the limits of earth, beyond the limits of the creation. As we are capable of understanding immensely more than we do understand, who can tell how far the understanding of men is capable of stretching itself? and as the understanding enlarges, the desire will enlarge with it. It must therefore be an incomprehensible object that must satisfy the soul; it will never be contented with that, and that only, to which it can see an end, it will never be satisfied with that happiness to which it can find a bottom. A man may seem to take contentment for a little while in a finite object, but after he has had a little experience, he finds that he wants something besides. This is very apparent from the experience of this restless craving world. Every one is inquiring, Who will show us any good?

2. Men in their fallen state, are in very great want of this happiness.

They were once in the enjoyment of it, but mankind are sunk to a very low estate; we are naturally poor, destitute creatures. We came naked into the world, and our souls as well as our bodies are in a wretched, miserable condition; we are so far from having food to eat suitable to our nature, that we are greedy after the husks which the swine do eat.

The poverty of man in a natural condition, appears in his discontented, craving spirit; it shows that the soul is very empty, when, like the horseleech, it cries, "Give, give, and saith not, It is enough." We are naturally like the prodigal, for we once were rich, but we departed from our father's house, and have squandered away our wealth, and are become poor, hungry, famishing wretches. Men in a natural condition may find something to gratify their senses, but there is nothing to feed the soul; that more noble and more essential part perishes for lack of food. They may fare sumptuously every day, they may pamper their bodies, but the soul cannot be fed from a sumptuous table; they may drink wine in bowls, yet the spiritual part is not refreshed. The superior faculties want to be supplied as well as the inferior. True poverty and true misery consist in the want of those things of which our spiritual part stands in need.

3. Those sinners who are thoroughly awakened, are sensible of their great want.

Multitudes of men are not sensible of their miserable, needy condition. There are many who are thus poor, and think themselves rich, and increased in goods. Indeed there are no natural men that have true contentment: they are all restless, and crying, "Who will show us any good?" but multitudes are not sensible how exceedingly necessitous is their condition. But the thoroughly awakened soul sees that he is very far from true happiness, that those things which he possesses will never make him happy; that for all his outward possessions he is wretched, and miserable, and poor, and blind, and naked. He becomes sensible of the short continuance and uncertainty of those things, and their insufficiency to satisfy a troubled conscience. He wants something else to give him peace and ease. If you would tell him that he might have a kingdom, it would not quiet him; he desires to have his sins pardoned, and to be at peace with his Judge. He is poor, and he becomes as a beggar; he comes and cries for help. He does not thirst, because he as yet sees where true happiness is to be found, but because he sees that he has it not, and cannot find it. He is without comfort, and does not know where to find it, but he longs for it. O, what would he not give, if he could find some satisfying peace and comfort!

Such are those hungry, thirsty souls that Christ so often invites to come to him. Isaiah 55:1, 2. "Ho, every one that thirsteth, come ye to the waters, and he that hath no money, come ye, buy and eat; yea, come, buy wine and milk without money and without price. Wherefore do ye spend money for that which is not bread, and your labor for that which satisfieth not? hearken diligently unto me, and eat ye that which is good, and let your soul delight itself in fatness." "If any man thirst, let him come unto me and drink; and he that is athirst, let him come and take of the water of life freely."

4. There is in Christ Jesus provision for the full satisfaction and contentment of such as these.

First, the excellency of Christ is such, that the discovery of it is exceedingly contenting and satisfying to the soul. The inquiry of the soul is after that which is most excellent. The carnal soul imagines that earthly things are excellent; one thinks riches most excellent, another has the highest esteem of honor, and to another carnal pleasure appears the most excellent; but the soul cannot find contentment in any of these things, because it soon finds an end to their excellency. Worldly men imagine, that there is true excellency and true happiness in those things which they are pursuing. They think that if they could but obtain them, they should be happy; and when they obtain them, and cannot find happiness, they look for happiness in something else, and are still upon the pursuit.

But Christ Jesus has true excellency, and so great excellency, that when they come to see it they look no further, but the mind rests there. It sees a transcendent glory and an ineffable sweetness in him; it sees that till now it has been pursuing shadows, but that now it has found the substance; that before it had been seeking happiness in the stream, but that now it has found the ocean. The excellency of Christ is an object adequate to the natural cravings of the soul, and is sufficient to fill the capacity. It is an infinite excellency, such an one as the mind desires, in which it can find no bounds; and the more the mind is used to it, the more excellent it appears. Every new discovery makes this beauty appear more ravishing, and the mind sees no end; here is room enough for the mind to go deeper and deeper, and never come to the bottom. The soul is exceedingly ravished when it first looks on this beauty, and it is never weary of it. The mind never has any satiety, but Christ's excellency is always fresh and new, and tends as much to delight, after it has been seen a thousand or ten thousand years, as when it was seen the first moment. The excellency of Christ is an object suited to the superior faculties of man, it is suited to entertain the faculty of reason and understanding, and there is nothing so worthy about which the understanding can be employed as this excellency; no other object is so great, noble, and exalted.

This excellency of Jesus Christ is the suitable food of the rational soul. The soul that comes to Christ, feeds upon this, and lives upon it; it is that bread which came down from heaven, of which he that eats shall not die; it is angels' food, it is that wine and milk that is given without money, and without price. This is that fatness in which the believing soul delights itself; here the longing soul may be satisfied, and the hungry soul may be filled with goodness. The delight and contentment that is to be found here, passeth understanding, and is unspeakable and full of glory. It is impossible for those who have tasted of this fountain, and know the sweetness of it, ever to forsake it. The soul has found the river of water of life, and it desires no other drink; it has found the tree of life, and it desires no other fruit.

Secondly, the manifestation of the love of Christ gives the soul abundant contentment. This love of Christ is exceedingly sweet and satisfying, it is better than life, because it is the love of a person of such dignity and excellency. The sweetness of his love depends very much upon the greatness of his excellency; so much the more lovely the person, so much the more desirable is his love. How sweet must the love of that person be, who is the eternal Son of God, who is of equal dignity with the Father! How great a happiness must it be to be the object of the love of him who is the Creator of the world, and by whom all things consist, and who is exalted at God's right hand, and made head over principalities and powers in heavenly places, who has all things put under his feet, and is King of kings and Lord of lords, and is the brightness of the Father's glory! Surely to be beloved by him, is enough to satisfy the soul of a worm of the dust.

This love of Christ is also exceedingly sweet and satisfying from the greatness of it; it is a dying love; such love as never was before seen, and such as no other can parallel. There have been instances of very great love between one earthly friend and another; there was a surpassing love between David and Jonathan. But there never was any such love as Christ has towards believers. The satisfying nature of this love arises also from the sweet fruits of it. Those precious benefits that Christ bestows upon his people, and those precious promises which he has given them, are the fruit of this love; joy and hope are the constant streams that flow from this fountain, from the love of Christ.

Third, there is provision for the satisfaction and contentment of the thirsty longing soul in Christ, as he is the way to the Father; not only from the fullness of excellency and grace which he has in his own person, but as by him we may come to God, may be reconciled to him, and may be made happy in his favor and love. The poverty and want of the soul in its natural state consist in its being separated from God, for God is the riches and the happiness of the creature. But we naturally are alienated from God; and God is alienated from us, our Maker is not at peace with us. But in Christ there is a way for a free communication between God and us; for us to come to God, and for God to communicate himself to us by his Spirit. John 14:6. "Jesus saith unto him, I am the way, and the truth, and the life: no man cometh unto the Father but by me." Ephesians 2:13, 18, 19. "But now in Christ Jesus, ye who sometimes were far off, are made nigh by the blood of Christ. For through him we both have access by one Spirit unto the Father. Now, therefore, ye are no more strangers and foreigners, but fellow-citizens with the saints, and of the household of God." Christ by being thus the way to the Father, is the way to true happiness and contentment. John 10:9. "I am the door: by me, if any man enter in, he shall be saved, and shall go in and out, and find pasture." Hence I would take occasion to invite needy, thirsty souls to come to Jesus. "In the last day, that great day of the feast, Jesus stood and cried, saying, If any man thirst, let him come unto me and drink." You that have not yet come to Christ, are in a poor, necessitous condition; you are in a parched wilderness, in a dry and thirsty land. And if you are thoroughly awakened, you are sensible that you are in distress and ready to faint for want of something to satisfy your souls. Come to him who is "as rivers of water in a dry place." There are plenty and fullness in him; he is like a river that is always flowing, you may live by it for ever, and never be in want. Come to him who has such excellency as is sufficient to give full contentment to your soul, who is a person of transcendent glory, and ineffable beauty, where you may entertain the view of your soul forever without weariness, and without being cloyed. Accept of the offered love of him who is the only-begotten Son of God, and his elect, in whom his soul delighteth. Through Christ, come to God the Father, from whom you have departed by sin. He is the way, the truth, and the life; he is the door, by which if any man enters he shall be saved.

III. There are quiet rest and sweet refreshment in Christ Jesus, for those that are weary. He is "as the shadow of a great rock in a weary land."

The comparison that is used in the text is very beautiful and very significative. The dry, barren, and scorched wilderness of Arabia is a very lively representation of the misery that men have brought upon themselves by sin. It is destitute of any inhabitants but lions and tigers and fiery serpents; it is barren and parched, and without any river or spring; it is a land of drought, wherein there is seldom any rain, a land exceedingly hot and uncomfortable. The scorching sunbeams that are ready to consume the spirits of travelers, are a fit representation of [the] terror of conscience, and the inward sense of God's displeasure. And there being no other shade in which travelers may rest, but only here and there that of a great rock, it is a fit representation of Jesus Christ, who came to redeem us from our misery. Christ is often compared to a rock, because he is a sure foundation to builders, and because he is a sure bulwark and defense. They who dwell upon the top of a rock, dwell in a most defensible place; we read of those whose habitation is the munitions of rocks. He may also be compared to a rock, as he is everlasting and unchangeable. A great rock remains steadfast, unmoved, and unbroken by winds and storms from age to age; and therefore God chose a rock to be an emblem of Christ in the wilderness, when he caused water to issue forth for the children of Israel; and the shadow of a great rock is a most fit representation of the refreshment given to weary souls by Jesus Christ.

1. *There is quiet rest and full refreshment in Christ for sinners that are weary and heavy laden with sin.* Sin is the most evil and odious thing, as well as the most mischievous and fatal; it is the most mortal poison; it, above all things, hazards life, and endangers the soul, exposes to the loss of all happiness, and to the suffering of all misery, and brings the wrath of God. All men have this dreadful evil hanging about them, and cleaving fast to the soul, and ruling

over it, and keeping it in possession, and under absolute command: it hangs like a viper to the heart, or rather holds it as a lion does his prey.

But yet there are multitudes, who are not sensible of their misery. They are in such a sleep that they are not very unquiet in this condition, it is not very burthensome to them, they are so sottish [drunkenly stupid] that they do not know what is their state, and what is like to become of them. But there are others who have their sense so far restored to them that they feel the pain, and see the approaching destruction, and sin lies like a heavy load upon their hearts; it is a load that lies upon them day and night, they cannot lay it down to rest themselves, but it continually oppresses them. It is bound fast unto them, and is ready to sink them down; it is a continual labor of heart, to support itself under this burden. Thus we read of them "that labor, and are heavy laden." Or rather, it is like the scorching heat in a dry wilderness, where the sun beats and burns all the day long; where they have nothing to defend them; where they can find no shade to refresh themselves. If they lay themselves down to rest, it is like lying down in the hot sands, where there is nothing to keep off the heat.

Here it may be proper to inquire who are weary and heavy laden with sin; and in what sense a sinner may be weary and burdened with sin. Sinners are not wearied with sin from any dislike to it, or dislike of it. There is no sinner that is burdened with sin in the sense in which a godly man carries his indwelling sin, as his daily and greatest burden, because he loathes it, and longs to get rid of it; he would fain be at a great distance from it, and have nothing more to do with it; he is ready to cry out as Paul did, "O wretched man that I am! who shall deliver me from the body of this death?" The unregenerate man has nothing of this nature, for sin is yet his delight, he dearly loves it. If he be under convictions, his love to sin in general is not mortified, he loves it as well as ever, he hides it still as a sweet morsel under his tongue.

But there is a difference between being weary and burdened *with* sin, and being weary *of* sin. Awakened sinners are weary with sin, but not properly weary of it.

Therefore, they are only weary of the guilt of sin, the guilt that cleaves to their consciences is that great burden. God has put the sense of feeling into their consciences, that were before as seared flesh, and it is guilt that pains them. The filthiness of sin and its evil nature, as it is an offence to a holy, gracious, and glorious God, is not a burden to them. But it is the connection between sin and punishment, between sin and God's wrath, that makes it a burden. Their consciences are heavy laden with guilt, which is an obligation to punishment; they see the threatening and curse of the law joined to their sins, and see that the justice of God and his vengeance are against them. They are burdened with their sins, not because there is any odiousness in them, but because there is Hell in them. This is the sting of sin, whereby it stings the conscience, and distresses and wearies the soul.

The guilt of such and such great sins is upon the soul, and the man sees no way to get rid of it, but he has wearisome days and wearisome nights; it makes him ready sometimes to say as the psalmist did,

> O that I had wings like a dove! for then would I fly away and be at rest. Lo, then would I wander far off, and remain in the wilderness. I would hasten my escape from the windy storm and tempest.

But when sinners come to Christ, he takes away that which was their burden, or their sin and guilt, that which was so heavy upon their hearts, that so distressed their minds.

First, he takes away the guilt of sin, from which the soul before saw no way how it was possible to be freed, and which, if it was not removed, led to eternal destruction. When the sinner comes to Christ, it is all at once taken away, and the soul is left free, it is lightened of its burden, it is delivered from its bondage, and is like a bird escaped from the snare of the fowler. The soul sees in Christ a way to peace with God, and a way by which the law may be answered, and justice satisfied, and yet he may escape; a wonderful way indeed, but yet a certain and a glorious one. And what rest does it give to the weary soul to see itself thus delivered, that the foundation of its anxieties and fears is wholly removed, and that God's wrath ceases, that it is brought into a state of peace with God, and that there is no more occasion to fear Hell, but that it is forever safe! How refreshing is it to the soul to be at once thus delivered of that which was so much its trouble and terror, and to be eased of that which was so much its burden! This is like coming to a cool shade after one has been traveling in a dry and hot wilderness, and almost fainting under the scorching heat. And then Christ also takes away sin itself, and mortifies that root of bitterness which is the cause of all the inward tumults and disquietudes that are in the mind, that make it like the troubled sea that cannot rest, and leaves it all calm. When guilt is taken away and sin is mortified, then the foundation of fear, and trouble, and pain is removed, and the soul is left in peace and serenity.

Secondly, Christ puts strength and a principle of new life into the weary soul that comes to him. The sinner, before he comes to Christ, is as a sick man that is weakened and brought low, and whose nature is consumed by some strong distemper: he is full of pain, and so weak that he cannot walk nor stand. Therefore, Christ is compared to a physician. "But when Jesus heard that, he said unto them, They that be whole, need not a physician, but they that are sick." When he comes and speaks the word, he puts a principle of life into him that was before as dead: he gives a principle of spiritual life and the beginning of eternal life; he invigorates the mind with a communication of his own life and strength, and renews the nature and creates it again, and makes the man to be a new creature.

So that the fainting, sinking spirits are now revived, and this principle of spiritual life is a continual spring of refreshment, like a well of living water. "Whosoever drinketh of the water that I shall give him, shall never thirst; but the water that I shall give him shall be in him a well of water springing up into everlasting life." Christ gives his Spirit, that calms the mind, and is like a refreshing breeze of wind. He gives that strength whereby he lifts up the hands that hang down, and strengthens the feeble knees.

Third, Christ gives to those who come to him such comfort and pleasure as are enough to make them forget all their former labor and travail. A little of true peace, a little of the joys of the manifested love of Christ, and a little of the true and holy hope of eternal life, are enough to compensate for all that toil and weariness, and to erase the remembrance of it from the mind. That peace which results from true faith passes understanding, and that joy is joy unspeakable. There is something peculiarly sweet and refreshing in this joy, that is not in other joys; and what can more effectually support the mind, or give a more rational ground of rejoicing, than a prospect of eternal glory in the enjoyment of God from God's own promise in Christ? If we come to Christ, we may not only be refreshed by resting in his shadow, but by eating his fruit: these things are the fruits of this tree. "I sat down under his shadow with great delight, and his fruit was sweet to my taste."

Before proceeding to the next particular of this proposition, I would apply myself to those that are weary; to move them to repose themselves under Christ's shadow.

The great trouble of such a state, one would think, should be a motive to you to accept of an offer of relief, and remedy. You are weary, and doubtless would be glad to be at rest; but here you are to consider:

First, that there is no remedy but in Jesus Christ; there is nothing else will give you true quietness. If you could fly into heaven, you would not find it there; if you should take the wings of the morning, and dwell in the uttermost parts of the earth, in some solitary place in the wilderness, you could not fly from your burden. So that if you do not come to Christ, you must either continue still weary and burdened, or, which is worse, you must return to your old dead sleep, to a state of stupidity; and not only so, but you must be everlastingly wearied with God's wrath.

Secondly, consider that Christ is a remedy at hand. You need not wish for the wings of a dove that you may fly afar off, and be at rest, but Christ is nigh at hand, if you were but sensible of it. Romans 10:6, 7, 8. "But the righteousness which is of faith speaketh on this wise, Say not in thine heart, Who shall ascend into heaven? (that is, to bring Christ down from above:) or, Who shall descend into the deep? (that is, to bring up Christ again from the dead.) But what saith it? The word is nigh thee, even in thy mouth, and in thy heart; that is, the word of faith which we preach." There is no need of doing any great work to come at this rest; the way is plain to it; it is but going to it, it is but sitting down under Christ's shadow. Christ requires no money to purchase rest of him, he calls to us to come freely, and for nothing. If we are poor and have no money, we may come. Christ sent out his servants to invite the poor, the maimed, the halt, and the blind. Christ does not want to be hired to accept of you, and to give you rest. It is his work as Mediator to give rest to the weary, it is the work that he was anointed for, and in which he delights. "The Spirit of the Lord God is upon me; because the Lord hath anointed me to preach good tidings unto the meek; he hath sent me to bind up the broken-hearted, to proclaim liberty to the captives, and the opening of the prison to them that are bound."

Third, Christ is not only a remedy for your weariness and trouble, but he will give you an abundance of the contrary, joy and delight. They who come to Christ, do not only come to a resting-place after they have been wandering in a wilderness, but they come to a banqueting-house where they may rest, and where they may feast. They may cease from their former troubles and toils, and they may enter upon a course of delights and spiritual joys.

Christ not only delivers from fears of Hell and of wrath, but he gives hopes of heaven, and the enjoyment of God's love. He delivers from inward tumults and inward pain from that guilt of conscience which is as a worm gnawing within, and he gives delight and inward glory. He brings us out of a wilderness of pits, and drought, and fiery flying spirits; and he brings us into a pleasant land, a land flowing with milk and honey. He delivers us out of prison, and lifts us off from the dunghill, and he sets us among princes, and causes us to inherit the throne of glory. Wherefore, if anyone is weary, if any is in prison, if anyone is in captivity, if anyone is in the wilderness, let him come to the blessed Jesus, who is as the shadow of a great rock in a weary land. Delay not, arise and come away.

2. There are quiet rest and sweet refreshment in Christ for God's people that are weary. The saints themselves, while they remain in this imperfect state, and have so much remains of sin in their hearts, are liable still to many troubles and sorrows, and much weariness, and have often need to resort anew unto Jesus Christ for rest. I shall mention three cases wherein Christ is a sufficient remedy.

First, there is rest and sweet refreshment in Christ for those that are wearied with persecutions. It has been the lot of God's church in this world for the most part to be persecuted. It has had now and then some lucid intervals of peace and outward prosperity, but generally it has been otherwise. This has accorded with the first prophecy concerning Christ; "I will put enmity between thee and the woman, and between thy seed and her seed." Those two seeds have been at enmity ever since the time of Abel. Satan has borne great malice against the church of God, and so have those that are his seed. And oftentimes God's people have been persecuted to an extreme degree, have been put to the most exquisite torments that wit or art could devise, and thousands of them have been tormented to death.

But even in such a case there are rest and refreshment to be found in Christ Jesus. When their cruel enemies have given them no rest in this world; when, as oftentimes has been the case, they could not flee, nor in any way avoid the rage of their adversaries, but many of them have been tormented gradually from day to day, that their torments might be lengthened; still rest has been found even then in Christ. It has been often found by experience; the martyrs have often showed plainly that the peace and calm of their minds were undisturbed in the midst of the greatest bodily torment, and have sometimes rejoiced and sung praises upon the rack and in the fire. If Christ is pleased to send forth his Spirit to manifest his love, and speaks friendly to the soul, it will support it even in the greatest outward torment that man can inflict. Christ is the joy of the soul, and if the soul be but rejoiced and filled with divine light, such joy no man can take away; whatever outward misery there be, the spirit will sustain it.

Secondly, there is in Christ rest for God's people, when exercised with afflictions. If a person labor under great bodily weakness, or under some disease that causes frequent and strong pains, such things will tire out so feeble a creature as man. It may to such an one be a comfort and an effectual support to think, that he has a Mediator, who knows by experience what pain is; who by his pain has purchased eternal ease and pleasure for him; and who will make his brief sufferings to work out a far more exceeding delight, to be bestowed when he shall rest from his labors and sorrows.

If a person be brought into great straits as to outward subsistence, and poverty brings abundance of difficulties and extremities; yet it may be a supporting, refreshing consideration to such an one to think, that he has a compassionate Savior, who when upon earth, was so poor that he had not where to lay his head, and who became poor to make him rich, and purchased for him durable riches, and will make his poverty work out an exceeding and eternal weight of glory.

If God in his providence calls his people to mourn over lost relations, and if he repeats his stroke and takes away one after another of those that were dear to him; it is a supporting, refreshing consideration to think, that Christ has declared that he will be in stead of all relations unto those who trust in him. They are as his mother, and sister, and brother; he has taken them into a very near relation to himself: and in every other afflictive providence, it is a great comfort to a believing soul to think that he has an intercessor with God, that by him he can have access with confidence to the throne of grace, and that in Christ we have so many great and precious promises, that all things shall work together for good, and shall issue in eternal blessedness. God's people, whenever they are scorched by afflictions as by hot sun-beams, may resort to him, who is as a shadow of a great rock, and be effectually sheltered, and sweetly refreshed.

Third, there is in Christ quiet rest and sweet refreshment for God's people, when wearied with the buffetings of Satan. The devil, that malicious enemy of God and man, does whatever lies in his power to darken and hinder, and tempt God's people, and render their lives uncomfortable. Often he raises needless and groundless scruples, and casts in doubts, and fills the mind with such fear as is tormenting, and tends to hinder them exceedingly in the Christian course; and he often raises mists and clouds of darkness, and stirs up corruption, and thereby fills the mind with concern and anguish, and sometimes wearies out the soul. So that they may say as the psalmist; "Many bulls have compassed me: strong bulls of Bashan have beset me round. They gaped upon me with their mouths, as a ravening and a roaring lion."

In such a case if the soul flies to Jesus Christ, they may find rest in him, for he came into the world to destroy Satan, and to rescue souls out of his hands. And he has all things put under his feet, whether they be things in heaven, or things on earth, or things in Hell, and therefore he can restrain Satan when he pleases. And that he is doubtless ready enough to pity us under such temptations, we may be assured, for he has been tempted and buffeted by Satan as well as we. He is able to succor those that are tempted, and he has promised that the will subdue Satan under his people's feet. Let God's people therefore, when they are exercised with any of those kinds of weariness, make their resort unto Jesus Christ for refuge and rest.

Reflections

1. *We may here see great reason to admire the goodness and grace of God to us in our low estate, that he has so provided for our help and relief.* We are by our own sin against God plunged into all sort of evil, and God has provided a remedy for us against every sort of evil, he has left us helpless in no calamity. We by our sin have exposed ourselves to wrath, to a vindictive justice; but God has done very great things that we might be saved from that wrath; he has been at infinite cost that the law might be answered without our suffering. We by our sins have exposed ourselves to terror of conscience, in expectation of the dreadful storm of God's wrath; but God has provided for us a hiding-place from the storm, he bids us enter into his chambers, and hide ourselves from indignation.

We by sin have made ourselves poor, needy creatures; but God has provided for us gold tried in the fire. We by sin have made ourselves naked; and when he passed by, he took notice of our want, and has provided us white raiment that we may be clothed. We have made ourselves blind, and God in mercy to us has provided eye-salve, that we may see. We have deprived ourselves of all spiritual food; we are like the prodigal son that perished with hunger, and would gladly have filled his belly with husks. God has taken notice of this our condition, and has provided for us a feast of fat things, and has sent forth his servants to invite the poor, the maimed, the halt, and the blind. We by sin have brought ourselves into a dry and thirsty wilderness; but God was merciful, and took notice of our condition, and has provided for us rivers of water, water out of the rock. We by sin have brought upon ourselves a miserable slavery and bondage; God has made provision for our liberty. We have exposed ourselves to weariness; God has provided a resting-place for us. We by sin have exposed ourselves to many outward troubles and afflictions; God has pitied us, and in Christ has provided true comfort for us. We have exposed ourselves to our grand enemy, even Satan, to be tempted and buffeted by him; God has pitied, and has provided for us a Savior and Captain of salvation, who has overcome Satan, and is able to deliver us. Thus God has in Christ provided sufficiently for our help in all kinds of evils.

How ought we to bless God for this abundant provision he has made for us, poor and sinful as we were, who were so undeserving and so ungrateful. He made no such provision for the fallen angels, who are left without remedy in all the woes and miseries into which they are plunged.

2. We should admire the love of Christ to men, that he has thus given himself to be the remedy for all their evil, and a fountain of all good. Christ has given himself to us, to be all things to us that we need. We want clothing, and Christ does not only give us clothing, but he gives himself to be our clothing, that we might put him on. Galatians 3:27. "For as many of you as have been baptized into Christ have put on Christ." Romans 13:14. "But put ye on the Lord Jesus Christ, and make not provision for the flesh, to fulfill the lusts thereof."

We want food, and Christ has given himself to be our food; he has given his own flesh to be our meat, and his blood to be our drink, to nourish our soul. Thus Christ tells us that he is the bread which came down from heaven, and the bread of life. "I am that bread of life. Your fathers did eat manna in the wilderness, and are dead. This is the bread which cometh down from heaven, that a man may eat thereof, and not die. I am the living bread which came down from heaven: if any man eat of this bread, he shall live for ever; and the bread that I will give is my flesh, which I will give for the life of the world." In order to our eating of his flesh, it was necessary that he should be slain, as the sacrifices must be slain before they could be eaten; and such was Christ's love to us, that he consented to be slain, he went as a sheep to the slaughter, that he might give us his flesh to be food for our poor, famishing souls.

We are in need of a habitation; we by sin have, as it were, turned ourselves out of house and home; Christ has given himself to be the habitation of his people. Psalm 90:1: "Lord, thou has been our dwelling-place in all generations." It is promised to God's people that they should dwell in the temple of God for ever, and should go no more out; and we are told that Christ is the temple of the new Jerusalem.

Christ gives himself to his people to be all things to them that they need, and all things that make for their happiness. Colossians 3:11: "Where there is neither Greek nor Jew, circumcision nor uncircumcision, barbarian, Scythian, bond, nor free; but Christ is all, and in all." And that he might be so, he has refused nothing that is needful to prepare him to be so.

When it was needful that he should be incarnate, he refused it not, but became man, and appeared in the form of a servant. When it was needful that he should be slain, he refused it not, but gave himself for us, and gave himself to us upon the cross.

Here is love for us to admire, for us to praise, and for us to rejoice in, with joy that is full of glory for ever.

The Excellency of Christ

August 1736. "Mr. Edwards selected this discourse because it. . .would properly follow others that were chiefly "awakening" discourses."(*Memoirs of Jonathan Edwards.*)

"And one of the elders saith unto me, 'Weep not: behold, the Lion of the tribe of Judah, the Root of David, hath prevailed to open the book, and to loose the seven seals thereof.' And I beheld, and, lo, in the midst of the throne, and of the four beasts, and in the midst of the elders, stood a Lamb, as it had been slain."—Revelation 5:5–6

The visions and revelations the apostle John had of the future events of God's providence, are here introduced with a vision of the book of God's decrees, by which those events were fore-ordained. This is represented (Revelation 5:1) as a book in the right hand of him who sat on the throne, "written within and on the back side, and sealed with seven seals." Books, in the form in which they were wont of old to be made, were broad leaves of parchment or paper, or something of that nature, joined together at one edge, and so rolled up together, and then sealed, or some way fastened together, to prevent their unfolding and opening. Hence we read of the roll of a book. (Jer. 36:2.)

It seems to have been such a book that John had a vision of here; and therefore it is said to be "written within and on the back side," i.e. on the inside pages, and also on one of the outside pages, namely, that which it was rolled in, in rolling the book up together. And it is said to be "sealed with seven seals," to signify that what was written in it was perfectly hidden and secret; or that God's decrees of future events are sealed, and shut up from all possibility of being discovered by creatures, till God is pleased to make them known. We find that seven is often used in Scripture as the number of perfection, to signify the superlative or most perfect degree of anything, which probably arose from this, that on the seventh day God beheld the works of creation finished, and rested and rejoiced in them, as being complete and perfect.

When John saw this book, he tells us, he

> saw a strong angel proclaiming with a loud voice, "Who is worthy to open the book, and to loose the seals thereof?" And no man in heaven, nor in earth, neither under the earth, was able to open the book, neither to look thereon.

And that he wept much, because "no man was found worthy to open and read the book, neither to look thereon." And then tells us how his tears were dried up, namely, that "one of the elders said unto him, 'Weep not, Behold the Lion of the tribe of Judah hath prevailed' " etc., as in the text. Though no man nor angel, nor any mere creature, was found either able to loose the seals, or worthy to be admitted to the privilege of reading the book, yet this was declared, for the comfort of this beloved disciple, that Christ was found both able and worthy. And we have an account in the succeeding chapters how he actually did it, opening the seals in order, first one, and then another, revealing what God had decreed should come to pass hereafter. And we have an account in this chapter, of his coming and taking the book out of the right hand of him that sat on the throne, and of the joyful praises that were sung to him in heaven and earth on that occasion.

Many things might be observed in the words of the text; but it is to my present purpose only to take notice of the two distinct appellations here given to Christ.

- *He is called a Lion.* Behold, the Lion of the tribe of Judah. He seems to be called the Lion of the tribe of Judah, in allusion to what Jacob said in his blessing of the tribe on his death-bed; who, when he came to bless Judah, compares him to a lion, Gen. 49:9. "Judah is a lion's whelp; from the prey, my son, thou art gone up: he stooped down, he couched as a lion, and as an old lion; who shall rouse him up?" And also to the standard of the camp of Judah in the wilderness on which was displayed a lion, according to the ancient tradition of the Jews. It is much on account of the valiant acts of David that the tribe of Judah, of which David was, is in Jacob's prophetical blessing compared to a lion; but more especially with an eye to Jesus Christ, who also was of that tribe, and was descended of David, and is in our text called "the Root of David"; and therefore Christ is here called "the Lion of the tribe of Judah."

- *He is called a Lamb.* John was told of a Lion that had prevailed to open the book, and probably expected to see a lion in his vision; but while he is expecting, behold a Lamb appears to open the book, an exceeding diverse kind of creature from a lion. A lion is a devourer, one that is wont to make terrible slaughter of others; and no creature more easily falls a prey to him than a lamb. And Christ is here represented not only as a Lamb, a creature very liable to be slain, but a "Lamb as it had been slain," that is, with the marks of its deadly wounds appearing on it.

That which I would observe from the words, for the subject of my present discourse, is this, namely:

- *There is an admirable conjunction of diverse excellencies in Jesus Christ.* The lion and the lamb, though very diverse kinds of creatures, yet have each their peculiar excellencies. The lion excels in strength, and in the majesty of his appearance and voice: the lamb excels in meekness and patience, besides the excellent nature of the creature as good for food, and yielding that which is fit for our clothing and being suitable to be offered in sacrifice to God. But we see that Christ is in the text compared to both, because the diverse excellencies of both wonderfully meet in him.

In handling this subject I would:

I. Show wherein there is an admirable conjunction of diverse excellencies in Christ.
II. Show how this admirable conjunction of excellencies appear in Christ's acts.
III. Make application.

I. I would show wherein there is an admirable conjunction of diverse excellencies in Jesus Christ, which appears in three things:

- There is a conjunction of such excellencies in Christ, as, in our manner of conceiving, are very diverse one from another.
- There is in him a conjunction of such really diverse excellencies, as otherwise would have seemed to us utterly incompatible in the same subject.

- Such diverse excellencies are exercised in him towards men that otherwise would have seemed impossible to be exercised towards the same object.

1. *There is a conjunction of such excellencies in Christ as, in our manner of conceiving, are very diverse one from another.* Such are the various divine perfections and excellencies that Christ is possessed of. Christ is a divine person, and therefore has all the attributes of God. The difference between these is chiefly relative, and in our manner of conceiving them. And those which, in this sense, are most diverse, meet in the person of Christ.

I shall mention two instances.

There do meet in Jesus Christ infinite highness and infinite condescension. Christ, as he is God, is infinitely great and high above all. He is higher than the kings of the earth; for he is King of kings, and Lord of lords. He is higher than the heavens, and higher than the highest angels of heaven. So great is he, that all men, all kings and princes, are as worms of the dust before him; all nations are as a drop in the bucket, and the light dust of the balance; yea, and angels themselves are as nothing before him. He is so high, that he is infinitely above any need of us; above our reach, that we cannot be profitable to him; and above our conceptions, that we cannot comprehend him. Prov. 30:4: "What is his name, and what is his Son's name, if thou canst tell?" Our understandings, if we stretch them never so far, cannot reach up to his divine glory. Job 11:8: "It is high as heaven, what canst thou do?" Christ is the Creator and great Possessor of heaven and earth. He is sovereign Lord of all. He rules over the whole universe, and doth whatsoever pleaseth him. His knowledge is without bound. His wisdom is perfect, and what none can circumvent. His power is infinite, and none can resist Him. His riches are immense and inexhaustible. His majesty is infinitely awful.

And yet he is one of infinite condescension. None are so low or inferior, but Christ's condescension is sufficient to take a gracious notice of them. He condescends not only to the angels, humbling himself to behold the things that are done in heaven, but he also condescends to such poor creatures as men; and that not only so as to take notice of princes and great men, but of those that are of meanest rank and degree, "the poor of the world," (James 2:5). Such as are commonly despised by their fellow creatures, Christ does not despise. 1 Corr. 1:28: "Base things of the world, and things that are despised, hath God chosen." Christ condescends to take notice of beggars (Luke 16:22) and people of the most despised nations. In Christ Jesus is neither "Barbarian, Scythian, bond nor free" (Col. 3:11). He that is thus high condescends to take a gracious notice of little children, Matt. 19:14: "Suffer little children to come unto me." Yea, which is more, his condescension is sufficient to take a gracious notice of the most unworthy, sinful creatures, those that have no good deservings, and those that have infinite ill deservings.

Yea, so great is his condescension, that it is not only sufficient to take some gracious notice of such as these, but sufficient for everything that is an act of condescension. His condescension is great enough to become their friend, to become their companion, to unite their souls to him in spiritual marriage. It is enough to take their nature upon him, to become one of them, that he may be one with them. Yea, it is great enough to abase himself yet lower for them, even to expose himself to shame and spitting; yea, to yield up himself to an ignominious death for them. And what act of condescension can be conceived of greater? Yet such an act as this, has his condescension yielded to, for those that are so low and mean, despicable and unworthy!

Such a conjunction of infinite highness and low condescension, in the same person, is admirable. We see, by manifold instances, what a tendency a high station has in men, to make them to be of a quite contrary disposition. If one worm be a little exalted above another, by having more dust, or a bigger dunghill, how much does he make of himself! What a distance does he keep from those that are below him! And a little condescension is what he expects should be made much of, and greatly acknowledged. Christ condescends to wash our feet; but how would great men, (or rather, the bigger worms) account themselves debased by acts of far less condescension!

There meet in Jesus Christ, infinite justice and infinite grace.

As Christ is a divine person, he is infinitely holy and just, hating sin, and disposed to execute condign punishment for sin. He is the Judge of the world, and the infinitely just Judge of it, and will not at all acquit the wicked, or by any means clear the guilty.

And yet he is infinitely gracious and merciful. Though his justice be so strict with respect to all sin, and every breach of the law, yet he has grace sufficient for every sinner, and even the chief of sinners. And it is not only sufficient for the most unworthy to show them mercy, and bestow some good upon them, but to bestow the greatest good; yea, it is sufficient to bestow all good upon them, and to do all things for them. There is no benefit or blessing that they can receive, so great but the grace of Christ is sufficient to bestow it on the greatest sinner that ever lived. And not only so, but so great is his grace, that nothing is too much as the means of this good. It is sufficient not only to do great things, but also to suffer in order to do it, and not only to suffer, but to suffer most extremely even unto death, the most terrible of natural evils; and not only death, but the most ignominious and tormenting, and every way the most terrible that men could inflict; yea, and greater sufferings than men could inflict, who could only torment the body. He had sufferings in his soul, that were the more immediate fruits of the wrath of God against the sins of those he undertakes for.

2. *There do meet in the person of Christ such really diverse excellencies, which otherwise would have been thought utterly incompatible in the same subject;* such as are conjoined in no other person whatever, either divine, human, or angelical; and such as neither men nor angels would ever have imagined could have met together in the same person, had it not been seen in the person of Christ. I would give some instances.

In the person of Christ do meet together infinite glory and lowest humility. Infinite glory, and the virtue of humility, meet in no other person but Christ. They meet in no created person; for no created person has infinite glory, and they meet in no other divine person but Christ. For though the divine nature be infinitely abhorrent to pride, yet humility is not properly predicable of God the Father, and the Holy Ghost, that exist only in the divine nature; because it is a proper excellency only of a created nature; for it consists radically in a sense of a comparative lowness and littleness before God, or the great distance between God and the subject of this virtue; but it would be a contradiction to suppose any such thing in God.

But in Jesus Christ, who is both God and man, those two diverse excellencies are sweetly united. He is a person infinitely exalted in glory and dignity. Phil. 2:6: "Being in the form of God, he thought it not robbery to be equal with God." There is equal honor due to him with the Father. John 5:23: "That all men should honor the Son, even as they honor the Father." God himself says to him, "thy throne, O God, is forever and ever," Heb. 1:8. And there is the same supreme respect and divine worship paid to him by the angels of heaven, as to God the Father, ver. 6: "Let all the angels of God worship him."

But however he is thus above all, yet he is lowest of all in humility. There never was so great an instance of this virtue among either men or angels, as Jesus. None ever was so sensible of the distance between God and him, or had a heart so lowly before God, as the man Christ Jesus. (Matt. 11:29.) What a wonderful spirit of humility appeared in him, when he was here upon earth, in all his behavior! In his contentment in his mean outward condition, contentedly living in the family of Joseph the carpenter, and Mary his mother, for thirty years together, and afterwards choosing outward meanness, poverty, and contempt, rather than earthly greatness; in his washing his disciples' feet, and in all his speeches and deportment towards them; in his cheerfully sustaining the form of a servant through his whole life, and submitting to such immense humiliation at death!

In the person of Christ do meet together infinite majesty and transcendent meekness. These again are two qualifications that meet together in no other person but Christ. Meekness, properly so called, is a virtue proper only to the creature: we scarcely ever find meekness mentioned as a divine attribute in Scripture; at least not in the New Testament; for thereby seems to be signified, a calmness and quietness of spirit, arising from humility in mutable beings that are naturally liable to be put into a ruffle by the assaults of a tempestuous and injurious world. But Christ, being both God and man, hath both infinite majesty and superlative meekness.

Christ was a person of infinite majesty. It is he that is spoken of, Psalm 45:3. "Gird thy sword upon thy thigh, O most mighty, with thy glory and thy majesty." It is he that is mighty, that rideth on the heavens, and his excellency on the sky. It is he that is terrible out of his holy places; who is mightier than the noise of many waters, yea, than the mighty waves of the sea: before whom a fire goeth, and burneth up his enemies round about; at whose presence the earth quakes, and the hills melt; who sitteth on the circle of the earth, and all the inhabitants thereof are as grasshoppers, who rebukes the sea, and maketh it dry and drieth up the rivers, whose eyes are as a flame of fire, from whose presence, and from the glory of whose power, the wicked shall be punished with everlasting destruction; who is the blessed and only Potentate, the King of kings, and Lord of lords, who hath heaven for his throne, and the earth for his footstool, and is the high and lofty One who inhabits eternity, whose kingdom is an everlasting kingdom, and of whose dominion there is no end.

And yet he was the most marvelous instance of meekness, and humble quietness of spirit, that ever was; agreeable to the prophecies of him, Matthew 21:4, 5:

> All this was done, that it might be fulfilled which was spoken by the prophet, saying, Tell ye the daughter of Zion, Behold, thy King cometh unto thee, meek, and sitting upon an ass, and a colt the foal of an ass.

And, agreeable to what Christ declares of himself, Matt. 11:29. "I am meek and lowly in heart." And agreeable to what was manifest in his behavior: for there never was such an instance seen on earth, of a meek behavior, under injuries and reproaches, and towards enemies; who, when he was reviled, reviled not again. He had a wonderful spirit of forgiveness, was ready to forgive his worst enemies, and prayed for them with fervent and effectual prayers. With what meekness did he appear in the ring of soldiers that were contemning and mocking him; he was silent, and opened not his mouth, but went as a lamb to the slaughter. Thus is Christ a Lion in majesty and a Lamb in meekness.

There meet in the person of Christ the deepest reverence towards God and equality with God. Christ, when on earth, appeared full of holy reverence towards the Father. He paid the most reverential worship to him, praying to him with postures of reverence. Thus we read of his "kneeling down and praying," Luke 22:41. This became Christ, as one who had taken on him the human nature, but at the same time he existed in the divine nature; whereby his person was in all respects equal to the person of the Father. God the Father hath no attribute or perfection that the Son hath not, in equal degree, and equal glory. These things meet in no other person but Jesus Christ.

There are conjoined in the person of Christ infinite worthiness of good, and the greatest patience under sufferings of evil.

He was perfectly innocent, and deserved no suffering. He deserved nothing from God by any guilt of his own, and he deserved no ill from men. Yea, he was not only harmless and undeserving of suffering, but he was infinitely worthy; worthy of the infinite love of the Father, worthy of infinite and eternal happiness, and infinitely worthy of all possible esteem, love, and service from all men.

And yet he was perfectly patient under the greatest sufferings that ever were endured in this world. (Heb. 12:2.) "He endured the cross, despising the shame." He suffered not from his Father for his faults, but ours; and he suffered from men not for his faults but for those things on account of which he was infinitely worthy of their love and honor, which made his patience the more wonderful and the more glorious. 1 Pet. 2:20:

> For what glory is it, if when ye be buffeted for your faults, ye shall take it patiently, but if when ye do well. and suffer for it, ye take it patiently; this is acceptable with God. For even hereunto were ye called; because Christ also suffered for us, leaving us an example, that we should follow his steps: who

> did no sin, neither was guile found in his mouth: who when he was reviled, reviled not again, when he suffered, he threatened not, but committed himself to him that judged righteously: who his own self bare our sins in his own body on the tree, that we being dead to sin, should live unto righteousness: by whose stripes ye were healed.

There is no such conjunction of innocence, worthiness, and patience under sufferings, as in the person of Christ.

In the person of Christ are conjoined an exceeding spirit of obedience, with supreme dominion over heaven and earth.

Christ is the Lord of all things in two respects: he is so, as God-man and Mediator, and thus his dominion is appointed, and given him of the Father. Having it by delegation from God, he is as it were the Father's vicegerent [ruler's administrative deputy]. But he is Lord of all things in another respect, namely, as he is (by his original nature) God; and so he is by natural right the Lord of all, and supreme over all as much as the Father. Thus, he has dominion over the world, not by delegation, but in his own right. He is not an "under God," as the Arians suppose, but to all intents and purposes, *supreme God.*

And yet in the same person is found the greatest spirit of obedience to the commands and laws of God that ever was in the universe; which was manifest in his obedience here in this world. John 14:31: "As the Father gave me commandment, even so I do." John 15:10: "Even as I have kept my Father's commandments, and abide in his love." The greatness of his obedience appears in its perfection, and in his obeying commands of such exceeding difficulty. Never anyone received commands from God of such difficulty, and that were so great a trial of obedience, as Jesus Christ. One of God's commands to him was, that he should yield himself to those dreadful sufferings that he underwent. See John 10:18. "No man taketh it from me, but I lay it down of myself." "This commandment received I of my Father." And Christ was thoroughly obedient to this command of God. Heb. 5:8: "Though he were a Son, yet he learned obedience by the things that he suffered." Philip. 2:8: "He humbled himself, and became obedient unto death, even the death of the cross." Never was there such an instance of obedience in man or angel as this, though he was at the same time supreme Lord of both angels and men.

In the person of Christ are conjoined absolute sovereignty and perfect resignation. This is another unparalleled conjunction.

Christ, as he is God, is the absolute sovereign of the world, the sovereign disposer of all events. The decrees of God are all his sovereign decrees;

and the work of creation, and all God's works of providence, are his sovereign works. It is he that worketh all things according to the counsel of his own will. Col. 1:16, 17: "By him, and through him, and to him, are all things." John 5:17: "The Father worketh hitherto, and I work." Matt. 8:3: "I will, be thou clean."

But yet Christ was the most wonderful instance of resignation that ever appeared in the world. He was absolutely and perfectly resigned when he had a near and immediate prospect of his terrible sufferings, and the dreadful cup that he was to drink. The idea and expectation of this made his soul exceeding sorrowful even unto death, and put him into such an agony, that his sweat was as it were great drops or clots of blood, falling down to the ground. But in such circumstances he was wholly resigned to the will of God. Matt 26:39: "O my Father, if it be possible, let this cup pass from me: nevertheless, not as I will, but as thou wilt." Verse 42: "O my Father, if this cup may not pass from me, except I drink it, thy will be done."

In Christ do meet together self-sufficiency, and an entire trust and reliance on God, which is another conjunction peculiar to the person of Christ.

As he is a divine person, he is self-sufficient, standing in need of nothing. All creatures are dependent on him, but he is dependent on none, but is absolutely independent. His proceeding from the Father, in his eternal generation, argues no proper dependence on the will of the Father; for that proceeding was natural and necessary, and not arbitrary.

But yet Christ entirely trusted in God: his enemies say that of him, "He trusted in God that he would deliver him," Matt. 27:43. And the apostle testifies, 1 Pet. 2:23, "That he committed himself God."

3. *Such diverse excellencies are expressed in him towards men, that otherwise would have seemed impossible to be exercised towards the same object; as particularly these three, justice, mercy, and truth.* The same that are mentioned in Psalm 85:10: "Mercy and truth are met together, righteousness and peace have kissed each other."

The strict justice of God, and even his revenging justice, and that against the sins of men, never was so gloriously manifested as in Christ. He manifested an infinite regard to the attribute of God's justice, in that, when he had a mind to save sinners, he was willing to undergo such extreme sufferings, rather than that their salvation should be to the injury of the honor of that attribute. And as he is the Judge of the world, he doth himself exercise strict justice: he will not clear the guilty, nor at all acquit the wicked in judgment.

Yet how wonderfully is infinite mercy towards sinners displayed in him! And what glorious and ineffable grace and love have been and are exercised by him, towards sinful men! Though he be the just Judge of a sinful world, yet he is also the Savior of the world. Though he be a consuming fire to sin, yet he is the light and life of sinners. Rom. 3:25, 26:

> Whom God hath set forth to be a propitiation, through faith in his blood, to declare his righteousness for the remission of sins that are past, through the forbearance of God; to declare, I say, at this time his righteousness, that he might be just, and the justifier of him which believeth in Jesus.

So the immutable truth of God, in the threatenings of his law against the sins of men, was never so manifested as it is in Jesus Christ, for there never was any other so great a trial of the unalterableness of the truth of God in those threatenings, as when sin came to be imputed to his own Son. And then in Christ has been seen already an actual complete accomplishment of those threatenings, which never has been nor will be seen in any other instance; because the eternity that will be taken up in fulfilling those threatenings on others, never will be finished. Christ manifested an infinite regard to this truth of God in his sufferings. And, in his judging the world, he makes the covenant of works, that contains those dreadful threatenings, his rule of judgment. He will see to it, that it is not infringed in the least jot or tittle: he will do nothing contrary to the threatenings of the law, and their complete fulfillment. And yet in him we have many great and precious promises, promises of perfect deliverance from the penalty of the law. And this is the promise that he hath promised us, even eternal life. And in him are all the promises of God yea, and Amen.

II. Having thus shown wherein there is an admirable conjunction of excellencies in Jesus Christ, I now proceed, secondly, to show how this admirable conjunction of excellencies appears in Christ's acts, namely:

- in his taking of human nature,
- in his earthly life,
- in his sacrificial death,
- in his exaltation in heaven,
- in his final subduing of all evil when he returns in glory.

1. *It appears in what Christ did in taking on him our nature.* In this act, his infinite condescension wonderfully appeared, that he who was God should become man; that the word should be made flesh, and should take on him a

nature infinitely below his original nature! And it appears yet more remarkably in the low circumstances of his incarnation: he was conceived in the womb of a poor young woman, whose poverty appeared in this, when she came to offer sacrifices of her purification, she brought what was allowed of in the law only in case of poverty, as Luke 2:24: "According to what is said in the law of the Lord, a pair of turtle-doves, or two young pigeons." This was allowed only in case the person was so poor that she was not able to offer a lamb. (Lev. 12:8.)

And though his infinite condescension thus appeared in the manner of his incarnation, yet his divine dignity also appeared in it; for though he was conceived in the womb of a poor virgin, yet he was conceived there by the power of the Holy Ghost. And his divine dignity also appeared in the holiness of his conception and birth. Though he was conceived in the womb of one of the corrupt race of mankind, yet he was conceived and born without sin; as the angel said to the blessed Virgin, Luke 1:35:

> The Holy Ghost shall come upon thee, and the power of the Highest shall overshadow thee, therefore also that holy thing which shall be born of thee, shall be called the Son of God.

His infinite condescension marvelously appeared in the manner of his birth. He was brought forth in a stable because there was no room for them in the inn. The inn was taken up by others, that were looked upon as persons of greater account. The Blessed Virgin, being poor and despised, was turned or shut out. Though she was in such necessitous circumstances, yet those that counted themselves her betters would not give place to her; and therefore, in the time of her travail, she was forced to betake herself to a stable; and when the child was born, it was wrapped in swaddling clothes, and laid in a manger. There Christ lay a little infant, and there he eminently appeared as a lamb.

But yet this feeble infant, born thus in a stable, and laid in a manger, was born to conquer and triumph over Satan, that roaring lion. He came to subdue the mighty powers of darkness, and make a show of them openly, and so to restore peace on earth, and to manifest God's good-will towards men, and to bring glory to God in the highest, according as the end of his birth was declared by the joyful songs of the glorious hosts of angels appearing to the shepherds at the same time that the infant lay in the manger; whereby his divine dignity was manifested.

2. *This admirable conjunction of excellencies appears in the acts and various passages of Christ's life.*

Though Christ dwelt in mean outward circumstances, whereby his condescension and humility especially appeared, and his majesty was veiled; yet his divine divinity and glory did in many of his acts shine through the veil, and it illustriously appeared, that he was not only the Son of man, but the great God.

Thus, in the circumstances of his infancy, his outward meanness appeared; yet there was something then to show forth his divine dignity, in the wise men's being stirred up to come from the east to give honor to him their being led by a miraculous star, and coming and falling down and worshiping him, and presenting him with gold, frankincense, and myrrh. His humility and meekness wonderfully appeared in his subjection to his mother and reputed father when he was a child. Herein he appeared as a lamb. But his divine glory broke forth and shone when, at twelve years old, he disputed with doctors in the temple. In that he appeared, in some measure, as the Lion of the tribe of Judah.

And so, after he entered on his public ministry, his marvelous humility and meekness was manifested in his choosing to appear in such mean outward circumstances; and in being contented in them, when he was so poor that he had nowhere to lay his head, and depended on the charity of some of his followers for his subsistence, as appears by Luke 8, at the beginning. How meek, condescending, and familiar his treatment of his disciples; his discourses with them, treating them as a father his children, yea, as friends and companions. How patient, bearing such affliction and reproach, and so many injuries from the scribes and Pharisees, and others. In these things he appeared as a Lamb.

And yet he at the same time did in many ways show forth his divine majesty and glory, particularly in the miracles he wrought, which were evidently divine works, and manifested omnipotent power, and so declared him to be the Lion of the tribe of Judah. His wonderful and miraculous works plainly showed him to be the God of nature; in that it appeared by them that he had all nature in his hands, and could lay an arrest upon it, and stop and change its course as he pleased. In healing the sick, and opening the eyes of the blind, and unstopping the ears of the deaf, and healing the lame, he showed that he was the God that framed the eye, and created the ear, and was the author of the frame of man's body. By the dead's rising at his command, it appeared that he was the author and fountain of life, and that "God the Lord, to whom belong the issues from death." By his walking on the sea in a storm, when the waves were raised, he showed himself to be that God spoken of in Job 9:8: "that treadeth on the waves of the sea." By his stilling the storm, and calming the rage of the sea, by his powerful command, saying, "Peace, be still," he showed that he has the command of the universe, and that he is that God who brings things to pass by the word of his power, who speaks and it is done, who commands and it stands fast; Psalm 115:7: "Who stilleth the noise of the seas, the noise of their waves." And Psalm 107:29: "That maketh the storm a calm, so that the waves thereof are still." And Psalm 139:8, 9:

> O Lord God of hosts, who is a strong Lord like unto thee, or to thy faithfulness round about thee? Thou rulest the raging of the sea: when the waves thereof arise, thou stillest them.

Christ, by casting out devils, remarkably appeared as the Lion of the tribe of Judah, and showed that he was stronger than the roaring lion, that seizes whom he may devour. He commanded them to come out, and they were forced to obey. They were terribly afraid of him; they fall down before him, and beseech him not so torment them. He forces a whole legion of them to forsake their hold, by his powerful word; and they could not so much as enter into the swine without his leave. He showed the glory of his omniscience, by telling the thoughts of men; as we have often an account. Herein he appeared to be that God spoken of, Amos 4:13: "That declareth unto man what is his thought." Thus, in the midst of his meanness and humiliation, his divine glory appeared in his miracles, John 2:11. "This beginning of miracles did Jesus in Cana of Galilee, and manifested forth his glory."

And though Christ ordinarily appeared without outward glory, and in great obscurity, yet at a certain time he threw off the veil, and appeared in his divine majesty, so far as it could be outwardly manifested to men in this frail state, when he was transfigured in the mount. The apostle Peter, 2 Pet. 1:16,17:

> was an eye-witness of his majesty, when he received from God the Father honor and glory, when there came such a voice to him from the excellent glory, "This is my beloved Son, in whom I am well pleased"; which voice that came from heaven they heard, when they were with him in the holy mount.

And at the same time that Christ was wont to appear in such meekness, condescension, and humility, in his familiar discourses with his disciples, appearing therein as the Lamb of God; he was also wont to appear as the Lion of the tribe of Judah, with divine authority and majesty, in his so sharply rebuking the scribes and Pharisees, and other hypocrites.

3. *This admirable conjunction of excellencies remarkably appears in his offering up himself a sacrifice for sinners in his last sufferings.*

As this was the greatest thing in all the works of redemption, the greatest act of Christ in that work; so in this act especially does there appear that admirable conjunction of excellencies that has been spoken of. Christ never so much appeared as a lamb, as when he was slain: "He came like a lamb to the slaughter," Isaiah 53:7. Then he was offered up to God as a lamb without blemish, and without spot: then especially did he appear to be the anti-type of the lamb of the Passover. 1 Cor 5:7: "Christ our Passover sacrificed for us." And yet in that act he did in an especial manner appear as the Lion of the tribe of Judah; yea, in this above all other acts, in many respects, as may appear in the following things.

Then was Christ in the greatest degree of his humiliation, and yet by that, above all other things, his divine glory appears.

Christ's humiliation was great, in being born in such a low condition, of a poor virgin, and in a stable. His humiliation was great, in being subject to Joseph the carpenter, and Mary his mother, and afterwards living in poverty, so as not to have [any]where to lay his head; and in suffering such manifold and bitter reproaches as he suffered, while he went about preaching and working miracles. But his humiliation was never so great as it was, in his last sufferings, beginning with his agony in the garden, till he expired on the cross. Never was he subject to such ignominy as then, never did he suffer so much pain in his body, or so much sorrow in his soul; never was he in so great an exercise of his condescension, humility, meekness, and patience, as he was in these last sufferings; never was his divine glory and majesty covered with so thick and dark a veil; never did he so empty himself and make himself of no reputation, as at this time.

And yet, never was his divine glory so manifested, by any act of his, as in yielding himself up to these sufferings. When the fruit of it came to appear, and the mystery and ends of it to be unfolded in its issue, then did the glory of it appear, then did it appear as the most glorious act of Christ that ever he exercised towards the creature. This act of his is celebrated by the angels and hosts of heaven with peculiar praises, as that which is above all others glorious, as you may see in the context, Revelation 5:9–12:

> And they sang a new song, saying, "Thou art worthy to take the book, and to open the seals thereof: for thou wast slain and hast redeemed us to God by thy blood, out of every kindred, and tongue, and people, and nation; and

> hast made us unto our God kings and priests: and we shall reign on the earth." And I beheld, and I heard the voice of many angels round about the throne, and the beasts, and the elders: and the number of them was ten thousand times ten thousand, and thousands of thousands, saying with a loud voice "Worthy is the Lamb that was slain, to receive power, and riches, and wisdom, and strength, and honor, and glory, and blessing."

He never in any act gave so great a manifestation of love to God, and yet never so manifested his love to those that were enemies to God, as in that act.

Christ never did anything whereby his love to the Father was so eminently manifested, as in his laying down his life, under such inexpressible sufferings, in obedience to his command and for the vindication of the honor of his authority and majesty; nor did ever any mere creature give such a testimony of love to God as that was.

And yet this was the greatest expression of his love to sinful men who were enemies to God, Rom. 5:10: "When we were enemies, we were reconciled to God, by the death of his Son." The greatness of Christ's love to such, appears in nothing so much as in its being dying love. That blood of Christ which fell in great drops to the ground, in his agony, was shed from love to God's enemies, and his own. That shame and spitting, that torment of body, and that exceeding sorrow, even unto death, which he endured in his soul, was what he underwent from love to rebels against God to save them from Hell, and to purchase for them eternal glory. Never did Christ so eminently show his regard to God's honor, as in offering up himself a victim to Justice. And yet in this above all, he manifested his love to them who dishonored God, so as to bring such guilt on themselves, that nothing less than his blood could atone for it.

Christ never so eminently appeared for *divine Justice, and yet never suffered so much* from *divine Justice, as when he offered up himself a sacrifice for our sins.*

In Christ's great sufferings did his infinite regard to the honor of God's justice distinguishingly appear, for it was from regard to that that he thus humbled himself.

And yet in these sufferings, Christ was the target of the vindictive expressions of that very justice of God. Revenging justice then spent all its force upon him, on account of our guilt; which made him sweat blood, and cry out upon the cross, and probably rent his vitals, [and] broke his heart, the fountain of blood, or some other blood vessels, and by the violent fermentation turned his blood to water. For the blood and water that issued out of his side, when pierced by the spear, seems to have been extravasated* blood, and so there might be a kind of literal fulfillment of Psalm 22:14. "I am poured out like water, and all my bones are out of joint: my heart is like wax, it is melted in the midst of my bowels." And this was the way and means by which Christ stood up for the honor of God's justice, namely, by thus suffering its terrible executions. For when he had undertaken for sinners, and had substituted himself in their room, divine justice could have its due honor no other way than by his suffering its revenges.

In this the diverse excellencies that met in the person of Christ appeared, namely, his infinite regard to God's justice, and such love to those that have exposed themselves to it, as induced him thus to yield himself a sacrifice to it.

Christ's holiness never so illustriously shone forth as it did in his last sufferings, and yet he never was to such a degree treated as guilty.

Christ's holiness never had such a trial as it had then, and therefore never had so great a manifestation. When it was tried in this furnace it came forth as gold, or as silver purified seven times. His holiness then above all appeared in his steadfast pursuit of the honor of God, and in his obedience to him. For his yielding himself unto death was transcendently the greatest act of obedience that ever was paid to God by anyone since the foundation of the world.

And yet then Christ was in the greatest degree treated as a wicked person would have been. He was apprehended and bound as a malefactor. His accusers represented him as a most wicked wretch. In his sufferings before his crucifixion, he was treated as if he had been the worst and vilest of mankind, and then, he was put to a kind of death, that none but the worst sort of malefactors were wont to suffer, those that were most abject in their persons, and guilty of the blackest crimes. And he suffered as though guilty from God himself, by reason of our guilt imputed to him; for he who knew no sin, was made sin for us; he was made subject to wrath, as if he had been sinful himself. He was made a curse for us.

Christ never so greatly manifested his hatred of sin, as against God, as in his dying to take away the dishonor that sin had done to God; and yet never was he to such a degree subject to the terrible effects of God's hatred of sin, and wrath against it, as he was then. In this appears those diverse excellencies meeting in Christ, namely, love to God, and grace to sinners.

**Extravasate*—to force the flow of blood (or lymph) from a vessel out into the surrounding tissue. *(American Heritage Dictionary.)*

He never was so dealt with, as unworthy, as in his last sufferings, and yet it is chiefly on account of them that he is accounted worthy.

He was therein dealt with as if he had not been worthy to live: they cry out, "Away with him! away with him! Crucify him."(John 19:15.) And they prefer Barabbas before him. And he suffered from the Father, as one whose demerits were infinite, by reason of our demerits that were laid upon him.

And yet it was especially by that act of his subjecting himself to those sufferings that he merited, and on the account of which chiefly he was accounted worthy of the glory of his exaltation. Philip. 2:8, 9: "He humbled himself, and became obedient unto death; wherefore God hath highly exalted him." And we see that it is on this account chiefly, that he is extolled as worthy by saints and angels in the context: "Worthy," say they, "is the Lamb that was slain." This shows an admirable conjunction in him of infinite dignity, and infinite condescension and love to the infinitely unworthy.

Christ in his last sufferings suffered most extremely from those towards whom he was then manifesting his greatest act of love.

He never suffered so much from his Father [as then], (though not from any hatred to him, but from hatred to our sins) for he then forsook him, or took away the comforts of his presence; and then "it pleased the Lord to bruise him, and put him to grief," as Isaiah 53:10. And yet he never gave so great a manifestation of love to God as then, as has been already observed.

So Christ never suffered so much from the hands of men as he did then; and yet never was in so high an exercise of love to men. He never was so ill treated by his disciples; who were so unconcerned about his sufferings, that they would not watch with him one hour, in his agony; and when he was apprehended, all forsook him and fled, except Peter, who denied him with oaths and curses. And yet then he was suffering, shedding his blood, and pouring out his soul unto death for them. Yea, he probably was then shedding his blood for some of them that shed his blood, for whom he prayed while they were crucifying him; and who were probably afterwards brought home to Christ by Peter's preaching. (Compare Luke 23:34, Acts 2:23, 36, 37, 41, and chap. 3:17, and chap. 4.) This shows an admirable meeting of justice and grace in the redemption of Christ.

It was in Christ's last sufferings, above all, that he was delivered up to the power of his enemies; and yet by these, above all, he obtained victory over his enemies.

Christ never was so in his enemies' hands, as in the time of his last sufferings. They sought his life before; but from time to time they were restrained, and Christ escaped out of their hands, and this reason is given for it, that his time was not yet come. But now they were suffered to work their will upon him, he was in a great degree delivered up to the malice and cruelty of both wicked men and devils. And therefore when Christ's enemies came to apprehend him, he says to them, Luke 22:53, "When I was daily with you in the temple ye stretched forth no hand against me: but this is your hour, and the power of darkness."

And yet it was principally by means of those sufferings that he conquered and overthrew his enemies. Christ never so effectually bruised Satan's head, as when Satan bruised his heel. The weapon with which Christ warred against the devil, and obtained a most complete victory and glorious triumph over him, was the cross, the instrument and weapon with which he thought he had overthrown Christ, and brought on him shameful destruction. Col. 2:14,15: "Blotting out the handwriting of ordinances, nailing it to his cross: and having spoiled principalities and powers, he made a show of them openly, triumphing over them in it." In his last sufferings, Christ sapped the very foundations of Satan's kingdom, he conquered his enemies in their own territories, and beat them with their own weapons, as David cut off Goliath's head with his own sword. The devil had, as it were, swallowed up Christ, as the whale did Jonah, but it was deadly poison to him, he gave him a mortal wound in his own bowels. He was soon sick of his morsel, and was forced to do by him as the whale did by Jonah. To this day he is heart-sick of what he then swallowed as his prey. In those sufferings of Christ was laid the foundation of all that glorious victory he has already obtained over Satan, in the overthrow of his heathenish kingdom in the Roman empire, and all the success the gospel has had since; and also of all his future and still more glorious victory that is to be obtained in the earth. Thus Samson's riddle is most eminently fulfilled, Judges 14:14. "Out of the eater came forth meat, and out of the strong came forth sweetness." And thus the true [actual] Samson does more towards the destruction of his enemies at his death than in his life. In yielding up himself to death, he pulls down the temple of Dagon,* and destroys many thousands of his enemies, even while they are making themselves sport in his sufferings. And so he whose type was the ark, pulls down Dagon, and breaks off his head and hands in his own temple, even while he is brought in there as Dagon's captive. (1 Samuel 5:1–4.)

Thus Christ appeared at the same time, and in the same act, as both a lion and a lamb. He appeared as a lamb in the hands of his cruel enemies;

*Dagon—the half-fish, half-man, god of the ancient Philistines.

as a lamb in the paws, and between the devouring jaws, of a roaring lion; yea, he was a lamb actually slain by this lion: and yet at the same time, as the Lion of the tribe of Judah, he conquers and triumphs over Satan; destroying his own destroyer; as Samson did the lion that roared upon him, when he rent him as he would a kid. And in nothing has Christ appeared so much as a lion, in glorious strength destroying his enemies, as when he was brought as a lamb to the slaughter. In his greatest weakness he was most strong; and when he suffered most from his enemies, he brought the greatest confusion on his enemies.

Thus this admirable conjunction of diverse excellencies was manifest in Christ, in his offering up himself to God in his last sufferings.

4. *It is still manifest in his acts, in his present state of exaltation in heaven.* Indeed, in his exalted state, he most eminently appears in manifestation of those excellencies, on the account of which he is compared to a lion; but still he appears as a lamb; Rev. 14:1. "And I looked, and lo, a Lamb stood on mount Zion"; as in his state of humiliation he chiefly appeared as a lamb, and yet did not appear without manifestation of his divine majesty and power, as the Lion of the tribe of Judah. Though Christ be now at the right-hand of God, exalted as King of heaven, and Lord of the universe; yet as he still is in the human nature, he still excels in humility. Though the man Christ Jesus be the highest of all creatures in heaven, yet he as much excels them all in humility as he doth in glory and dignity, for none sees so much of the distance between God and him as he does. And though he now appears in such glorious majesty and dominion in heaven, yet he appears as a lamb in his condescending, mild, and sweet treatment of his saints there, for he is a Lamb still, even amidst the throne of his exaltation, and he that is the Shepherd of the whole flock is himself a Lamb, and goes before them in heaven as such. Rev. 7:17:

> For the Lamb, which is in the midst of the throne, shall feed them, and shall lead them unto living fountains of waters, and God shall wipe away all tears from their eyes.

Though in heaven every knee bows to him, and though the angels fall down before him adoring him, yet he treats his saints with infinite condescension, mildness, and endearment. And in his acts towards the saints on earth, he still appears as a lamb, manifesting exceeding love and tenderness in his intercession for them, as one that has had experience of affliction and temptation. He has not forgot what these things are, nor has he forgot how to pity those that are subject to them. And he still manifests his lamb-like excellencies, in his dealings with his saints on earth, in admirable forbearance, love, gentleness, and compassion. Behold him instructing, supplying, supporting, and comforting them; often coming to them, and manifesting himself to them by his Spirit, that he may sup with them, and they with him. Behold him admitting them to sweet communion, enabling them with boldness and confidence to come to him, and solacing their hearts. And in heaven Christ still appears, as it were, with the marks of his wounds upon him, and so appears as a Lamb as it had been slain, as he was represented in vision to St. John, in the text, when he appeared to open the book sealed with seven seals, which is part of the glory of his exaltation.

5. *And lastly, this admirable conjunction of excellencies will be manifest in Christ's acts at the last judgment.*

He then, above all other times, will appear as the Lion of the tribe of Judah in infinite greatness and majesty, when he shall come in the glory of his Father, with all the holy angels, and the earth shall tremble before him, and the hills shall melt. This is he (Rev. 20:11): "that shall sit on a great white throne, before whose face the earth and heaven shall flee away." He will then appear in the most dreadful and amazing manner to the wicked. The devils tremble at the thought of that appearance, and when it shall be, the kings, and the great men, and the rich men, and the chief captains. and the mighty men, and every bond-man and every free-man, shall hide themselves in the dens, and in the rocks of the mountains, and shall cry to the mountains and rocks to fall on them, to hide them from the face and wrath of the Lamb. And none can declare or conceive of the amazing manifestations of wrath in which he will then appear towards these, or the trembling and astonishment the shrieking and gnashing of teeth, with which they shall stand before his judgment-seat, and receive the terrible sentence of his wrath.

And yet he will at the same time appear as a Lamb to his saints; he will receive them as friends and brethren, treating them with infinite mildness and love. There shall be nothing in him terrible to them, but towards them he will clothe himself wholly with sweetness and endearment. The church shall be then admitted to him as his bride; that shall be her wedding-day. The saints shall all be sweetly invited to come with him to inherit the kingdom, and reign in it with him to all eternity.

III. I would now show how the aforesaid teaching is of benefit to us, in that it gives us insight into the names of Christ in Scripture, it encourages us to accept him as our Savior, it encourages us to accept him as our Friend.

1. *From this doctrine we may learn one reason why Christ is called by such a variety of names, and held forth under such a variety of representations, in Scripture.* It is the better to signify and exhibit to us that variety of excellencies that meet together and are conjoined in him. Many appellations are mentioned together in one verse, Isaiah 9:6:

> For unto us a Child is born, unto us a Son is given, and the government shall be upon his shoulder: and his name shall be called Wonderful, Counselor, the mighty God, the everlasting Father, the Prince of Peace.

It shows a wonderful conjunction of excellencies, that the same person should be a Son, born and given, and yet be the everlasting Father, without beginning or end, that he should be a Child, and yet be he whose name is Counselor, and the mighty God; and well may his name, in whom such things are conjoined, be called wonderful.

By reason of the same wonderful conjunction, Christ is represented by a great variety of sensible things, that are on some account excellent. Thus in some places he is called a Sun, as Mal. 4:2, in others a Star, Numb. 24:17. And he is especially represented by the Morning star, as being that which excels all other stars in brightness, and is the forerunner of the day, Rev. 22:16. And, as in our text, he is compared to a lion in one verse, and a lamb in the next, so sometimes he is compared to a roe or young hart, another creature most diverse from a lion. So in some places he is called a rock, in others he is compared to a pearl. In some places he is called a man of war, and the Captain of our Salvation, in other places he is represented as a bridegroom. In the second chapter of Canticles, the first verse, he is compared to a rose and a lily, that are sweet and beautiful flowers; in the next verse but one, he is compared to a tree bearing sweet fruit. In Isaiah 53:2 he is called a Root out of a dry ground; but elsewhere, instead of that, he is called the Tree of Life, that grows (not in a dry or barren ground, but) "in the midst of the paradise of God." (Rev. 2:7.)

2. *Let the consideration of this wonderful meeting of diverse excellencies in Christ induce you to accept of him, and close with him as your Savior.* As all manner of excellencies meet in him, so there are concurring in him all manner of arguments and motives, to move you to choose him for your Savior, and everything that tends to encourage poor sinners to come and put their trust

in him: his fullness and all-sufficiency as a Savior gloriously appear in that variety of excellencies that has been spoken of.

Fallen man is in a state of exceeding great misery, and is helpless in it; he is a poor weak creature, like an infant cast out in its blood in the day that it is born. But Christ is the lion of the tribe of Judah; he is strong, though we are weak; he hath prevailed to do that for us which no creature else could do. Fallen man is a mean despicable creature, a contemptible worm; but Christ, who has undertaken for us, is infinitely honorable and worthy. Fallen man is polluted, but Christ is infinitely holy; fallen man is hateful, but Christ is infinitely lovely; fallen man is the object of God's indignation, but Christ is infinitely dear to him. We have dreadfully provoked God, but Christ has performed that righteousness which is infinitely precious in God's eyes.

And here is not only infinite strength and infinite worthiness, but infinite condescension, and love and mercy, as great as power and dignity. If you are a poor, distressed sinner, whose heart is ready to sink for fear that God never will have mercy on you, you need not be afraid to go to Christ, for fear that he is either unable or unwilling to help you. Here is a strong foundation, and an inexhaustible treasure, to answer the necessities of your poor soul, and here is infinite grace and gentleness to invite and embolden a poor, unworthy, fearful soul to come to it. If Christ accepts of you, you need not fear but that you will be safe, for he is a strong Lion for your defense. And if you come, you need not fear but that you shall be accepted; for he is like a Lamb to all that come to him, and receives then with infinite grace and tenderness. It is true he has awful majesty, he is the great God, and infinitely high above you; but there is this to encourage and embolden the poor sinner, that Christ is man as well as God; he is a creature, as well as the Creator, and he is the most humble and lowly in heart of any creature in heaven or earth. This may well make the poor unworthy creature bold in coming to him. You need not hesitate one moment; but may run to him, and cast yourself upon him. You will certainly be graciously and meekly received by him. Though he is a lion, he will only be a lion to your enemies, but he will be a lamb to you. It could not have been conceived, had it not been so in the person of Christ, that there could have been so much in any Savior, that is inviting and tending to encourage sinners to trust in him. Whatever your circumstances are, you need not be afraid to come to such a Savior as this. Be you ever so wicked a creature, here is worthiness enough; be you ever so poor, and mean, and ignorant a creature, there is no danger of being despised, for though he be so much greater than you, he is also immensely more humble than you. Anyone of you that is a father or mother, will not despise one of your own children that comes to you in distress: much less danger is there of Christ's despising you, if you in your heart come to him.

Here let me a little expostulate with the poor, burdened, distressed soul.

What are you afraid of, that you dare not venture your soul upon Christ? Are you afraid that he cannot save you, that he is not strong enough to conquer the enemies of your soul? But how can you desire one stronger than "the almighty God"? as Christ is called, Isa. 9:6. Is there need of greater than infinite strength? Are you afraid that he will not be willing to stoop so low as to take any gracious notice of you? But then, look on him, as he stood in the ring of soldiers, exposing his blessed face to be buffeted and spit upon by them! Behold him bound with his back uncovered to those that smote him! And behold him hanging on the cross! Do you think that he that had condescension enough to stoop to these things, and that for his crucifiers, will be unwilling to accept of you, if you come to him? Or, are you afraid that if he does accept you, that God the Father will not accept of him for you? But consider, will God reject his own Son, in whom his infinite delight is, and has been, from all eternity, and who is so united to him, that if he should reject him he would reject himself?

What is there that you can desire should be in a Savior, that is not in Christ? Or, wherein should you desire a Savior should be otherwise than Christ is? What excellency is there wanting? What is there that is great or good; what is there that is venerable or winning; what is there that is adorable or endearing; or, what can you think of that would be encouraging, which is not to be found in the person of Christ? Would you have your Savior to be great and honorable, because you are not willing to be beholden to a mean person? And, is not Christ a person honorable enough to be worthy that you should be dependent on him? Is he not a person high enough to be appointed to so honorable a work as your salvation? Would you not only have a Savior of high degree, but would you have him, notwithstanding his exaltation and dignity, to be made also of low degree, that he might have experience of afflictions and trials, that he might learn by the things that he has suffered, to pity them that suffer and are tempted? And has not Christ been made low enough for you? and has he not suffered enough? Would you not only have him possess experience of the afflictions you now suffer, but also of that amazing wrath that you fear hereafter, that he may know how to pity those that are in danger, and afraid of it? This Christ has had experience of, which experience gave him a greater sense of it, a thousand times, than you have, or any man living has. Would you have your Savior to be one who is near to God, that so his mediation might be prevalent with him? And can you desire him to be nearer to God than Christ is, who is his only-begotten Son, of the same essence with the Father? And would you not only have him near to God, but also near to you, that you may have free access to him? And would you have him nearer to you than to be in the same nature, united to you by a spiritual union, so close as to be fitly represented by the union of the wife to the husband, of the branch to the vine, of the member to the head; yea, so as to be one spirit? For so he will be united to you, if you accept of him. Would you have a Savior that has given some great and extraordinary testimony of mercy and love to sinners, by something that he has done, as well as by what he says? And can you think or conceive of greater things than Christ has done? Was it not a great thing for him, who was God, to take upon him human nature: to be not only God, but man thenceforward to all eternity? But would you look upon suffering for sinners to be a yet greater testimony of love to sinners, than merely doing, though it be ever so extraordinary a thing that he has done? And would you desire that a Savior should suffer more than Christ has suffered for sinners? What is there wanting, or what would you add if you could, to make him more fit to be your Savior?

But further, to induce you to accept of Christ as your Savior, consider two things particularly.

[Consider] how much Christ appears as the Lamb of God in his invitations to you to come to him and trust in him. With what sweet grace and kindness does he, from time to time, call and invite you, as Prov. 8:4: "Unto you, O men, I call, and my voice is to the sons of men." And Isaiah 55:1–3: "Ho, every one that thirsteth, come ye to the waters, and he that hath no money, come ye, buy and eat yea come, buy wine and milk without money, and without price." How gracious is he here in inviting everyone that thirsts, and in so repeating his invitation over and over, "Come ye to the waters, come, buy and eat—yea come!" Mark the excellency of that entertainment which he invites you to accept of, "Come, buy wine and milk!" Your poverty, having nothing to pay for it, shall be no objection, "Come, he that hath no money, come without money, and without price!" What gracious arguments and expostulations he uses with you!

> Wherefore do ye spend money for that which is not bread? and your labor for that which satisfieth not? Hearken diligently unto me, and eat ye that which is good, and let your soul delight itself in fatness.

As much as to say:

> It is altogether needless for you to continue laboring and toiling for that which can never serve your turn, seeking rest in the world, and in your own righteousness—I have made abundant provision for you, of that which is really good, and will fully satisfy your desires, and answer your end, and I stand ready to accept of you: you need not be afraid. If you will come to me, I will engage to see all your wants supplied, and you made a happy creature.

As he promises in the third verse, "Incline your ear, and come unto me: hear, and your soul shall live, and I will make an everlasting covenant with you, even the sure mercies of David." And so Prov. 9 at the beginning, how gracious and sweet is the invitation there! "Whoso is simple, let him turn in hither"; let you be never so poor, ignorant, and blind a creature, you shall be welcome. And in the following words Christ sets forth the provision that he has made for you, "Come, eat of my bread, and drink of the wine which I have mingled."

You are in a poor famishing state, and have nothing wherewith to feed your perishing soul; you have been seeking something, but yet remain destitute. Hearken, how Christ calls you to eat of his bread, and to drink of the wine that he hath mingled! And how much like a lamb does Christ appear in Matt. 9:28 30:

> Come unto me, all ye that labor and are heavy laden, and I will give you rest. Take my yoke upon you, and learn of me, for I am meek and lowly in heart, and ye shall find rest to your souls. For my yoke is easy, and my burden is light.

O thou poor distressed soul! whoever thou art, consider that Christ mentions thy very case when he calls to them who labor and are heavy laden! How he repeatedly promises you rest if you come to him! In the 28th verse he says, "I will give you rest." And in the 29th verse, "Ye shall find rest to your souls." This is what you want. This is the thing you have been so long in vain seeking after. O how sweet would rest be to you, if you could but obtain it! Come to Christ, and you shall obtain it.

And hear how Christ, to encourage you, represents himself as a lamb! He tells you, that he is meek and lowly in heart, and are you afraid to come to such a one! And again, Rev. 3:20, "Behold, I stand at the door and knock: if any man hear my voice, and open the door, I will come in to him, and I will sup with him and he with me." Christ condescends not only to call you to him, but he comes to you; he comes to your door, and there knocks. He might send an officer and seize you as a rebel and vile malefactor, but instead of that, he comes and knocks at your door, and seeks that you would receive him into your house, as your Friend and Savior. And he not only knocks at your door, but he stands there waiting, while you are backward and unwilling. And not only so, but he makes promises what he will do for you, if you will admit him, what privileges he will admit you to; he will sup with you, and you with him. And again, Rev. 22:16,17:

> I am the root and the offspring of David, and the bright and morning star. And the Spirit and the bride say, "Come." And let him that heareth, say, "Come." And let him that is athirst come. And whosoever will let him take of the water of life freely.

How does Christ here graciously set before you his own winning attractive excellency! And how does he condescend to declare to you not only his own invitation, but the invitation of the Spirit and the bride, if by any means he might encourage you to come! And how does he invite every one that will, that they may "take of the water of life freely," that they may take it as a free gift, however precious it be, and though it be the Water of life.

If you do come to Christ, he will appear as a Lion, in his glorious power and dominion, to defend you. All those excellencies of his, in which he appears as a lion, shall be yours, and shall be employed for you in your defense, for your safety, and to promote your glory, he will be as a lion to fight against your enemies. He that touches you, or offends you, will provoke his wrath, as he that stirs up a lion. Unless your enemies can conquer this Lion, they shall not be able to destroy or hurt you; unless they are stronger than he, they shall not be able to hinder your happiness. Isaiah 31:4:

> For thus hath the Lord spoken unto me, like as the lion and the young lion roaring on his prey, when a multitude of shepherds is called forth against him, he will not be afraid of their voice, nor abase himself for the noise of them; so shall the Lord of hosts come down to fight for mount Zion, and for the hill thereof.

3. *Let what has been said be improved to induce you to love the Lord Jesus Christ, and choose him for your friend and portion.* As there is such an admirable meeting of diverse excellencies in Christ, so there is everything in him to render him worthy of your love and choice, and to win and engage it. Whatsoever there is or can be desirable in a friend, is in Christ, and that to the highest degree that can be desired.

Would you choose for a friend a person of great dignity? It is a thing taking with men to have those for their friends who are much above them; because they look upon themselves honored by the friendship of such. Thus, how taking would it be with an inferior maid to be the object of the dear love of some great and excellent prince. But Christ is infinitely above you, and above all the princes of the earth; for he is the King of kings. So honorable a person as this offers himself to you, in the nearest and dearest friendship.

And would you choose to have a friend not only great but good? In Christ infinite greatness and infinite goodness meet together, and receive luster and glory one from another. His greatness is rendered lovely by his goodness. The greater anyone is without goodness, so much the greater evil; but when infinite goodness is joined with greatness, it renders it a glorious and adorable greatness. So, on the other hand, his infinite goodness receives luster from his greatness. He that is of great understanding and ability, and is withal of a good and excellent disposition, is deservedly more esteemed than a lower and lesser being with the same kind inclination and good will. Indeed goodness is excellent in whatever subject it be found; it is beauty and excellency itself, and renders all excellent that are possessed of it; and yet most excellent when joined with greatness. The very same excellent qualities of gold render the body in which they are inherent more precious, and of greater value, when joined with greater than when with lesser dimensions.

And how glorious is the sight, to see him who is the great Creator and supreme Lord of heaven and earth, full of condescension, tender pity and mercy, towards the mean and unworthy! His almighty power, and infinite majesty and self-sufficiency, render his exceeding love and grace the more surprising And how do his condescension and compassion endear his majesty, power, and dominion, and render those attributes pleasant, that would otherwise be only terrible! Would you not desire that your friend, though great and honorable, should be of such condescension and grace, and so to have the way opened to free access to him, that his exaltation above you might not hinder your free enjoyment of his friendship? And would you choose not only that the infinite greatness and majesty of your friend should be, as it were, mollified and sweetened with condescension and grace; but would you also desire to have your friend brought nearer to you? Would you choose a friend far above you, and yet as it were upon a level with you too? Though it be taking with men to have a near and dear friend of superior dignity, yet there is also an inclination in them to have their friend a sharer with them in circumstances. Thus is Christ. Though he be the great God, yet he has, as it were, brought himself down to be upon a level with you, so as to become man as you are, that he might not only be your Lord, but your brother, and that he might be the more fit to be a companion for such a worm of the dust. This is one end of Christ's taking upon him man's nature, that his people might be under advantages for a more familiar converse with him than the infinite distance of the divine nature would allow of. And upon this account the church longed for Christ's incarnation, Cant. 8:1. "O that thou wert my brother that sucked the breast of my mother! When I should find thee without, I would kiss thee, yea, I should not be despised." One design of God in the gospel is to bring us to make God the object of our undivided respect, that he may engross our regard every way, that whatever natural inclination there is in our souls, he may be the center of it; that God may be all in all. But there is an inclination in the creature, not only to the adoration of a Lord and Sovereign, but to complacence in someone as a friend, to love and delight in someone that may be conversed with as a companion. And virtue and holiness do not destroy or weaken this inclination of our nature. But so hath God contrived in the affair of our redemption, that a divine person may be the object even of this inclination of our nature. And in order hereto, such a one is come down to us, and has taken our nature, and is become one of us, and calls himself our friend, brother, and companion. Psalm 122:8: "For my brethren and companions' sake, will I now say, 'Peace be within thee.' "

But is it not enough in order to invite and encourage you to free access to a friend so great and high, that he is one of infinite condescending grace, and also has taken your own nature, and is become man? But would you, further to embolden and win you, have him a man of wonderful meekness and humility? Why, such a one is Christ! He is not only become man for you, but far the meekest and most humble of all men, the greatest instance of these sweet virtues that ever was, or will be. And besides these, he has all other human excellencies in the highest perfection. These, indeed, are no proper addition to his divine excellencies. Christ has no more excellency in his person, since his incarnation, than he had before; for divine excellency is infinite, and cannot be added to. Yet his human excellencies are additional manifestations of his glory and excellency to us, and are additional recommendations of him to our esteem and love, who are of finite comprehension. Though his human excellencies are but communications and reflections of his divine, and though this light, as reflected, falls infinitely short of the divine fountain of light in its immediate glory; yet the reflection shines not without its proper advantages, as presented to our view and affection. The glory of Christ in the qualifications of his human nature, appears to us in excellencies that are of our own kind, and are exercised in our own way and manner, and so, in some respect, are peculiarly fitted to invite our acquaintance and draw our affection. The glory of

Christ as it appears in his divinity, though far brighter, more dazzles our eyes, and exceeds the strength of our sight or our comprehension; but, as it shines in the human excellencies of Christ, it is brought more to a level with our conceptions, and suitableness to our nature and manner, yet retaining a semblance of the same divine beauty, and a savor of the same divine sweetness. But as both divine and human excellencies meet together in Christ, they set off and recommend each other to us. It tends to endear the divine majesty and holiness of Christ to us, that these are attributes of one in our nature, one of us, who is become our brother, and is the meekest and humblest of men. It encourages us to look upon these divine perfections, however high and great; since we have some near concern in and liberty freely to enjoy them. And on the other hand, how much more glorious and surprising do the meekness, the humility, obedience, resignation, and other human excellencies of Christ appear, when we consider that they are in so great a person, as the eternal Son of God, the Lord of heaven and earth!

By your choosing Christ for your friend and portion, you will obtain these two infinite benefits.

Christ will give himself to you, with all those various excellencies that meet in him, to your full and everlasting enjoyment. He will ever after treat you as his dear friend; and you shall ere long be where he is, and shall behold his glory, and dwell with him, in most free and intimate communion and enjoyment.

When the saints get to heaven, they shall not merely see Christ, and have to do with him as subjects and servants with a glorious and gracious Lord and Sovereign, but Christ will entertain them as friends and brethren. This we may learn from the manner of Christ's conversing with his disciples here on earth: though he was their Sovereign Lord, and did not refuse, but required, their supreme respect and adoration, yet he did not treat them as earthly sovereigns are wont to do their subjects. He did not keep them at an awful distance, but all along conversed with them with the most friendly familiarity, as a father amongst a company of children, yea, as with brethren. So he did with the twelve, and so he did with Mary, Martha, and Lazarus. He told his disciples, that he did not call them servants, but friends, and we read of one of them that leaned on his bosom: and doubtless he will not treat his disciples with less freedom and endearment in heaven. He will not keep them at a greater distance for his being in a state of exaltation; but he will rather take them into a state of exaltation with him. This will be the improvement Christ will make of his own glory, to make his beloved friends partakers with him, to glorify them in his glory, as he says to his

Father, John 17:22, 23. "And the glory which thou hast given me, have I given them, that they may be one, even as we are one I in them," etc. We are to consider, that though Christ is greatly exalted, yet he is exalted, not as a private person for himself only, but as his people's head; he is exalted in their name, and upon their account, as the first fruits, and as representing the whole harvest. He is not exalted that he may be at a greater distance from them, but that they may be exalted with him. The exaltation and honor of the head is not to make a greater distance between the head and the members, but the members have the same relation and union with the head they had before, and are honored with the head; and instead of the distance being greater, the union shall be nearer and more perfect. When believers get to heaven, Christ will conform them to himself, as he is set down in his Father's throne, so they shall sit down with him on his throne, and shall in their measure be made like him.

When Christ was going to heaven, he comforted his disciples with the thought, that after a while, he would come again and take them to himself, that they might be with him. And we are not to suppose that when the disciples got to heaven, they found him keeping a greater distance than he used to do. No, doubtless, be embraced them as friends, and welcomed them to his and their Father's house, and to his and their glory. They who had been his friends in this world, who had been together with him here, and had together partaken of sorrows and troubles, are now welcomed by him to rest, and to partake of glory with him. He took them and led them into his chambers, and showed them all his glory; as he prayed, John 17:24. "Father, I will that they also whom thou hast given me, be with me, that they may behold the glory which thou hast given me." And he led them to his living fountains of waters, and made them partake of his delights, as he prays John 17:13. "That my joy may be fulfilled in themselves," and set them down with him at his table in his kingdom, and made them partake with him of his dainties, according to his promise, Luke 22:30, and led them into his banqueting house, and made them to drink new wine with him in the kingdom of his heavenly Father, as he foretold them when he instituted the Lord's supper, Matt. 26:29.

Yea, the saints' conversation with Christ in heaven shall not only be as intimate, and their access to him as free, as of the disciples on earth, but in many respects much more so; for in heaven, that vital union shall be perfect, which is exceeding imperfect here. While the saints are in this world, there are great remains of sin and darkness to separate or disunite them from Christ, which shall then all be removed. This is not a time for that full acquaintance, and those glorious manifestations of love, which Christ designs for his people hereafter; which seems to be signified by his speech to Mary Magdalene, when ready to embrace him, when she met him after his resurrection; John 20:17. "Jesus saith unto her, 'Touch me not; for I am not yet ascended to my Father.' "

When the saints shall see Christ's glory and exaltation in heaven, it will indeed possess their hearts with the greater admiration and adoring respect, but it will not awe them into any separation, but will serve only to heighten their surprise and joy, when they find Christ condescending to admit them to such intimate access, and so freely and fully communicating himself to them. So that if we choose Christ for our friend and portion, we shall hereafter be so received to him, that there shall be nothing to hinder the fullest enjoyment of him, to the satisfying the utmost cravings of our souls. We may take our full swing at gratifying our spiritual appetite after these holy pleasures. Christ will then say, as in Cant. 5:1. "Eat, O friends, drink, yea, drink abundantly, O beloved." And this shall be our entertainment to all eternity! There shall never be any end of this happiness, or anything to interrupt our enjoyment of it, or in the least to molest us in it!

By your being united to Christ, you will have a more glorious union with and enjoyment of God the Father, than otherwise could be. For hereby the saints' relation to God becomes much nearer; they are the children of God in a higher manner than otherwise could be. For, being members of God's own Son, they are in a sort partakers of his relation to the Father: they are not only sons of God by regeneration, but by a kind of communion in the sonship of the eternal Son. This seems to be intended, Gal. 4:4–6:

> God sent forth his Son, made of a woman, made under the law, to redeem them that are under the law, that we might receive the adoption of sons. And because ye are sons, God hath sent forth the Spirit of his Son into your hearts, crying, "Abba, Father."

The church is the daughter of God not only as he hath begotten her by his word and Spirit but as she is the spouse of his eternal Son.

So we, being members of the Son, are partakers in our measure of the Father's love to the Son, and complacence in him. John 17:23: "I in them, and thou in me. Thou hast loved them as thou hast loved me." And ver. 26: "That the love wherewith thou hast loved me, may be in them." And chap. 16:27: "The Father himself loveth you, because ye have loved me, and have believed that I came out from God." So we shall, according to our capacities, be partakers of the Son's enjoyment of God, and have his joy fulfilled in ourselves, John 17:13. And by this means we shall come to an immensely higher, more intimate and full enjoyment of God, than otherwise could have been. For there is doubtless an infinite intimacy between the Father and the Son which is expressed by his being in the bosom of the Father. And saints being in him, shall, in their measure and manner, partake with him in it, and of the blessedness of it.

And thus is the affair of our redemption ordered, that thereby we are brought to an immensely more exalted kind of union with God, and enjoyment of him, both the Father and the Son, than otherwise could have been. For Christ being united to the human nature, we have advantage for a more free and full enjoyment of him, than we could have had if he had remained only in the divine nature. So again, we, being united to a divine person, as his members, can have a more intimate union and intercourse with God the Father, who is only in the divine nature, than otherwise could be. Christ, who is a divine person, by taking on him our nature, descends from the infinite distance and height above us, and is brought nigh to us; whereby we have advantage for the full enjoyment of him. And, on the other hand, we, by being in Christ a divine person, do as it were ascend up to God, through the infinite distance, and have hereby advantage for the full enjoyment of him also.

This was the design of Christ, that he, and his Father, and his people, might all be united in one. John 17:21–23:

> That they all may be one, as thou, Father, art in me, and I in thee—that they also may be one in us; that the world may believe that thou hast sent me. And the glory which thou hast given me, I have given them, that they may be one, even as we are one; I in them and thou in me, that they may be made perfect in one.

Christ has brought it to pass, that those whom the Father has given him should be brought into the household of God, that he and his Father, and his people, should be as one society, one family; that the church should be, as it were, admitted into the society of the blessed Trinity.

Jesus Christ the Same Yesterday, Today, and Forever

April 1738.

"Jesus Christ, the same yesterday, today, and forever."—Hebrews 13:8

The exhortation which the apostle gives the Christian Hebrews in the verse preceding this is to remember and follow the good instructions and examples of their ministers. "Remember them who have the rule over you, who have spoken unto you the Word of God; whose faith follow, considering the end of their conversation." The last part of this exhortation is to follow their faith. By following their faith, the apostle seems to intend adhering to the Christian faith and those wholesome doctrines which their pastors taught them, and not depart from them, as many in that day had done, to heretical tenets. And the enforcement of the doctrine is in these words, "Considering the end of their conversation, Jesus Christ, the same yesterday, today, and for ever." Christ is the end of their conversation, he is the end of their conversation in their office, the end of the doctrines which they taught, and the end of all their administrations, and all their labors in all their work. And as he was so, they ought to follow their faith, or cleave steadfastly to the doctrines they had taught them, and not depart to other doctrines. For Jesus Christ was the same, yesterday, today, and forever.

If they still professed to be Christians or the followers of Jesus Christ, then they should still cleave to the same doctrines that they were taught in their first conversion. They should still follow the faith of them who had first indoctrinated them in Christianity. For Jesus Christ was the same now that he was then, and therefore, Christianity was obviously the same thing. It was not one thing now and another when they were first converted, or even like to any other thing than it always had been. Surely therefore, when Christ and Christianity were thus unchangeable, he would therefore have them not fickle and changeable in their faith, not depart from their former faith, nor be carried about with diverse and strange doctrines, as it follows in the next verse.

When it is said that Christ is the same yesterday, today, and forever, by *yesterday* is meant *all time past;* by *today, the time present;* and by *forever, all that is future,* from the present time to eternity.

Doctrine.

Jesus Christ is the same now that he ever has been and ever will be. Christ is thus unchangeable in two respects.

I. [He is unchangeable] in his divine nature.

As Christ is one of the persons of the Trinity, he is God, and so has the divine nature, or the Godhead dwelling in him, and all the divine attributes belong to him, of which immutability or unchangeableness is one. Christ in his human nature was not absolutely unchangeable, though his human nature, by reason of its union with the divine, was not liable to those changes to which it was liable, [if he were] as a mere creature. As for instance, it was indestructible and imperishable. Having the divine nature to uphold it, it was not liable to fall and commit sin, as Adam and the fallen angels did, but yet the human nature of Christ, when he was upon earth, was subject to many changes. It had a beginning. It was conceived in the womb of the Virgin. It was in a state of infancy, and afterwards changed from that state to a state of manhood, and this was attended not only with a change on his body, by his increasing in stature, but also on his mind. For we read that he not only increased in stature but also in wisdom. (Luke 2:52.) And the human nature of Christ was subject to sorrowful changes, though not to sinful ones. He suffered hunger, and thirst, and cold. And at last he suffered dreadful changes by having his body tortured and destroyed, and his soul poured out unto death. And afterwards became subject to a glorious change at his resurrection and ascension. And that his human nature was not liable to sinful changes, as Adam's or the angels', was not owing to anything in his human nature, but to its relation to the divine nature which upheld it. But the divine nature of Christ is absolutely unchangeable, and not liable to the least alteration or variation in any respect. It is the same now as it was before the world was created. It was the same after Christ's incarnation as before, when Christ was born in a stable, and laid in a manger, and underwent many changes on earth, and at last suffered that dreadful agony in the garden, and suffered on the cross. It made no real alteration in the divine nature. And afterwards when Christ was glorified, and sat on the right hand of the Majesty of high, it made no alteration in his divine nature.

II. Christ is unchangeable in his office.

He is unchangeable as the Mediator and Savior of his church and people. That unchangeableness of Christ in his office of Mediator, appears in several things.

1. This office never ceases to give place to any other to come in his room [place]. Christ is the only Mediator between God and man that ever has been or ever shall be. He is an everlasting Savior. There have been typical mediators, many that have continued but a little while, and then have passed away, and others have come in their room. But the great *anti-type* continues forever. There have been prophets that have been raised up, and these have died, and others have succeeded them. Moses was not suffered to continue by reason of death. And the dispensation which he introduced was abolished to give place to another which Christ should introduce. Moses gives place to Christ, but Christ never gives place to any other.

John the Baptist was a great prophet. He was Christ's forerunner; like the morning star, the forerunner of the sun, he shone bright a little while, but his ministry by degrees ceased, and gave way to the ministry of Christ, as the morning star by little and little goes out as the sun rises. (John 3:30.) John the Baptist says, "He must increase, but I must decrease." But Christ's ministry never ceases.

So the ancient legal priests, they had but a changeable and short-lived priesthood. Aaron died, and his son Eleazar succeeded in his room. And so there were many priests, one after another. But Christ continues a priest forever. (Heb. 7:23, 24.) And they truly were many priests; and they were not suffered to continue by reason of death. But Christ, because he continueth ever, hath an unchangeable priesthood. These legal priests succeeded one another by inheritance. The father died and the son succeeded him, and then he died and *his* son succeeded him. But it is observed that Christ, in his priesthood, "is without father and without mother, without descent." He had no ancestor that went before him in his priesthood, or any posterity that should succeed him in it. It that respect, Melchizedek is a type of Christ, of whom the Scriptures give us an account, that he was a priest, but seems not to have been a priest by inheritance, as the sons of Aaron were: as Heb. 7:3,

> without father, and without mother, and without descent, having neither beginning of days, nor end of life, but made like unto the Son of God, abideth a priest continually.

And therefore it is said of Christ, Psa. 110:4, "The Lord hath sworn and will not repent. Thou art a priest forever after the order of Melchizedek."

Those things that appertain to Christ's priesthood are everlasting. The tabernacle at which the priests of old officiated was a tabernacle that men pitched, and therefore a tabernacle that was taken down. It was the holy of holies of old. But Christ is a minister of the true tabernacle and the true sanctuary, which the Lord has built, and not man. (Heb. 8:2.) The holy of holies he entered into was *heaven.* He is priest in a tabernacle which shall never be taken down, and in a temple that shall never be demolished. So the altar on which he offers incense, the priestly garments or robes in which he officiates, are not of a corruptible nature.

And so Christ is everlasting with reference to his kingly office. David and Solomon were great kings, and eminent types of Christ. But death put an end of their kingdom and greatness. Earthly monarchies that ever have been, those that have ruled over the bigger part of the known world, as particularly the Grecian and Roman monarchies, they have come to an end, but Christ's is an everlasting Kingdom, his throne is forever and ever. Heb. 1:8, "Thy throne, O God, is forever and ever; a scepter righteousness is the scepter of thy kingdom." Though all other kingdoms shall be demolished, Christ's kingdom shall stand forever. (Dan. 7:13, 14.)

2. Christ is at all times equally sufficient for the office he has undertaken. He undertook the office from eternity, and he was sufficient for it from eternity. He has been in the exercise of his office from the fall of man, and remains equally sufficient throughout all ages. His power and his wisdom, his love, his excellency, and worthiness is at all times equally sufficient for the salvation of sinners, and for the upholding and glorifying of believers. He is forever able to save, because he lives forever. His life is an endless and unchangeable life. He is made not after the law of a carnal commandment, but after the power of an endless life. (Heb. 7:16.) He is at all times equally accepted as a Mediator in the sight of the Father, who is ever well pleased in him. He is always equally worthy and lovely in his eyes. He is daily his delight, rejoicing always before him. The sacrifice that he has offered, and the righteousness that he has performed, is at all times equally sufficient. His blood is as sufficient to cleanse away sin now, as when it was warm from his wounds.

3. *He is now, and ever will be, the same that he ever has been in the disposition and will which he exercises in his office.* He is not changeable in his disposition, as men are that are called to any office or business, which causes them to appear and act very differently in their offices at some times, from what they do at others. But Jesus Christ is, in this respect, the same yesterday, today, and forever. He is ever disposed to execute his office in a holy manner. He ever has been, still is, and ever will be disposed to execute it so as to glorify his Father, to discountenance sin, and to encourage holiness. He ever exercised the same grace and mercy in his office. He undertook the office of a Mediator from eternity with delight. He then delighted in the thoughts of saving sinners, and he still delights in it. He never has altered from the disposition to accomplish it.

When man actually fell and became a rebel and an enemy, an enemy to his Father and himself; still it was his delight to do the part of a Mediator for him. And when he came into the world, and came to his last agony, when the bitter cup that he was to drink was set before him, and he had an extraordinary view of it, so that the sight of it made "his soul exceeding sorrowful even unto death," and caused him to "sweat as it were great drops of blood;" still he retained his disposition to do the part of a Mediator for sinners, and delighted in the thoughts of it. So, even when he was enduring the cross, the salvation of sinners was a joy set before him, Heb. 12:2. And he never alters from his readiness to receive and embrace all that do in faith come to him. He is always equally willing to receive such. His love is unchangeable. He loved from eternity. (Jer. 31:3.) He loved with an everlasting love; and it will be to eternity. John 13:1, "Having loved his own, he loved them unto the end."

4. *Christ is the same yesterday, today, and forever, as the end which he aims at in his office.* His supreme end in it is the glory of God, as particularly in

vindicating the honor of his majesty, justice, and holiness, and the honor of his holy law. For this end did he undertake to stand as a Mediator between God and man, and to suffer for men, viz. that the honor of God's justice, majesty, and law may be vindicated in his sufferings. And he also undertook the office to glorify the free grace of God. And his special end in his undertaking was the salvation and happiness of the elect. These two ends he has in his eye, in all parts of the work of his office. And these two ends he unchangeably aims at. These he sought on entering into covenant with the Father from eternity. These he has sought from the beginning of the world to this time, and these he ever will seek. He does not sometimes pursue one end, and then alter his mind and pursue another. But he ever pursues the same ends.

5. Christ ever acts by the same rules in the execution of his mediatorial office. The rules that Christ acts by, in the execution of his office, are contained in a twofold covenant.

First, the covenant of redemption, or the eternal covenant that was between the Father and the Son, wherein Christ undertook to stand as Mediator with fallen man, and was appointed thereto of the Father. In that covenant, all things concerning Christ's execution of his mediatorial office were agreed between Christ and his Father, and established by them. And this covenant or eternal agreement is the highest rule that Christ acts by in his office. And it is a rule that he never in the least departs from. He never does anything, more or less, than is contained in that eternal covenant. Christ does the work that God gave him to do in that covenant, and no other. He saves those, and those only, that the Father gave him in that covenant to save. And he brings them to such a degree of happiness as was therein agreed. To this rule, Christ is unchangeable in his regard. It stands good with Christ in every article of it, yesterday, today, and forever.

Secondly, another covenant that Christ has regard to in the execution of his mediatorial office is that covenant of grace which God established with man. Though indeed this be less properly the rule by which Christ acts as Mediator than the covenant of redemption, yet it may be called a rule. God does, as it were, make his promises which he makes to his creatures, his rule to act by: *i.e.* all his actions are in an exact conformity to his promises, and he never departs in the least degree from them, as is the case with men with regard to what they make the rule of their actions. Yet it is not a rule to God in the same sense as a rule is to a created agent, which must be considered as something antecedent to the purposes of the agent, and that by which his purposes are regulated. But God's promises are consequent on his purposes, and are no other than the expressions of them. And the covenant of grace is not essentially different from the covenant of redemption. It is but an expression of it. It is only that covenant of redemption partly revealed to mankind for their encouragement, faith, and comfort. And therefore the fact that Christ never departs from the covenant of redemption, infers that he will never depart from the covenant of grace. For all that was promised to men in the covenant of grace was agreed on between the Father and the Son in the covenant of redemption. However, there is one thing wherein Christ's unchangeableness in his office appears: that he never departs from the promises that he has made to man. There is the same covenant of grace in all ages of the world. The covenant is not essentially different now from what it was under the Old Testament, and even before the flood. And it always will remain the same. It is therefore called an everlasting covenant, Isa. 55:3.

And as Christ does not alter his covenant, so he unchangeably fulfills it. He never departs in the least jot or tittle. Though he has given exceedingly great and precious promises to those that believe in him, he ever fulfills them all. Heaven and earth shall sooner pass away, than one jot or one tittle of his promises shall fail, till all be fulfilled. It is especially on account of his unchangeableness with respect to his promises, that he styles himself, "*I am that I am,*" and is called "Jehovah," Exo. 3:14, and 6:3. Christ revealed himself to the children of Israel, in their Egyptian bondage, by this name, to encourage the people that he would fulfill his promises made to Abraham, Isaac, and Jacob.

6. *He is in many respects unchangeable in the acts which he exercises in his office.* He is unchangeable in his acceptance of those that believe in him, and never will reject them. And he is unchangeable in his complacency and delight in them. He is unchangeable in his intercession for his church and people. He ever lives to make intercession. (Heb. 7:25.) His intercession before God in heaven is a continual intercession. It is a constant presentation of his will before the Father for the salvation and happiness of those that are his in the virtue of his blood. And as Christ is unchangeable in his intercession, so he is unchangeable in upholding and preserving those that are his, and ordering all things for their good, until they are brought to his heavenly glory. He is constant and unchangeable in taking care of them in all respects, and will hereafter receive them to a constant and unchangeable enjoyment of himself.

Application

I. We learn from the truth taught in the text, how fit Christ was to be appointed as the surety of fallen man.

Adam, the first surety of mankind, failed in his work, because he was a mere creature, and so a mutable being. Though he had so great a trust committed to him, as the care of the eternal welfare of all his posterity, yet, not being unchangeable, he failed, and transgressed God's holy covenant. He was led aside, and drawn away by the subtle temptation of the devil. He, being a changeable being, his subtle adversary found means to turn him aside, and so he fell, and all his posterity fell with him. It appeared, therefore, that we stood in need of a surety that was unchangeable, and could not fail in his work. Christ, whom God appointed to this work, to be to us a second Adam, is such an one that is the same yesterday, today, and forever, and therefore was not liable to fail in his undertaking. He was sufficient to be depended on as one that would certainly stand all trials, and go through all difficulties, until he had finished the work that he had undertaken, and actually wrought out eternal redemption for us.

II. This truth may be well applied to the awakening of those who profess to be Christians, and this on several accounts.

You may be hence assured that Christ will fulfill his threatenings that he has denounced against unbelievers. There are many awful threatenings which Christ has denounced against wicked men. Christ has threatened woe to this wicked world, Mat. 18:7, and has declared, concerning all that do not believe, that they shall be damned. This is that which Christ gave in charge to his disciples before his ascension, when he sent them forth to preach and teach all nations. Mark 16:15, 16,

> Go ye into all the world, and preach the gospel to every creature. He that believeth shall be saved, and he that believeth not shall be damned.

So Christ declares that every tree that bringeth not forth good fruit, shall be hewn down, and cast into the fire. (Mat. 7:18.)

And he has especially threatened an awful punishment to gospel sinners. He has declared that every branch in him that beareth not fruit shall be cut off, and cast forth, and gathered up and burnt. And that, however wicked men and false Christians may dwell among the godly, as tares grow among wheat, yet when the harvest comes, and the wheat is gathered into the barn, the tares shall be gathered into bundles and burnt. (Mat. 13:30.) And in the explication of the parable, he says that, at the day of judgment,

> the Son of man shall send forth his angels, and they shall gather out of his kingdom all things that offend, and them that do iniquity, and shall cast them into a furnace of fire, where shall be wailing and gnashing of teeth (verse 41, 42.)

So he declares in Mat. 7:22–23, concerning those visible Christians that say to him, "Lord, Lord," and that do not do the will of his Father which is in heaven, that he will hereafter profess unto them, that he never knew them, and that he will say unto them, "Depart from me, ye that work iniquity;" and that those that build their house on the sand shall fall, and that great shall be their fall; and that such as these shall see many coming from the east, and from the west, and from the north, and from the south, and sitting down with Abraham, and Isaac, and Jacob, in the kingdom of God, and themselves thrust out.

And he teaches in his parables that unprofitable servants, and those that as professing Christians come to the gospel feast without the wedding garment, shall be bound hand and foot and cast into outer darkness, where [there] shall be weeping and gnashing of teeth. He often denounces woe on hypocrites, and threatens concerning such as begin a life of religion and do not finish, and are not thorough and persevering in it, that they shall come to shame. That those who are foolish virgins, that take their lamps and take no oil with them, shall at last be shut from the marriage when others enter in with the bridegroom, and that when they come to the door, they shall find it shut, and shall cry, "Lord, Lord, open to us," in vain.

And that at the day of judgment, Christ shall separate the righteous from the wicked, as a shepherd divideth his sheep from the goats, setting the righteous on the right hand, and the wicked on the left. And that he shall say to the wicked, "Depart, accursed, into everlasting fire, prepared for the devil and his angels." And that the wicked shall go away into everlasting punishment. And particularly he has threatened concerning them that have not a spirit of self-denial, that do not cut off a right hand or a right foot, nor pluck out a right eye, that they shall go with two hands, or two feet, or two eyes, into Hell-fire, into the fire that never shall be quenched, where the worm dieth not, and the fire is not quenched. And that those that have not a spirit to sell all for his sake, and that do not in comparison of him hate father, and mother, and wife, and every earthly relative and earthly possession, shall not be acknowledged of him as his disciples.

And concerning those that are ashamed of religion before men, that of them, will he be ashamed before his Father and before the angels. And concerning those that are of a revengeful spirit, and not of a spirit of forgiveness, that they shall not be forgiven: and concerning all that are of a malicious spirit, and not of a spirit of Christian love and meekness, that are of an angry, wrathful, and scornful disposition, that say to their brother, "Raca," or "Thou fool;" that they shall be in danger of everlasting punishment proportioned to the heinousness of their crimes. And concerning worldly-minded men, he has declared that 'tis impossible for those that trust in riches to enter into the kingdom of God. Concerning such he has said, "Woe unto you that are rich, for ye have received your consolation; and woe unto you that are full, for ye shall hunger."

And concerning such as are addicted to carnal mirth and jollity, he says, "Woe unto you that laugh now, for ye shall mourn and weep." And he has abundantly declared concerning gospel sinners, that their punishment shall be far more dreadful than that of the worst of the heathen. That it shall be more tolerable even for Sodom and Gomorrah in the day of judgment, than for them. And he has declared that those, that are once cast into Hell, shall in no wise come out thence, until they have paid the uttermost farthing.

Such things as these did Christ threaten against the ungodly when he was here upon earth. And by the doctrine of the text you learn that he now is and ever will be the same that he was then. He has not at all altered, no, nor ever will. But these dreadful things that he has threatened, he will surely fulfill. Christ was no more disposed to threaten, than to fulfill his threatenings. Christ is as holy, and his nature and will is as ever to sin now as ever it was. And he is as strictly [strict] just now as he was then.

Therefore, let no Christless person flatter himself, that, continuing such, he shall by any means escape punishment. Christ's threatenings are the threatenings of one, that is the same yesterday, today, and forever. And what he has threatened with his mouth he will fulfill with his hands. When Christ appears at the day of judgment, and you shall stand at his bar to be judged, you will find him, in judging, just what he was, and just what you find him in your Bibles, in threatening.

III. The truth in the text may be applied by way of *reproof*.

1. *To those that have been heretofore under awakenings, but have now become senseless and careless.* This doctrine shows your folly. You act as if Christ were altered, as though he were not now so dreadful a Judge, and

his displeasure not so much to be feared, as heretofore. Time was when you were afraid of the displeasure and wrath of Christ. You were afraid of the dreadful sentence from his mouth, "Depart, ye cursed, into everlasting fire." And why is it so much otherwise with you now? Is not the wrath of this Judge as much to be dreaded now, as ever it was? Time was, when those threatenings, that Christ has denounced against sinners, were terrible things to you. And why do you make so light of them now? Is this your great Judge grown weaker than he was, and less able to fulfill his threatenings? Are you less in his hands than you were, or do you imagine that Christ is become more reconciled to sin, and has not such a disposition to execute vengeance for it as he had?

Time was, that you seemed to feel yourself to be in lamentable circumstances that you had not an interest in Christ, and to have a great mind to get an interest in him. You sought it, and prayed to God daily for it, and took considerable pains, and went and asked others what you should do to obtain an interest in Christ. Why is it that you are so much more careless about it now? Is Christ altered? Is an interest in him less valuable, or less necessary, now, than it was then? Was acceptance with him worth earnestly seeking, and praying, and striving for then, and is it good for nothing now? Did you stand in great need of it then, and can you do well enough without it now?

Time was when you seemed to be much concerned about your having been guilty of so much sin against God and Christ, and, it may be, wept about it in your prayers. But now, you are not concerned about it. The thought of your having so often and so greatly offended him does not so much trouble you, but that you can be easy and quiet, and have your heart taken up about one vanity or another, without being very much disturbed with the thoughts of your sins. Then you used to be careful to avoid sin. You were watchful to avoid those things that were forbidden in God's holy word. You were careful that you did not sin by profaning the Sabbath, or by unsuitably spending the time in God's house, or by neglecting the duties of reading and prayer. You were careful of your behavior among men, lest you should transgress. If you suspected anything to be sinful then, you dared not do it.

But now there is no such care upon your spirit, there is no such watch maintained, you have no such guard upon you. But when you are tempted to do or omit anything, it is not a thought coming with weight upon your heart, "Is this sinful or not?" "Is this contrary to the mind and will of God, or not?" You do not dwell long on such kind of thoughts as these. You are grown very bold, and live in neglects and practices that are sinful, and that you have light enough to know to be so. [It is] just as if you thought that Christ's disposition with respect to sin was altered, and that he was less an enemy to sin now than he was then. Instead of being less an enemy to sin than you then thought he was, and instead of being a less dreadful Judge of ungodly men than you then imagined, or had a sense of in your heart, he is a thousand times *more so*. For then, when you were most awakened and convinced, you conceived but very little of what is in reality. You apprehended very imperfectly the enmity of Christ's nature against sin, and the dreadfulness of his wrath against the ungodly. It was but a little sense you had of it. His wrath is infinitely more dreadful than ever you have yet had any conception of.

And though Christ be unchangeable, yet you are not. You are changed for the worse since the time when you were awakened. Christ is equally an enemy of sin, and you are become more sinful than you then were. Christ's wrath is in itself equally dreadful as it then was. But you have far more reason to dread it than you had then, for you are in much greater danger of it. And, if you do not repent, [you] are much nearer to the execution of it. And not only so, but you are now exposed to much more of that wrath. Christ's wrath hung over your head then, and so it does now, but with this difference, that now much more of that wrath hangs over you than did then. You hung over the pit of Hell then, and so you do now. But with this difference, that you have ever since been kindling and enraging the flames of that fiery gulf over which you hang, so that they are vastly fiercer than they were then. And the moth of time has been nibbling at that slender thread ever since, and has much nearer gnawed it off than it had then. And your heart is far more hardened than it was. And the devil has faster hold of you, and the way to escape is more blocked up. And your case upon many accounts is inexpressibly more doleful, however much more careless and unconcerned you are about your own circumstances.

2. *This doctrine reproves all that have entered into the bonds of the Christian covenant, and have proved false to it.* If Christ be the same yesterday, today, and forever, and is always the same towards us in fulfilling as he is in promising, then surely we ought to be so towards him. If he never breaks covenant with his people, then they are greatly to be reproved who are false and treacherous in their dealings with him. Therefore this reproves a covenant people that depart from Christ, and break covenant with him, as we in this land have done, having greatly revolted and degenerated both from the

pure profession and religious practice of the first times of the country. Though Christ and his doctrine, and the religion that he taught, are always the same, yet this country has great multitudes in it that are driven to and fro by every wind of doctrine, and has now for a long time been exceedingly corrupted by the prevalency of many evil customs and practices.

And by this doctrine is every particular person reproved that does not take care to keep covenant with Christ. We are in general under the solemn bonds of our baptismal covenant. And that covenant that was sealed in our baptism, most of us have explicitly owned, and expressly and solemnly promised to walk in, in a way of obedience to all the commands of God, as long as we live. And have, time after time, in the most solemn manner, sealed this covenant anew, by taking the body and blood of Christ upon it at the Lord's supper. They bring dreadful guilt on themselves who are not careful to fulfill such vows. They that have solemnly vowed to obey Christ in all his commandments as long as they live, and have sealed these vows by eating and drinking at the Lord's Supper with far greater solemnity than if they sealed it with as many solemn oaths, yet live in ways of sin, live in the neglect of several commanded duties, and in the commission of forbidden sin, or at least do not make it the care of their lives strictly to keep Christ's commands—surely such persons render themselves very guilty.

3. *This doctrine reproves those that have been seemingly pious and have fallen away to ways of sin.* Who these persons are, their own consciences are better able to judge than those that are about them. There are many here present, that in times past have been seemingly pious—and let everyone inquire at the mouth of his own conscience whether his seeming piety holds on, [or] whether it be not come to an end. If you find reason, by a serious and strict examination, to conclude that you are one of them, consider how vile is your treatment of him who is the same yesterday, today, and forever, and who never is false to any to whom he once manifests his favor. How greatly does God complain of such short-lived religion in the Scriptures! Hos. 6:4:

> O Ephraim, what shall I do unto thee? O Judah, what shall I do unto thee? for your goodness is as a morning cloud, and as the early dew it goeth away.

Psa. 78:56–57:

> They tempted and provoked the most high God, and kept not his testimonies, but turned back and dealt unfaithfully like their fathers; they were turned aside like a deceitful bow.

4. Hereby the truly godly are greatly to be reproved for their declension [decline]. There are many such here, as I charitably hope, and many of them I fear have been guilty of great declension in religion. Formerly they were lively and animated in religion, now they are dull and indifferent. Formerly their hearts went up on high after God, but now after the world. They carried themselves for a while very exemplary, but have since behaved in such a manner as to wound religion. Why will you be guilty of such a departure from your Redeemer, who changes not with regard to you? His love he formerly manifested towards you, but it does not change. It has ever held up to the same height. His faithfulness never has failed to you. Why then does your love so languish towards him, and why are you so unfaithful to him? He keeps up the same care and watchfulness towards you, to preserve you, to provide for you, to defend you from your enemies—and why will you suffer your care and strictness to serve and please Christ, and honor him, to fail in any measure?

When you were first converted, your heart seemed to be wrapt up in love to Christ, and delight in him and his praises. You were then continually meditating on Christ and the things of Christ, and your meditations on him were sweet. And you were then much in speaking of those things, and you delighted to speak of them. And why is it so much otherwise with you now? Is Christ less excellent than he was then? Is he less worthy of your love?

5. This doctrine affords matter of reproof to us of this town, for our declining is much from what we have lately been. That we have exceedingly declined in religion is most manifest, and what all confess. A little while ago Christ was the great object of regard among us. The hearts of the people in general were greatly engaged about Christ, as though Christ had been all, and the world nothing. There was then a great deal of conversation among all sorts of persons, and in all companies, of Christ. They who thought they had no interest in Christ were full of concern how to obtain an interest in him. And they were almost ready to neglect their worldly concerns, as though Christ was all they needed. And with regard to those that thought they had obtained an interest in Christ, their thoughts and their conversation seemed also to be very much taken up about Christ. They were much engaged in talking of the excellency of Christ, and seemed to be full of the grace and dying love of Christ. And one and another of you expressed the strong sense you had of one perfection and excellency and another of Christ['s], and of the glory of the works that he has done, and of the sweetness of the words that he speaks. The town seemed to be full of the praises of Christ. You expressed to one another how you earnestly longed to praise him and bless his name forever and ever, and how you desired that others should help you to praise him. The benefits procured by Christ were then greatly valued in the town, and both Christ and his benefits were then precious among us. And multitudes seemed to be concerned what they should do for the honor of Christ, how they should live to his glory, and do something for the advancement of his kingdom in the world.

But now, how much otherwise is it. How little is Christ set by, in comparison of what he has been. How much is he neglected, how much is he dropped out of people's common discourse and conversation! How have many of you left off earnestly following after Christ, to pursue after the world? One to pursue after riches, another to be engrossed by amusement and diversion, another by fine clothes and gay apparel. And all sorts, young and old, have gone their way wandering in a great measure from Christ: as though Christ was not as excellent now as he was then, as though his grace and dying love were not as wonderful now as they were then, as though Christ were not now as much preferable to the world, as worthy to be loved, and to be praised, to be thought of, and talked of; and as though he was not as worthy that we should be concerned to honor him, and live to his praise, as ever he was. If Christ be as much altered as the town is altered, he is altered very much indeed. Are we so foolish as to think that he, that is the same yesterday, today, and forever, is so much altered from what he was three years ago?

IV. The truth taught in the text may be applied by way of *encouragement.*

1. To sinners whose minds are burdened and exercised with concern about the state of their souls, to come to Christ, and put their trust in him for salvation. If Christ is now and ever will be, the same that he ever was, then here is great encouragement for you to come to him, as will appear by considering two things:

First, how Christ has invited you to come to him with promises that he will accept of you if you do so. Christ in his word often invites those that are in your circumstances, whether we consider your circumstances as a lost sinner, or as a sinner under anxiety and concern about your condition. If we consider your circumstances merely as a lost sinner, Christ invites you. For he is often inviting and calling on sinners to come to him. Pro. 8:4, "Unto you, O men, I call, and my voice is to the sons of men." And chap. 9:4, 5, "Whoso is simple, let him turn in hither; and ye that want understanding, come, eat of my bread, and drink of the wine that I have mingled." Rev. 3:20, "Behold, I stand at the door and knock." Rev. 22:17, "The Spirit and the bride say, 'Come.' " Or if we consider your circumstances as a sinner burdened in your soul with concern about your condition, such are especially invited by Christ. Mat. 11:28, "Come unto me, all ye that labor and are heavy laden, and I will give you rest." And Isa. 55:1, "Ho every one that thirsteth, come ye to the waters." And John 7:37, "If any man thirst, let him come unto me and drink."

That Christ is the same yesterday, today, and forever, shows what a joint encouragement these invitations are for you to come to Christ in two ways:

- *It shows that as Christ invited such sinners, when these invitations were spoken and penned, so he does now, for he is the same now that he was then.* So that you are to look on the invitations that you find in your Bible, not only as invitations that were made then when they were first spoken or written, but that are made now. Christ makes them now as much as he made them then. Those invitations which proceeded out of Christ's mouth when he was on earth are made to you now as much as if they now this moment proceeded from Christ's mouth. For there is no alteration in Christ. He is the same as ever he has been. So that when you read or hear any of the invitations of Christ, you may look upon them as if they now came from his blessed lips.
- *It shows that if you come to Christ, he will surely prove to be the same in* accepting *that he is in* inviting. Christ will be consistent with himself. He will not appear one way in calling and inviting you, and then another way in his treatment of you when you come to accept of his invitation. Christ will not appear with two faces, with a pleasant winning face in inviting, and with a frowning countenance in his treatment of persons that come at his call. For he is ever the same. You see that Christ is exceedingly gracious and sweet in his invitations. And he surely will be as gracious and sweet in his acceptance of you, if you close with his call. And then Christ does not merely *invite,* he also *promises,* that if you accept of his invitation, he will not reject you. John 6:37, "Him that cometh unto me I will in no wise cast out." He that is the same yesterday, today, and forever, will be found the same in *fulfilling* that he is in *promising.*

Secondly, [consider] how Christ has treated those that have come to him heretofore. Christ in times past has graciously received those that have come to him. He has made them welcome. He has embraced them in the arms of his love. He has admitted them to a blessed and eternal union with himself and has given them a right to all the privileges of the sons of God. And he is the same still that he has been heretofore. We have an account in Scripture of many that came to him. We have an account in the history of Christ's life of many that accepted his calls, and we have an account in the book of the Acts of the Apostles, of multitudes that believed in him.

But we read of *none* that ever were rejected by him. And we ourselves have seen many that we have reason to think Christ has accepted on their coming to him, many that have been great sinners, many that have been old hardened sinners, many that had been backsliders, and many that had been guilty of quenching the Spirit of God. And he is the same still. He is as ready to receive such sinners now as he was then. Christ never yet rejected any that came to him. He has always been the same in this respect. He is so now, and so he surely will be still.

2. There is in this doctrine great encouragement to all persons to look to Christ under all manner of difficulties and afflictions, and that especially from what appeared in Christ when he was here. We have an account in the history of Christ of great numbers under a great variety of afflictions and difficulties, resorting to him for help. And we have no account of his rejecting one person who came to him in a friendly manner for help, under any difficulty whatever. But on the contrary, the history of his life is principally filled up with miracles that he wrought for the relief of such. When they came to him, he presently relieved them, and always did it freely without money or price. We never read of his doing anything for any person as hired to it, by any reward that was offered him. And he helped persons fully, he completely delivered them from those difficulties under which they labored. And by the doctrine of the text we learn that though he is not now upon earth, but in heaven, yet he is the same that he was then. He is as able to help, and he is as ready to help under every kind of difficulty.

Here is great encouragement for persons who are sick to look to Christ for healing, and for their near friends to carry their case to Christ; for how ready was Christ, when on earth, to help those that looked to him under such difficulties! And how sufficient did he appear to be for it, commonly healing by laying on his hand, or by speaking a word! And we read of his healing all manner of sickness and all manner of disease among the people. Persons under the most terrible and inveterate diseases were often healed.

And Christ is the same still. And here is great encouragement for mourners to look to Christ for comfort. We read of Christ's pitying such, as in the case of the widow of Nain, [in] Luke 7:12, 13 etc.

> And so he wept with those that wept, and groaned in spirit, and wept with compassion for Martha and Mary, when he saw their sorrow for the loss of their brother Lazarus," John 11:32, etc.

And he is the same still. He is as ready to pity those that are in affliction now as he was then.

And here is great encouragement for those that are exercised with the temptations of Satan. For how often do we read of Christ casting out Satan from those of whom he had the strongest possession! And Christ is the same still. And whoever are under spiritual darkness, from the consideration of their own sinfulness, have encouragement hence to look to Christ for comfort. For if they do so, he will be ready to say to them, as he did to the paralytic, "Son, be of good cheer; thy sins are forgiven thee." For he is still the same that he was then.

V. The truth taught in the text may be applied by way of *consolation* to the godly.

You may consider that you have in him an unchangeable Savior, who, as he has loved you and undertaken for you from eternity, and in time has died for you before you were born, and has since converted you by his grace, and brought you out of a blind, guilty, and undone condition, savingly home to himself; so he will carry on his work in your heart; he will perfect what is yet lacking in you, in order to your complete deliverance from sin, and death, and all evil, and to your establishment in complete and unalterable blessedness. From the unchangeableness of your Savior, you may see how he thinks of that chain in Rom. 8:29–30:

> For whom he did foreknow, them he also did predestinate, and whom he did predestinate, them he also called, and whom he called, them he also justified, and whom he justified, them he also glorified.

The Savior has promised you very great and precious blessings in this world. And things which eye has not seen, nor ear heard, nor the heart of man conceived, in the world to come. And from his unchangeableness you may be assured that the things which he has promised he will also perform.

You may from this doctrine see the unchangeableness of his love. And therefore, when you consider how great love he seemed to manifest, when he yielded himself up to God a sacrifice for you, in his agony and bloody sweat in the garden, and when he went out to the place of his crucifixion bearing his own cross, you may rejoice that his love now is the same that it was then.

And so when you think of past discoveries which Christ has made of himself in his glory, and in his love to your soul, you may comfort yourself that he is as glorious, and his love to you is as great, as it was in the time of these discoveries.

You may greatly comfort yourself that you have an unchangeable friend in Christ Jesus. Constancy is justly looked upon as a most necessary and most desirable qualification in a friend. That he be not fickle, and so that his friendship cannot be depended on, as that of a steady sure friend. How excellent his [Jesus'] friendship is, you may learn from his manner of treating his disciples on earth, whom he graciously treated as a tender father his children, meekly instructing them, most friendly conversing with them, and being ready to pity them, and help them, and forgive their infirmities. And then you may consider this doctrine, and how it thence appears that he is the same still that he was then, and ever will be the same.

From the unchangeableness of your Savior, you may be assured of your continuance in a state of grace. As to yourself, you are so changeable, that, if left to yourself, you would soon fall utterly away. There is no dependence on your unchangeableness. But Christ is the same, and therefore, when he has begun a good work in you he will finish it. As he has been the author, he will be the finisher of your faith. Your love to Christ is in itself changeable. But his to you is unchangeable, and therefore he will never suffer your love to him utterly to fail. The apostle gives this reason why the saints' love to Christ cannot fail, viz. that his love to them never can fail.

From the unchangeableness of Christ you may learn the unchangeableness of his intercession, how he will never cease to intercede for you. And from this you may learn the unalterableness of your heavenly happiness. When once you have entered on the happiness of heaven, it never shall be taken from you, because Christ, your Savior and friend, who bestows it on you, and in whom you have it, is unchangeable. He will be the same forever and ever, and therefore so will be your happiness in heaven. As Christ is an unchangeable Savior, so he is your unchangeable portion. That may be your rejoicing, that however your earthly enjoyments may be removed, Christ can never fail. Your dear friends may be taken away and you [may] suffer many losses. And at last you must part with all those things. Yet you have a portion, a precious treasure, more worth, ten thousand times, than all these things. That portion cannot fail you, for you have it in him, who is the same yesterday, today, and forever.

Christ Exalted

Or: Jesus Christ Gloriously Exalted Above All Evil in the Work of Redemption

Lecture, dated August 1738.

"For he must reign, till he hath put all enemies under his feet. The last enemy that shall be destroyed, is death."—1 Corinthians 15:25, 26

The apostle in this chapter particularly opposes some among the Christian Corinthians who denied the resurrection of the dead and infested the church with their doctrine.

There were two sorts of persons in that age who were especially great opposers of the doctrine of the resurrection. One among the *Jews* were the Sadducees, of whom we read, Acts 23:8: "For the Sadducees say that there is no resurrection, either angel or spirit." And we have the same account in other places. Among the *heathen* that were the chief opposers of this doctrine were their philosophers. The doctrine of the resurrection of the dead was not consistent with their philosophy, by the principles of which, it was impossible that one who was deprived of the habit of life, would ever receive it again. And therefore they ridiculed the doctrine when the apostle preached it among them at Athens. (Acts 17.) Probably the church at Corinth received this corruption from the philosophers, and not the Sadducees. For Corinth was near to Athens, and the place of the chief resort of the philosophers of Greece.

The apostle, in opposing this error, first insists on Christ's resurrection from the dead, and next on the resurrection of all the saints at the end of the world. And in the verses next before the text, shows how both are connected, or that one arises or follows from the other. And then adds,

> then cometh the end, when he shall have delivered up the kingdom to God, even the Father; when he shall have put down all rule, and all authority, and power. For he must reign till he hath put all enemies under his feet. The last enemy that shall be destroyed is death.

Observe,

I. Here is one thing wherein appears the glory of that exaltation and dominion, that Christ has as our redeemer, viz. *that it issues in the subjection of all enemies under his feet.* It is not said all *his* enemies, possibly because those that shall be put under his feet are not only his enemies, but also the enemies of his Father and of his people. Their being *under his feet* denotes their being perfectly subdued, and his being gloriously exalted over them. It shall be thus with respect to God's and his, and his people's enemies universally, not one excepted; which universality is signified here two ways; *all enemies*—and the very *last enemy*: when there shall be but one enemy left, that shall also be put under his feet.

II. We may learn what is here meant by enemies by the particular instance here given as the last that shall be destroyed, viz. *death.* Which shows that by enemies, is not meant *persons* only, that set themselves in opposition to God and his people, but *evils*; whatever is against God and his people, and opposes Christ or his saints, whether they be persons or things.

I. How evil of all kinds has prevailed and highly exalted itself in the world.

Evil, of all kinds, has risen to an exceeding height in the world, and highly exalted itself against God, and Christ, and the church. This will appear by the following particulars.

1. Satan has highly exalted himself, and greatly prevailed. He is vastly superior in his natural capacity and abilities to mankind. He was originally one of the highest rank of creatures, but proudly exalted himself in rebellion against God in heaven. We are told, that *pride* was *the condemnation of the devil.* (1 Tim. 3:6) He became proud of his own superior dignity and mighty abilities, and the glory which his Creator had put upon him. And [he] probably thought it too much to submit to the Son of God, and attempted to exalt his throne above him. And he prevailed to draw away vast multitudes of the heavenly hosts into an open rebellion against God.

And after he was cast down from heaven, he proudly exalted himself in this world, and prevailed to do great things. By his subtle temptations he procured the fall of our first parents, and so brought about the ruin of their whole race. He procured their ruin in body and soul, and the death of both, and that they should be exposed to all manner of calamity in this world, and to eternal ruin hereafter. He so far prevailed, that he drew men off from the service of their Maker, and set up himself to be the god of this world. And in a little time, [he] drew the world into that almost universal corruption, which brought on the flood of water, through which it was destroyed. And after that, he drew on all nations, except the posterity of Jacob, from the worship of the true God, and darkened all the world with heathenism, and held them under this darkness for a great many ages, he himself being worshiped as God almost all over the world. The nations of the earth offered sacrifices to him and multitudes offered up their children. And during that time, he often so far prevailed against the people of God, that he had almost swallowed them up. The church was often brought to the very brink of ruin.

And when Christ himself appeared in the world, how did he exalt himself against him! And prevailed so far, as to influence men to hate and despise him all the days of his life. And at last he persuaded one of his own disciples to betray him. Accordingly, he was delivered into the hands of men, to be mocked, buffeted, spit upon, and treated with the greatest ignominy that unrestrained malice could devise. And, at last procured that he should be put to the most cruel and ignominious kind of death. And since that, he has greatly exalted himself against the gospel and kingdom of Christ. He has procured that the church, for the most part, has been the subject of great persecution; has often brought it to the brink of utter destruction; has accomplished great works in setting up those great kingdoms of antichrist and Mahomet; and darkened great part of the world, that was once enlightened with the gospel of Christ, with worse than heathen darkness. And he has infected the Christian world with multitudes of heresies and false ways of worship, and greatly promoted atheism and infidelity. Thus highly has the devil exalted himself against God and Christ, and the elect. And so far he prevailed.

2. *Guilt is another evil which has come to a great height in the world.* All guilt is an evil of a dreadful nature. The least degree of it is enough utterly to undo any creature. It is a thing that reaches unto heaven, and cries to God, and brings down his wrath. The guilt of any one sin is so terrible an evil that it prevails to bind over the guilty person to suffer everlasting burnings. And so is it in some respect infinite, in that it obliges to that punishment which has no end. And so it is infinitely terrible.

But this kind of evil has risen to a most amazing height in this world. Where not only some persons are guilty, but all, in all nations and ages, are naturally guilty wretches. And they who live to act any time in the world, are not only guilty of one sin, but of thousands, and thousands of thousands. What multiplied and what aggravated sins are some men guilty of! What guilt lies on some particular persons! How much more on some particular populous cities! How much more still on this wicked world! How much does the guilt of the world transcend all account, all expression, all power of numbers or measures! And above all, how vast is the guilt of the world, in all ages, from the beginning to the end of it! To what a pitch has guilt risen! The world, being, as it were, on every side, loaded with it, as with mountains heaped on mountains, above the clouds and stars of heaven.

And guilt, when it was imparted to Christ, greatly prevailed against him—though in himself innocent, and the eternal Son of God—even so as to hold him prisoner of justice for a while, and to open the flood-gates of God's wrath upon him, and bring his waves and billows over him.

3. *Corruption and wickedness of heart is another thing that has risen to an exceeding height in the world.* Sin has so far prevailed that it has become universal. All mere men are become sinful and corrupt creatures. Let us attend to St. Paul's description of the world (Rom. 3:9–18):

> Jews and Gentiles are all under sin. As is written, "There is none righteous, no not one; there is none that understandeth, there is none that seeketh after God. They are all gone out of the way, they are together become unprofitable, there is none that doeth good, no, not one."

And not only is every one corrupt, but they are all-over corrupt, in every power, faculty, and principle. Every part is depraved. Which is here represented by the several parts of the body being corrupt, as the throat, the tongue, the lips, the mouth, the feet.

> Their throat is an open sepulcher, with their tongues they have used deceit, the poison of asps is under their lips; whose mouth is full of cursing and bitterness: their feet are swift to shed blood.

And not only is every part corrupt, but exceeding corrupt, being possessed with dreadful principles of corruption. horribly evil dispositions and principles of sin, that may be represented by the poison of asps, which makes men like vipers and devils, principles of all uncleanness, pride, deceit, injustice, enmity, malice, blasphemy, murder. Here their *throats* are compared to an *open sepulcher,* and their *mouth* is said to be full of *cursing and bitterness,* and destruction and misery are said to be in their ways.

And there are those principles of sin not only that are very bad, but every kind. Here is no sort of wickedness, but there is a seed of it in men. And these seeds and principles have not only a being in men's hearts, but are there in great strength. They have the absolute possession and dominion over men so that they are *sold under sin.* Yea, wicked principles, and those only, are in the heart. *The imagination of the thoughts of their heart is evil only.* There are bad principles only, and no good ones. "There is no fear of God before their eyes." Thus the hearts of all men are *deceitful and desperately wicked* (Jer. 17:9).

And if we look, not only at the natural corruption of the heart, but at the contracted habits of sin, by wicked education and customs, how full shall we find the world of wickedness, in this respect! How have men, by bad customs in sinning, broken down all restraints upon natural corruption, and as it were abandoned themselves to wickedness! So far has corruption and wickedness prevailed in the world, and so high has it risen, that it is become a great and universal deluge, that overtops all things, and prevails with that strength, that it is like the raging waves of the tempestuous ocean, which are ready to bear down all before them.

4. *Many of the devil's instruments have greatly prevailed and have been exalted to an exceeding height in the world.* It has been so in almost all ages of the world. Many of the devil's instruments have prospered and prevailed till they have got to the head of great kingdoms and empires, with vast riches and mighty power. Those four great heathen monarchies that rose in the world before Christ are spoken of in Scripture as kingdoms set up in opposition to the kingdom of Christ. So they are represented in the interpretation of Nebuchadnezzar's dream (Dan. 2:35, 36). These monarchies were exceeding powerful.

The two last ruled over the greater part of the then known world. And the last especially, viz. the Roman empire, was exceeding mighty. So that it is said to be diverse from all kingdoms, and that it would devour the whole earth, and tread it down, and break it in pieces (Dan. 7:23). It is represented by the fourth beast, which was dreadful and terrible, and strong exceedingly, and had great iron teeth, that devoured and brake in pieces, and stamped the residue with his feet (Dan. 7:7). These four kingdoms all persecuted the church of God in their turns, especially the last. One of the governors of this monarchy put Christ to death. And afterwards one emperor after another made dreadful havoc of the church, making a business of it, with the force of all the empire, to torment and destroy the Christians, endeavoring, if possible, to root out the Christian name from under heaven.

And in those latter ages, how have those two great instruments of the devil, viz. antichrist and Mahomet, prevailed, and to what a pitch of advancement have they arrived, ruling over vast empires, with mighty wealth, pride and power, so that the earth has been, as it were, subdued by them. Antichrist has set up himself as the vicar of Christ, and has for many ages usurped the power of God, "sitting in the temple of God, and showing himself that he is God; and exalting himself above all that is called God, or that is worshiped." And how dreadfully has he ravaged the church of God, being drunk with the blood of the saints, and the martyrs of Jesus. And has often, as it were, deluged the world in Christian blood, he with the utmost cruelty that human wit and malice could invent. And at this day, many other instruments of the devil, many heretics, atheists, and other infidels, are exerting themselves against Christ and his church, with great pride and contempt.

5. Affliction and misery have also prevailed and risen to an unspeakable height in the world. The spiritual misery which the elect are naturally in is great. They are miserable captives of sin and Satan, and under obligations to suffer eternal burnings. This misery all mankind are naturally in. And spiritual troubles and sorrows have often risen to a great height in the elect. The troubles of a wounded spirit and guilty conscience, have been felt with intolerable and insupportable weight. "A wounded spirit who can bear?" (Proverbs 18:14). And the darkness that has risen to God's people after conversion, through the temptations and buffetings of the devil, and the hidings of God's face, and manifestations of his anger, have been very terrible. And temporal afflictions have often risen exceeding high. The church of God has, for the most part, all along, been a seat of great affliction and tribulation.

But the height to which the evil of affliction has risen, nowhere appears so much as in the afflictions that Christ suffered. The evil of affliction and sorrow exalted itself so high, as to seize the Son of God himself, and to cause him to be all in a bloody sweat, and to make his soul exceeding sorrowful, even unto death. It caused him to cry out, "My God, my God, why hast thou forsaken me?" Affliction never prevailed to such a degree in this world, as in Christ, whose soul was, as it were, overwhelmed in an ocean of it.

6. *Death is an evil which has greatly prevailed and made dreadful havoc in this world.* How does it waste and devour mankind, one age after another, sparing none, high or low, rich or poor, good or bad! Wild beasts have destroyed many. Many cruel princes have taken away the lives of thousands, and laid waste whole countries. But death devours all. None are suffered to escape. And the bodies of the saints as well as other, fall a prey to this great devourer. Yea, so high did this enemy rise, that he took hold on Christ himself, and swallowed him among the rest. He became the prey of this great, insatiable monster. By his means, was his bodily frame destroyed, and laid dead in the dark and silent grave. And death still goes on destroying thousands every day. And therefore the grave is one of those things which Agur says, never has enough (Pro. 30:16). So have evils of every kind prevailed, and to such a degree have they exalted themselves in the world.

II. How Jesus Christ, in the work of redemption, appears gloriously above all these evils.

It was not the will of the infinitely wise and holy Governor of the world that things should remain in this confusion, this reign of evil, which had prevailed and exalted itself to such a height. But he had a design of subduing it, and delivering an elect part of the world from it, and exalting them to the possession of the greatest good, and to reign in the highest glory, out of a state of subjection to all these evils. And he chose his Son as the person most fit for an undertaking that was infinitely too great for any mere creature. And he has undertaken the work of our redemption. And though these evils are so many and so great, and have prevailed to such a degree, and have risen to such a height, and have been, as it were, all combined together; yet wherein they have exalted themselves, Christ, in the work of redemption, appears above them. He has gloriously prevailed against them all, and brings them under his feet, and rides forth, in the chariots of salvation, over their heads, or leading them in triumph at his chariot wheels. He appears in this work infinitely higher and mightier than they, and sufficient to carry his people above them, and utterly to destroy them all.

1. *Christ appears gloriously above all evil in what he did to procure redemption for us in his state of humiliation, by the righteousness he wrought out, and the atonement he made for sin.* The evils mentioned never seemed so much to prevail against him as in his sufferings. But in them, the foundation was laid for their overthrow. In them he appeared above *Satan*. Though Satan never exalted himself so high as he did in procuring these sufferings of Christ; yet, then, Christ laid the foundation for the utter overthrow of his kingdom. He slew Satan, as it were, with his own weapon, the spiritual David cut off this Goliath's head with his own sword, and he triumphed over him in his cross. "Having spoiled principalities and powers, he made a show of them openly, triumphing over them in *it*," (Col. 2:15) *i.e.* in his cross, mentioned in the preceding words. Then the wisdom of Christ appeared gloriously above the subtlety of Satan. Satan, that old serpent, used a great deal of subtlety to procure Christ's death. And doubtless, when he had accomplished it, thought he had obtained a complete victory, being then ignorant of the contrivance of our redemption. But so did the wisdom of Christ order things that Satan's subtlety and malice should be made the very means of undermining the foundations of his kingdom. And so he wisely led him into the pit that he had dug.

In this also Christ appeared gloriously above the guilt of men. For he offered a sacrifice that was sufficient to do away all the guilt of the whole world. Though the guilt of man was like the great mountains, whose heads are lifted up to the heavens; yet his dying love, and his merits, appeared as a mighty deluge that overflowed the highest mountains, or like a boundless ocean that swallows them up, or like an immense fountain of light that with the fullness and redundancy of its brightness, swallows up men's greatest sins, as little motes are swallowed up and hidden in the disk of the sun.

In this Christ appeared above all of the *corruption* of man, in that hereby he purchased holiness for the chief of sinners. And Christ in undergoing such extreme affliction, got the victory over all *misery*; and laid a foundation for its being utterly abolished, with respect to his elect. In dying he became the plague and destruction of death. When death slew him, it slew itself. For Christ, through death, destroyed him that had the power of death, even the devil (Heb. 2:14). By this he laid the foundation of the glorious resurrection of all his people to an immortal life.

2. Christ appears gloriously exalted above all evil, in his resurrection and ascension into heaven. When Christ rose from the dead, then it appeared that he was above death, which, though it had taken him captive, could not hold him.

Then he appeared above the devil. Then this Leviathan that had swallowed him was forced to vomit him up again, as the Philistines that had taken captive the ark were forced to return it, Dagon being fallen before it, with his head and hands broken off, and only the stumps left. Then he appeared above our guilt. For he was justified in his resurrection (Rom. 4:4, 25; 1 Tim. 3:16). In his resurrection he appeared above all affliction. For though he had been subject to much affliction and overwhelmed in it, he then emerged out of it, as having gotten the victory, never to conflict with any more sorrow.

When he ascended up into heaven, he rose far above the reach of the devil and all his instruments, who had before had him in their hands. And now has he sat down at the right hand of God, as being made head over all things to the church, in order to a complete and perfect victory over sin, Satan, death, and all his enemies. It was then said to him, "Sit thou on my right hand, until I make thine enemies thy footstool," (Psa. 110:1). He entered into a state of glory, wherein he is exalted far above all these evils, as the forerunner of his people, and to make intercession for them, till they also are brought to be with him, in like manner exalted above all evil.

3. Christ appears gloriously above all evil, in his work in the hearts of the elect, in their conversion and sanctification. This is what the application of redemption, so far as it is applied in this world, consists in, which is done by the Holy Ghost as the Spirit of Christ. In this work of Christ in the hearts of his elect, he appears glorious above Satan. For the strong man armed is overcome, and all his armor, wherein he trusted, is taken from him, and his spoil divided. In this work, the lamb is, by the spiritual David taken out of the mouth of the lion and bear. The poor captive is delivered from his mighty and cruel enemies.

In this Christ appears gloriously above the *corruption* and wickedness of the heart, above its natural darkness in dispelling it, and letting in light, and above its enmity and opposition, by prevailing over it, drawing it powerfully and irresistibly to himself, and turning a heart of stone into a heart of flesh, above the obstinacy and perverseness of the will, by making them willing in the day of his power. In this he appears above all their lusts. For all sin is mortified in this work, and the soul is delivered from the power and dominion of it. In this work the grace of Christ gloriously triumphs over men's *guilt*. He comes over the mountains of their sins, and visits them with his salvation.

And God is wont often in their work, either in the beginning or progress of it, to give his people those spiritual comforts, in which he gloriously appears to be above all affliction and sorrow. And often gives them to triumph over the devil, and his powerful and cruel instruments. Many saints, by the influences of Christ's Spirit on their hearts, have rejoiced and triumphed, when suffering the greatest torments and cruelties of their persecutors. And in this work Christ sometimes gloriously appears above death, in carrying his people far above the fears of it, and making them to say, "O death, where is thy sting? O grave, where is thy victory?"

4. Christ gloriously appears above all these aforementioned evils, in his glorifying the souls of departed saints in heaven. In this he gives a glorious victory over death. Death by it is turned from an enemy into a servant. And their death, by the glorious change that passes in the state of their souls, is become a resurrection, rather than a death. Now Christ exalts the soul to a state of glory, wherein it is perfectly delivered from Satan and all his temptations, and all his instrument, and from all remains of sin and corruption, and from all affliction. "They shall hunger no more, neither thirst any more, neither shall the sun light on them, nor any heat—and God shall wipe away all tears from their eyes," (Rev. 7:16, 17).

5. Christ appears gloriously above these evils, in what he does in his providence in the world, as head and redeemer of his church. He appears gloriously above Satan and all his instruments in upholding his church, even from its first establishment, through all the powerful attempts that have been made against it by earth and Hell. Hereby fulfilling his promise, "That the gates of Hell should never prevail against it," (Mat. 16:18).

Christ gloriously triumphed over these his enemies, in a remarkable success of his gospel, soon after his ascension, when many thousands in Jerusalem, and all parts of the world, were so soon turned from darkness unto light, and from the power of Satan unto God, and in causing his word to go on and prosper, and his church to increase and prevail against all the opposition of the heathen world, when they united all their power to put a stop to it, and root it out. So that, in spite of all that the philosophers, and wise men, and emperors and princes could do, the gospel in a little time overthrew Satan's old heathenish kingdom in the whole Roman empire, which was then the main part of the world. And so brought about the greatest and most glorious revolution. Instead of one single nation, now the greater part of the nations of the known world were become God's people.

And Christ's exaltation above all evil in his government of the world, in his providence, as the Redeemer of his people, has since gloriously appeared in reviving his church by the reformation from popery, after it had for many ages lain in a great measure hid, and dwelt in a wilderness, under anti-Christian persecution.

And he will yet far more gloriously triumph over Satan and all his instruments, in all the mighty kingdoms that have been set up in opposition to the kingdom of Christ, at the time of the fall of antichrist, and the beginning of those glorious times so much spoken of in Scripture prophecy.

> Then shall the stone that has been cut out without hands smite all these kingdoms, and break them to pieces; and they shall become like the chaff of the summer threshing-floors, and the wind shall carry them away, that no place should be found for them: and the stone which smote them shall become a great mountain, and fill the whole earth. (Dan. 2:34, 35)

> Then shall the God of heaven set up a kingdom, which shall never be destroyed; and it shall break in pieces, and consume all these kingdoms, and it shall stand forever. (Dan. 2:44)

> And then the kingdoms of this world shall become the kingdoms of our Lord and of his Christ, and he shall reign forever and ever. (Rev. 11:15)

Though great and might empires have been set up one after another in the world, in opposition to the kingdom of Christ, during the succession of so many ages; yet, Christ's kingdom shall be the last and the universal kingdom, which he has given him, as the heir of the world. Whatever great works Satan has wrought, the final issue and event of all, in the winding up of things in the last ages of the world, shall be the glorious kingdom of Christ through the world; a kingdom of righteousness and holiness, of love and peace, established everywhere. Agreeable to the ancient prediction,

> I saw in the night visions, and behold, one like the Son of man, came with the clouds of heaven, and came to the Ancient of days, and they brought him near before him. And there was given him dominion and glory, and a kingdom, that all people, nations, and languages should serve him: his dominion is an everlasting dominion, which shall not pass away, and his kingdom that which shall not be destroyed. And the kingdom and dominion, and the greatness of the kingdom under the whole heaven, shall be given to the people of the saints of the Most High, whose kingdom is an everlasting kingdom, and all dominions shall serve and obey him. (Dan. 7:13, 14, 27)

Then shall Christ appear gloriously exalted indeed above all evil. And then shall all the saints in earth and heaven gloriously triumph in him, and sing, "Hallelujah, salvation, and glory, and honor, and power unto the Lord our God; for true and righteous are his judgments; for he hath judged the great whore, which did corrupt the earth with her fornication, and hath avenged the blood of his servants at her hand. Hallelujah: for the Lord God omnipotent reigneth," (Rev. 19:1, 2, 6).

6. *Christ will appear gloriously above all evil in the consummation of the redemption of his elect church at the end of the world.* Then will be completed the whole work of redemption with respect to all that Christ died for, both in its interpretation and application; and not till then. And then will Christ's exaltation above all evil be most perfectly and fully manifest. Then shall the conquest and triumph be completed with respect to all of them. Then shall all the devils, and all their instruments, be brought before Christ, to be judged and condemned. And then shall be completed their destruction in their consummate and everlasting misery; when they shall be all cast into the lake of fire, no more to range, and usurp dominion in the world, or have liberty to make opposition against God and Christ. They shall forever be shut up, thence forward only to suffer. Then shall death be totally destroyed. All the saints shall be delivered everlastingly from it. Even their bodies shall be taken from the power of death by a glorious resurrection.

Then shall all guilt, and all sin and corruption, and all affliction, all sighs and tears, be utterly and eternally abolished, concerning every one of the elect, they being all brought to one complete body, to their consummate and immutable glory. And all this as the fruit of Christ's blood, and as an accomplishment of his redemption.

Then all that evil, which has so prevailed, and so exalted itself, and usurped and raged, and reigned, shall be perfectly and forever thrust down and destroyed, with respect to all the elect. And all will be exalted to a state wherein they will be forever immensely above all these things.

> And there shall be no more death, neither sorrow nor crying, neither shall there be any more pain: for the former things are passed away. (Rev. 21:4)

III. The subject improved and applied.

1. *In this we may see how the glory of the Lord Jesus Christ appears in the work of redemption.* It was because the Father had from eternity a design of exceedingly glorifying his Son, that he appointed him to be the person that should thus triumph over the evil in the world. The work of redemption is

the most glorious of all God's works that are made known to us. The glory of God most remarkably shines forth in it. And this is one thing wherein its glory eminently appears, that therein Christ appears so gloriously above Satan and all his instruments, above all guilt, all corruption, all affliction, above death, and above all evil. And more especially, because evil has so exalted itself in the world, as we have heard, and exalted itself against Christ in particular.

Satan has ever had a peculiar enmity against the Son of God. Probably his first rebellion, which was his condemnation, was his proudly taking it in disdain, when God declared the decree in heaven, that his Son in man's nature, should be the King of heaven, and that all the angels should worship him. However that was, yet it is certain that his strife has ever been especially against the Son of God. The enmity has always been between the seed of the woman, and the serpent. And therefore that war which the devil maintains against God is represented by the devil and his angels fighting against Michael and his angels (Rev. 12:7). This Michael is Christ (Dan. 10:21 and 12:1).

God had appointed his Son to be the heir of the world. But the devil has contested this matter with him, and has strove to set himself up as God of the world. And how exceedingly has the devil exalted himself against Christ! How did he oppose him as he dwelt among the Jews, in his tabernacle and temple! And how did he oppose him when on earth! And how has he opposed him since his ascension! What great and mighty works has Satan brought to pass in the world! How many Babels has he built up to heaven, in his opposition to the Son of God! How exceeding proud and haughty has he appeared in his opposition! How have he and his instruments, and sin, affliction, and death, of which he is the father, raged against Christ? But yet Christ, in the work of redemption, appears infinitely above them all. In this work he triumphs over them, however they have dealt proudly, and they all appear under his feet. In this the glory of the Son of God, in the work of redemption, remarkably appears.

The beauty of good appears with the greatest advantage, when compared with its contrary, and appears vastly above it, in its greatest height. The glory of Christ, in this glorious exaltation over so great evil, that so exalted itself against him, the more remarkable appears, in that he is thus exalted out of so low a state. Though he appeared in the world as a little child; yet how does he triumph over the most gigantic enemies of God and men! He who was "a man of sorrows, and acquainted with grief," is a man of war, and triumphed over his enemies in all their power. He who was meek and lowly of heart, has triumphed over those proud foes. And he is exalted over them all, in that which appears most despicable, even his cross.

2. *Here is matter of exceeding great encouragement for all sinful miserable creatures in the world of mankind to come to Christ.* For let them be as sinful as they will, and ever so miserable; Christ, in the work of redemption, is gloriously exalted above all their sin and misery.

How high soever their guilt has risen, though mountains have been heaping on mountains all the days of their lives, till the pile appears towering up to heaven, and above the very stars; yet Christ in the work of redemption appears gloriously exalted above all this height. Though they are overwhelmed in a mighty deluge of woe and misery, a deluge that is not only above all their heads, but above the heads of the highest mountains, and they do not see how it is possible that they should escape; yet they have no reason to be discouraged from looking to Christ for help, who in the work of redemption, appears gloriously above the deluge of evil. Though they see dreadful corruption in their hearts, though their lusts appear like giants, or like the raging waves of the sea; yet they need not despair of help, but may look to Christ, who appears in the work of redemption, gloriously above all this corruption.

If they apprehend themselves to be miserable captives of Satan, and find him too strong an adversary for them, and the devil is often tempting and buffeting them, and triumphing over them with great cruelty; if it seems to them that the devil has swallowed them up, and his got full possession of them, as the whale had of Jonah; yet there is encouragement for them to look again, as Jonah did, towards God's holy temple, and to trust in Christ for deliverance from Satan, who appears so gloriously exalted above him in the work of redemption.

If they are ready to sink with darkness and sorrows, distress of conscience, or those frowns of God upon them, so that God's waves and billows seem to pass over them; yet they have encouragement enough to look to Christ for deliverance. These waves and billows have before exalted themselves against Christ, and he appeared to be infinitely above them. And if they are afraid of death, if it looks exceeding terrible, as an enemy that would swallow them up; yet let them look to Christ who has appeared so gloriously above death, and their fears will turn into joy and triumph.

3. *What cause have they who have an interest in Christ, to glory in their Redeemer!* They are often beset with many evils, and many mighty enemies surround them on every side, with open mouths ready to devour them. But

they need not fear any of them. They may glory in Christ, the rock of their salvation, who appears so gloriously above them all. They may triumph over Satan, over this evil world, over guilt, and over death. For as their Redeemer is mighty, and is so exalted above all evil, so shall they also be exalted in him, They are now, in a sense, so exalted. For nothing can hurt them. Christ carries them, as on eagle's wings, high out of the reach of all evils, so that they cannot come near them, to do them any real harm. And, in a little time, they shall be carried so out of their reach, that they shall not be able even to molest them anymore, forever.

True Saints, When Absent from the Body, Are Present with the Lord

"Preached on the day of the funeral of the Rev. Mr. David Brainerd, missionary to the Indians, from the Honorable Society in Scotland for the Propagation of Christian Knowledge, and pastor of a church of Christian Indians in New Jersey; who died at Northampton in New England, October 9, 1747, in the 30th year of his age, and was interred on the 12th following." (*Works of Jonathan Edwards.*)

"We are confident, I say, and willing rather to be absent from the body, and to be present with the Lord."—2 Corinthians 5:8

The apostle in this place is giving a reason why he went on with so much boldness and immovable steadfastness, through such labors, sufferings, and dangers of his life, in the service of his Lord; for which his enemies, the false teachers among the Corinthians, sometimes reproached him as being beside himself, and driven on by a kind of madness. In the latter part of the preceding chapter, the apostle informs the Christian Corinthians that the reason why he did thus, was that he firmly believed the promises that Christ had made to his faithful servants of a glorious future eternal reward, and knew that these present afflictions were light, and but for a moment, in comparison of that far more exceeding and eternal weight of glory. The same discourse is continued in this chapter; wherein the apostle further insists on the reason he had given of his constancy in suffering, and exposing himself to death in the work of the ministry, even the more happy state he expected after death. And this is the subject of the text; wherein may be observed,

- *The great future privilege, which the apostle hoped for; that of being present with Christ.* The words, in the original, properly signify dwelling with Christ, as in the same country or city, or making a home with Christ.
- *When the apostle looked for this privilege, viz., when he should be absent from the body.* Not to wait for it till the resurrection, when soul and body should be united again. He signifies the same thing in his epistle to the Philippians, chap. 1:22, 23: "But if I live in the flesh, this is the fruit of my labor. Yet what I shall choose, I wot [know—from "wit"] not. For I am in a strait between two; having a desire to depart, and to be with Christ."
- *The value the apostle set on this privilege.* It was such, that for the sake of it, he chose to be absent from the body. He was willing rather, or (as the word properly signifies) it were more pleasing to him, to part with the present life, and all its enjoyments, and be possessed of this great benefit, than to continue here.
- *The present benefit, which the apostle had by his faith and hope of this future privilege, and of his great value for it, viz., that hence he received courage, assurance, and constancy of mind, agreeable to the proper import of the word that is rendered, we are confident.* The apostle is now giving a reason of that fortitude and immovable stability of mind, with which he went through those extreme labors, hardships and dangers, which he mentions in this discourse; so that, in the midst of all, he did not faint, was not discouraged, but had constant light, and inward support, strength, and comfort in the midst of all: agreeable to the 10th verse of the foregoing chapter, "For which cause, we faint not; but though our outward man perish, yet the inward man is renewed day by day." And the same is expressed more particularly in the 8th, 9th, and 10th verses, of that chapter:

  > We are troubled on every side, yet not distressed; we are perplexed, but not in despair; persecuted, but not forsaken; cast down, but not destroyed; always bearing about in the body, the dying of the Lord Jesus, that the life also of Jesus might be made manifest in our mortal flesh.

And in the next chapter, verses 4–10:

> In all things approving ourselves as the ministers of God, in much patience, in afflictions, in necessities, in distresses, in stripes, in imprisonments, in tumults, in labors, in watchings, in fastings, by pureness, by knowledge, by long-suffering, by kindness, by the Holy Ghost, by love unfeigned, by the word of truth, by the power of God, by the armor of righteousness on the right hand and on the left, by honor and dishonor, by evil report and good report: as deceivers, and yet true; as unknown, and yet well known; as dying, and behold, we live; as chastened, and not killed; as sorrowful, yet always rejoicing; as poor, yet making many rich; as having nothing, and yet possessing all things.

Among the many useful observations there might be raised from the text, I shall at this time only insist on that which lies most plainly before us in the words, viz., this: the souls of true saints, when they leave their bodies at death, go to be with Christ.

Departed souls of saints go to be with Christ, in the following respects.

I. They go to dwell in the same blessed abode with the glorified human nature of Christ.

The human nature of Christ is yet in being. He still continues, and will continue to all eternity, to be both God and man. His whole human nature remains: not only his human soul, but also his human body. His dead body rose from the dead; and the same [body] that was raised from the dead, is exalted and glorified at God's right hand; that which was dead is now alive, and lives for evermore.

And therefore there is a certain place, a particular part of the external creation, to which Christ is gone, and where he remains. And this place is that which we call the highest heaven, or the heaven of heavens; a place beyond all the visible heavens. Eph. 4:9, 10:

> Now that he ascended, what is it but that he also descended first into the lower parts of the earth? He that descended, is the same also that ascended up far above all heavens.

This is the same which the apostle calls the third heaven, 2 Cor. 12:2, reckoning the aerial heaven as the first, the starry heaven as the second, and the highest heaven as the third. This is the abode of the holy angels; they are called "the angels of heaven," Matt. 24:36; "The angels which are in heaven," Mark 13:32; "The angels of God in heaven," Matt. 22:30 and Mark 12:25. They are said "always to behold the face of the Father which is in heaven;" Matt. 18:10. And they are elsewhere often represented as before the throne of God, or surrounding his throne in heaven, and sent from thence, and descending from thence on messages to this world. And thither it is that the souls of departed saints are conducted, when they die. They are not reserved in some abode distinct from the highest heaven; a place of rest, which they are kept in, till the day of judgment; such as some imagine, which they call the hades of the happy: but they go directly to heaven itself. This is the saints' home, being their Father's house: they are pilgrims and strangers on the earth, and this is the other and better country that they are traveling to, Heb. 11:13–26. This is the city they belong to. Philip. 3:20, "Our conversation or (as the word properly signifies), citizenship, is in heaven." Therefore this undoubtedly is the place the apostle has respect to in my text, when he says, "We are willing to forsake our former house, the body, and to dwell in the same house, city or country, wherein Christ dwells;" which is the proper import of the words of the original. What can this house, or city, or country be, but that house, which is elsewhere spoken of, as their proper home, and their Father's house, and the city and country to which they properly belong, and whither they are traveling all the while they continue in this world, and the house, city, and country where we know the human nature of Christ is? This is the saints' rest; here their hearts are while they live; and here their treasure is. "The inheritance incorruptible, and undefiled, and that fadeth not away, that is designed for them, is reserved in heaven" (1 Pet. 1:4); and therefore they never can have their proper and full rest till they come here. So that undoubtedly their souls, when absent from their bodies (when the Scriptures represent them as in a state of perfect rest), arrive hither.

Those two saints, that left this world, to go to their rest in another world, without dying, viz., Enoch and Elijah, went to heaven. Elijah was seen ascending up to heaven, as Christ was. And to the same resting place, is there all reason to think, that those saints go, that leave the world, to go to their rest, by death. Moses, when he died in the top of the mount, ascended to the same glorious abode with Elias [Elijah], who ascended without dying. They are companions in another world; as they appeared together at Christ's transfiguration. They were together at that time with Christ in the mount, when there was a specimen or sample of his glorification in heaven. And doubtless they were also together afterwards, with him, when he was, actually, fully glorified in heaven. And thither undoubtedly it was, that the soul of Stephen ascended, when he expired. The circumstances of his death demonstrate it, as we have an account of it, Acts 7:55, etc.:

> He, being full of the Holy Ghost, looked up steadfastly into heaven, and saw the glory of God, and Jesus standing on the right hand of God, and said, "Behold, I see the heavens opened, and the Son of man"

(i.e. Jesus, in his human nature),

> "standing on the right hand of God." Then they cried out with a loud voice, and stopped their ears, and ran upon him with one accord, and cast him out of the city, and stoned him. . . . And they stoned Stephen, [and he was] calling upon God, and saying, "Lord Jesus, receive my spirit."

Before his death he had an extraordinary view of the glory that his Savior had received in heaven, not only for himself, but for him, and all his faithful followers; that he might be encouraged, by the hopes of this glory, cheerfully to lay down his life for his sake. Accordingly he dies in the hope of this, saying, "Lord Jesus, receive my spirit." By which doubtless he meant, "receive my spirit to be with thee, in that glory, wherein I have now seen thee, in heaven, at the right hand of God." And thither it was that the soul of the penitent thief on the cross ascended. Christ said to him, "today shalt thou be with me in paradise." Paradise is the same with the third heaven; as appears by 2 Cor. 12:2–4. There that which is called the third heaven in the second verse, in the fourth verse is called paradise. The departed souls of the apostles and prophets are in heaven; as is manifest from Rev. 18:20: "Rejoice over her, thou heaven, and ye holy apostles and prophets."

The church of God is distinguished in Scripture, from time to time, into these two parts; that part of it that is in heaven, and that which is in earth; Eph. 3:14, 15, "Jesus Christ, of whom the whole family in heaven and earth is named." Col. 1:20:

> And having made peace through the blood of his cross, by him to reconcile all things to himself, by him, I say, whether they be things in earth or things in heaven.

Now what things in heaven are they, for whom peace has been made by the blood of Christ's cross, and who have by him been reconciled to God, but the saints in heaven? In like manner we read, Eph. 1:10, of God's gathering "together in one, all things in Christ, both which are in heaven, and which are on earth, even in him." The spirits of just men made perfect are in the same city of the living God, and heavenly Jerusalem, with the innumerable company of angels, and Jesus the Mediator of the new covenant; as is manifest by Heb. 12:22–24. The church of God is often in Scripture called by the name Jerusalem; and the apostle speaks of the Jerusalem which is above, or which is in heaven, as the mother of us all; but if no part of the church be in heaven, or none but Enoch and Elias, it is not likely that the church would be called the Jerusalem which is in heaven.

II. The souls of true saints, when they leave their bodies at death, go to be with Christ, as they go to dwell in the immediate, full and constant sight or view of him.

When we are absent from our dear friends, they are out of sight; but when we are with them, we have the opportunity and satisfaction of seeing them. So while the saints are in the body, and are absent from the Lord, *he* is in several respects out of sight: 1 Pet. 1:8, "Whom having not seen, ye love: in whom, though now ye see him not, yet believing," etc. They have indeed, in this world, a spiritual sight of Christ; but they see through a glass darkly, and with great interruption; but in heaven they see him face to face (1 Cor. 13:12). "The pure in heart are blessed; for they shall see God" (Matt. 5:8). Their beatifical vision of God is in Christ, who is that brightness or effulgence of God's glory, by which his glory shines forth in heaven, to the view of saints and angels there, as well as here on earth. This is the Sun of righteousness, that is not only the light of this world, but is also the sun that enlightens the heavenly Jerusalem; by whose bright beams it is that the glory of God shines forth there, to the enlightening and making happy all the glorious inhabitants. "The Lamb is the light thereof; and so the glory of God doth lighten it," Rev. 21:23.

No one sees God the Father immediately, who is the King eternal, immortal, invisible; Christ is the image of that invisible God, by which he is seen by all elect creatures. The only begotten Son that is in the bosom of the Father, he hath declared him, and manifested him. No one has ever immediately seen the Father, but the Son; and no one else sees the Father any other way, than by the Son's revealing him. And in heaven, the spirits of just men made perfect do see him as he is. They behold his glory. They see the glory of his divine nature, consisting in all the glory of the Godhead, the beauty of all his perfections; his great majesty, almighty power, his infinite wisdom, holiness, and grace, and they see the beauty of his glorified human nature, and the glory which the Father hath given him, as God-man and Mediator. For this end, Christ desired that his saints might "be with him, that they might behold his glory," John 17:24. And when the souls of the saints leave their bodies, to go to be with Christ, they behold the marvelous glory of that great work of his, the work of redemption, and of the glorious way of salvation by him; desire to look into. They have a most clear view of the unfathomable depths of the manifold wisdom and knowledge of God; and the most bright displays of the infinite purity and holiness of God, that do appear in that way and work; and see in a much clearer manner than the saints do here, what is the breadth and length, and depth and height of the grace and love of Christ, appearing in his redemption. And as they see the unspeakable riches and glory of the attribute of God's grace, so they most clearly behold and understand Christ's eternal and unmeasurable dying love to them in particular. And in short, they see every thing in Christ that tends to kindle and inflame love, and every thing that tends to gratify love, and every thing that tends to satisfy them: and that in the most clear and glorious manner, without any darkness or delusion, without any impediment or interruption. Now the saints, while in the body, see something of Christ's glory and love; as we, in the dawning of the morning, see something of the reflected light of the sun mingled with darkness; but when separated from the body, they see their glorious and loving Redeemer, as we see the sun when risen, and showing his whole disk above the horizon, by his direct beams, in a clear hemisphere, and with perfect day.

III. The souls of true saints, when absent from the body, go to be with Jesus Christ, as they are brought into a most perfect conformity to, and union with, him.

Their spiritual conformity is begun while they are in the body; here beholding, as in a glass, the glory of the Lord, they are changed into the same image; but when they come to see him as he is, in heaven, then they become like him in another manner. That perfect sight will abolish all remains of deformity, disagreement, and sinful unlikeness; as all darkness is abolished before the full blaze of the sun's meridian light: it is impossible that the least degree of obscurity should remain before such light; so it is impossible the least degree of sin and spiritual deformity should remain, in such a view of the spiritual beauty and glory of Christ, as the saints enjoy in heaven; when they see that Sun of righteousness without a cloud, they themselves shine forth as the sun, and shall be as little suns, without a spot.

For then is come the time when Christ presents his saints to himself, in glorious beauty; "not having spot, or wrinkle, or any such thing;" and having holiness without a blemish. And then the saints' union with Christ is perfected. This also is begun in this world. The relative union is both begun and perfected at once, when the soul first closes with Christ by faith: the real union, consisting in the union of hearts and affections, and in the vital union, is begun in this world and perfected in the next. The union of the heart of a believer to Christ, is begun when his heart is drawn to Christ, by the first discovery of divine excellency, at conversion; and consequent on this drawing and closing of his heart with Christ, is established a vital union with Christ; whereby the believer becomes a living branch of the true vine, living by a communication of the sap and vital juice of the stock and root; and a member of Christ's mystical body, living by a communication of spiritual and vital influences from the head, and by a kind of participation of Christ's own life. But while the saints are in the body, there is much remaining distance between Christ and them: there are remainders of alienation, and the vital union is very imperfect; and so consequently is the communication of spiritual life and vital influences: there is much between Christ and believers to keep them asunder, much indwelling sin, much temptation, a world of carnal objects, to keep off the soul from Christ, and hinder a perfect coalescence.

But when the soul leaves the body, all these clogs and hindrances shall be removed, every separating wall shall be broken down, and every impediment taken out of the way, and all distance shall cease; the heart shall be wholly and forever attached and bound to him, by a perfect view of his glory. And the vital union shall then be brought to perfection; the soul shall live perfectly in and upon Christ, being perfectly filled with his spirit, and animated by his vital influences; living, as it were, only by Christ's life, without any remainder of spiritual death, or carnal life.

IV. Departed souls of saints are with Christ, as they enjoy a glorious and immediate intercourse and converse with him.

While we are present with our friends, we have opportunity for that free and immediate conversation with them, which we cannot have in absence from them. And therefore, by reason of the vastly more free, perfect, and immediate intercourse with Christ, which the saints enjoy when absent from the body, they are fitly represented as present with him.

The most intimate intercourse becomes that relation that the saints stand in to Jesus Christ; and especially becomes that most perfect and glorious union they shall be brought into with him in heaven. They are not merely Christ's servants, but his friends, John 15:15. His brethren and companions, Psalm 122:8; "yea, they are the spouse of Christ." They are espoused or betrothed to Christ while in the body; but when they go to heaven, they enter into the king's palace, their marriage with him is come, and the king brings them into his chambers indeed. They then go to dwell with Christ constantly, to enjoy the most perfect converse with him. Christ conversed in the most friendly manner with his disciples on earth; he admitted one of them to lean on his bosom: but they are admitted much more fully and freely to converse with him in heaven.

Though Christ be there [in heaven] in a state of glorious exaltation, reigning in the majesty and glory of the sovereign Lord and God of heaven and earth, angels and men; yet this will not hinder intimacy and freedom of intercourse, but rather promote it. For he is thus exalted, not only for himself, but for them; he is instated [installed] in this glory of head over all things for their sakes, that they might be exalted and glorified; and when they go to heaven where he is, they are exalted and glorified with him; and shall not be kept at a more awful distance from Christ, but shall be admitted nearer, and to a greater intimacy. For they shall be unspeakably more fit for it, and Christ in more fit circumstances to bestow on them this blessedness. Their seeing the great glory of their friend and Redeemer, will not awe them to a distance, and make them afraid of a near approach; but on the contrary, will most powerfully draw them near, and encourage and engage them to holy freedom. For they will know that it is he that is their own Redeemer, and beloved friend and bridegroom; the very same that loved them with a dying love, and redeemed them to God by his blood. Matt. 14:27: "It is I; be not afraid." Rev. 1:17, 18: "Fear not: I am he that liveth, and was dead."

And the nature of this glory of Christ that they shall see, will be such as will draw and encourage them; for they will not only see infinite majesty and greatness, but infinite grace, condescension, and mildness, and gentleness and sweetness, equal to his majesty. For he appears in heaven, not only as "the Lion of the tribe of Judah, but as the Lamb, and the Lamb in the midst of the throne," (Rev. 5:5, 6); and this Lamb in the midst of the throne shall be their shepherd, to "feed them, and lead them to living fountains of water" (Rev. 7:17); so that the sight of Christ's great kingly majesty will be no terror to them; but will only serve the more to heighten their pleasure and surprise. When Mary was about to embrace Christ, being full of joy at the sight of him again alive after his crucifixion, Christ forbids her to do it for the present, because he was not yet ascended. John 20:16, 17:

> Jesus saith unto her, "Mary." She turned herself, and saith unto him, "Rabboni," which is to say, Master. Jesus saith unto her, "Touch me not: for I am not yet ascended to my Father: but go to my brethren, and say unto them, 'I ascend unto my Father, and your Father, and to my God and your God.' "

As if he had said,

> This is not the time and place for that freedom your love to me desires: this is appointed in heaven after my ascension. I am going thither; and you that are my true disciples, shall, as my brethren and companions, soon be there with me in my glory. And then there shall be no restraint. That is the place appointed for the most perfect expressions of complacence and endearment, and full enjoyment of mutual love.

And accordingly the souls of departed saints with Christ in heaven, shall have Christ as it were unbosomed unto them, manifesting those infinite riches of love towards them, that have been there from eternity; and they shall be enabled to express their love to him, in an infinitely better manner than ever they could while in the body. Thus they shall eat and drink abundantly, and swim in the ocean of love, and be eternally swallowed up in the infinitely bright, and infinitely mild and sweet beams of divine love; eternally receiving that light, eternally full of it, and eternally compassed round with it, and everlastingly reflecting it back again to the fountain of it.

V. The souls of the saints, when they leave their bodies at death, go to be with Christ, as they are received to a glorious fellowship with Christ in his blessedness.

As the wife is received to a joint possession of her husband's estate, and as the wife of a prince partakes with him in his princely possessions and honors; so the church—the spouse of Christ, when the marriage comes, and she is received to dwell with him in heaven—shall partake with him in his glory. When Christ rose from the dead, and took possession of eternal life; this was not as a private person, but as the public head of all his redeemed people. He took possession of it for them, as well as for himself; and "they are quickened together with him, and raised up together." And so when he ascended into heaven, and was exalted to great glory there, this also was as a public person. He took possession of heaven, not only for himself, but his people, as their forerunner and head, that they might ascend also, "and sit together in heavenly places with him"(Eph. 2:5, 6). "Christ writes upon them his new name" (Rev. 3:12); i.e., he makes them partakers of his own glory and exaltation in heaven. His new name is that new honor and glory that the Father invested him with, when he set him on his own right hand. As a prince, when he advances anyone to new dignity in his kingdom, gives him a new title, Christ and his saints shall be glorified together (Rom. 8:17).

The saints in heaven have communion, or a joint participation, with Christ in his glory and blessedness in heaven, in the following respects, more especially.

1. *They partake with him in the ineffable delights he has in heaven, in the enjoyment of his Father.* When Christ ascended into heaven, he was received to a glorious and peculiar joy and blessedness in the enjoyment of his Father, who, in his passion, hid his face from him; such an enjoyment as became the relation he stood in to the Father, and such as was a meet reward for the great and hard service he had performed on earth. Then "God showed him the path of life, and brought him into his presence, where is fullness of joy, and to sit on his right hand, where there are pleasures for evermore," as is said of Christ, Psalm 16:11. Then the Father "made him most blessed forever. He made him exceeding glad with his countenance;" as in Psalm 21:6. The saints, by virtue of their union with Christ, and being his members, do, in some sort partake of his childlike relation to the Father; and so are heirs with him of his happiness in the enjoyment of his Father; as seems to be intimated by the apostle, in Gal. 4:4–7. The spouse of Christ, by virtue of her espousals to that only-begotten Son of God, is, as it were, a partaker of his filial relation to God, and becomes the king's daughter, Psalm 14:13, and so partakes with her divine husband in his enjoyment of "his Father and her Father, his God and her God." A promise of this seems to be implied in those words of Christ to Mary, John 20:17. Thus Christ's faithful servants "enter into the joy of their Lord," Matt. 25:21, 23, and "Christ's joy remains in them;" agreeably to those words of Christ, John 15:11.

Christ from eternity is, as it were, in the bosom of the Father, as the object of his infinite complacence. In him is the Father's eternal happiness. Before the world was, he was with the Father, in the enjoyment of his infinite love; and had infinite delight and blessedness in that enjoyment; as he declares of himself in Prov. 8:30: "Then I was by him as one brought up with him. And I was daily his delight, rejoicing always before him." And when

Christ ascended to the Father after his passion, he went to him, to the enjoyment of the same glory and blessedness in the enjoyment of his love; agreeably to his prayer the evening before his crucifixion, John 17:5: "And now, O Father, glorify me with thine own self, with the glory I had with thee before the world was." And in the same prayer, he manifests it to be his will, that his true disciples should be with him in the enjoyment of that joy and glory, which he then asked for himself, verse 13: "That my joy might be fulfilled in themselves" and verse 22, "And the glory which thou gavest me, I have given them." This glory of Christ, which the saints are to enjoy with him, is that which he has in the enjoyment of the Father's infinite love to him; as appears by the last words of that prayer of our Lord, verse 26: "That the love wherewith thou hast loved me, may be in them, and I in them." The love which the Father has to his Son is great indeed: the Deity does, as it were, wholly and entirely flow out in a stream of love to Christ; and the joy and pleasure of Christ is proportionably great. This is the stream of Christ's delights, the river of his infinite pleasure; which he will make his saints to drink of with him, agreeably to Psal. 36:8, 9:

> They shall be abundantly satisfied with the fatness of thy house. Thou shalt make them drink of the river of thy pleasures. For with thee is the fountain of life. In thy light shall we see light.

The saints shall have pleasure in partaking with Christ in his pleasure, and shall see light in his light. They shall partake with Christ of the same river of pleasure, shall drink of the same water of life, and of the same new wine in Christ's Father's kingdom, Matt. 26:29. That new wine is especially that joy and happiness that Christ and his true disciples shall partake of together in glory, which is the purchase of Christ's blood, or the reward of his obedience unto death. Christ, at his ascension into heaven, received everlasting pleasures at his Father's right hand, and in the enjoyment of his Father's love, as the reward of his own death, or obedience unto death. But the same righteousness is reckoned to both head and members; and both shall have fellowship in the same reward, each according to their distinct capacity.

That the saints in heaven have such a communion with Christ in his joy, and do so partake with him in his own enjoyment of the Father, does greatly manifest the transcendent excellency of their happiness, and their being admitted to a vastly higher privilege in glory than the angels.

2. *The saints in heaven are received to a fellowship or participation with Christ in the glory of that dominion to which the Father hath exalted him.* The saints—when they ascend to heaven as Christ ascended, and are made to sit

together with him in heavenly places, and are partakers of the glory of his exaltation—are exalted to reign with him. They are through him made kings and priests, and reign with him, and in him, over the same kingdom. As the Father hath appointed unto him a kingdom, so he has appointed to them. The Father has appointed the Son to reign over his own kingdom, and the Son appoints his saints to reign in his.

The Father has given to Christ to sit with him on his throne, and Christ gives to the saints to sit with him on his throne, agreeably to Christ's promise, Rev. 3:21. Christ, as God's Son, is the heir of his kingdom, and the saints are joint heirs with Christ: which implies, that they are heirs of the same inheritance, to possess the same kingdom, in and with him, according to their capacity. Christ, in his kingdom, reigns over heaven and earth; he is appointed the heir of all things; and so all things are the saints'; "whether Paul, or Apollos, or Cephas, or the world, or life, or death, or things present, or things to come," all are theirs; because they are Christ's, and united to him, (1 Cor. 3:21–23). The angels are given to Christ as a part of his dominion: they are all given to wait upon him as ministering spirits to him. So also they are all, even the highest and most dignified of them, ministering spirits, to minister to them who are the heirs of salvation. They are Christ's angels, and they are also *their* angels. Such is the saints' union with Christ, and their interest in him, that what he possesses, they possess, in a much more perfect and blessed manner than if all things were given to them separately, and by themselves, to be disposed of according to their discretion. They are now disposed of so as, in every respect, to be most for their blessedness, by an infinitely better discretion than their own; and in being disposed of by their head and husband, between whom and them there is the most perfect union of hearts, and so the most perfect union of wills, and who are most perfectly each other's.

As the glorified spouse of this great King reigns with and in him, in his dominion over the universe, so more especially does she partake with him in the joy and glory of his reign in his kingdom of grace; which is more peculiarly the kingdom that he possesses as Head of the church, and is that kingdom wherein she is more especially interested. It was especially to reign in this kingdom, that God the Father exalted him to his throne in heaven: he set his King on his holy hill of Zion, especially that he might reign over Zion, or over his church, in his kingdom of grace; and that he might be under the best advantages to carry on the designs of his love in this lower world. And therefore undoubtedly the saints in heaven are partakers with Christ in the joy and glory of the advancement and prosperity of his kingdom of grace on earth, and success of his gospel here, which he looks on as the peculiar glory of his reign.

The good shepherd rejoices when he finds but one sheep that was lost; and his friends and neighbors in heaven rejoice with him on that occasion. That part of the family that is in heaven is surely not unacquainted with the affairs of that part of the same family that is on earth. They that are with the King and are next to him, the royal family, that dwell in his palace, are not kept in ignorance of the affairs of his kingdom. The saints in heaven are with the angels, the King's ministers, by which he manages the affairs of his kingdom, and who are continually ascending and descending from heaven to the earth, and one or other of them daily employed as ministering spirits to each individual member of the church below: besides the continual ascending of the souls of departed saints from all parts of the militant church.

On these accounts the saints in heaven must needs be under a thousand times greater advantage than we here for a full view of the state of the church on earth, and a speedy, direct, and certain acquaintance with all its affairs in every part. And that which gives them much greater advantage for such an acquaintance than the things already mentioned, is their being constantly in the immediate presence of Christ, and in the enjoyment of the most perfect intercourse with him, who is the King who manages all these affairs, and has an absolutely perfect knowledge of them. Christ is the head of the whole glorified assembly; they are mystically his glorified body: and what the head sees, it sees for the information of the whole body, according to its capacity: and what the head enjoys, is for the joy of the whole body.

The saints, in leaving this world, and ascending to heaven, do not go out of sight of things appertaining to Christ's kingdom on earth; but, on the contrary, they go out of a state of obscurity, and ascend above the mists and clouds into the clearest light: to a pinnacle in the very center of light, where everything appears in clear view. They have as much greater advantage to view the state of Christ's kingdom, and the works of the new creation here, than while they were in this world, as a man that ascends to the top of a high mountain has a greater advantage to view the face of the earth, than he had while he was in a deep valley, or thick forest below, surrounded on every side with those things that impeded and limited his sight. Nor do they view as indifferent or unconcerned spectators, any more than Christ himself is an unconcerned spectator.

The happiness of the saints in heaven consists very much in beholding the glory of God appearing in the work of redemption: for it is by this chiefly that God manifests his glory, the glory of his wisdom, holiness, grace, and other perfections, to both saints and angels; as is apparent by many Scriptures. And therefore undoubtedly their happiness consists very much in beholding the progress of this work in its application and success, and the steps by which infinite power and wisdom bring it to its consummation. And the saints in heaven are under unspeakably greater advantage to take the pleasure of beholding the progress of this work on earth than we are, that are here; as they are under greater advantages to see and understand the marvelous steps that Divine Wisdom takes in all that is done, and the glorious ends he obtains, the opposition Satan makes, and how he is baffled and overthrown. They can better see the connection of one event with another, and the beautiful order of all things that come to pass in the church in different ages, that to us appear like confusion. Nor do they only view these things, and rejoice in them, as a glorious and beautiful sight, but as persons interested, as Christ is interested; as possessing these things in Christ, and reigning with him, in this kingdom.

Christ's success in his work of redemption, in bringing home souls to himself, applying his saving benefits by his Spirit, and the advancement of the kingdom of grace in the world, is the reward especially promised to him by his Father in the covenant of redemption, for the hard and difficult service he performed while in the form of a servant; as is manifest by Isaiah 53:10–12.

But the saints shall be rewarded with him: they shall partake with him in the joy of this reward; for this obedience that is thus rewarded is reckoned to them as they are his members, as was before observed. This was especially the joy that was set before Christ, for the sake of which he endured the cross and despised the shame. And his joy is the joy of all heaven. They that are with him in heaven are under much the greatest advantages to partake with him in this joy; for they have a perfect communion with him, through whom, and in fellowship with whom, they enjoy and possess their whole inheritance, all their heavenly happiness; as much as the whole body has all its pleasure of music by the ear, and all the pleasure of its food by the mouth and stomach; and all the benefit and refreshment of the air by the lungs.

The saints while on earth pray and labor for the same thing that Christ labored for, viz., the advancement of the kingdom of God among men, the promoting of the prosperity of Zion, and flourishing of religion in this world; and most of them have suffered for that end as Christ did, have been made partakers with their head in his sufferings, and "filled up (as the apostle expresses it) that which is behind of the sufferings of Christ:" and therefore they shall partake with him of the glory and joy of the end obtained. Rom. 8:17, "We are joint heirs with Christ; if so be that we suffer with him, that we may be also glorified together." 2 Tim. 2:12, "If we suffer with him, we shall also reign with him."

Christ, when his sufferings were past, and he left the earth and ascended into heaven, was so far from having done with kingdom in this world, that it was as it were but then begun: and he ascended for that very end, that he might more fully possess and enjoy this kingdom, that he might reign in it, and be under the best advantages for it; as much as a king ascends a throne in order to reign over his people, and receive the honor and glory of his dominion. No more have the saints done with Christ's kingdom on earth, when they leave the earth and ascend into heaven.

> Christ came [i.e., ascended] with clouds of heaven, and came to the Ancient of days, and was brought near before him, to the very end, that he might receive dominion, and glory, and a kingdom, that all people, nations and languages, should serve him. (Dan. 7:13, 14)

Which shall be eminently fulfilled after the ruin of Antichrist, which is especially the time of Christ's kingdom. And the same is the time when "the kingdom and dominion, and greatness of the kingdom under the whole heaven, shall be given to the people of the saints of the Most High God;" as verse 27, in the same chapter. It is because they shall reign in and with Christ, the Most High, as seems intimated in the words that follow; "whose kingdom is an everlasting kingdom, and all dominions shall serve and obey him." This verse is true, not only of the saints on earth, but also the saints in heaven. Hence the saints in heaven, having respect to this time, do sing, in Rev. 5:10, "We shall reign on the earth."

And agreeably hereto, it is afterwards represented, that when the aforementioned time comes, the souls of them that in former ages had *suffered* with Christ, do *reign* with Christ; having, as it were given to them new life and joy, in that spiritual blessed resurrection, which shall then be of the church of God on earth; and thus it is that it is said, Matt. 5:5, "The meek (those that meekly and patiently suffer with Christ, and for his sake) shall inherit the earth:" they shall inherit it, and reign on earth with Christ. Christ is the heir of the world; and when the appointed time of his kingdom comes, his inheritance shall be given him, and then the meek, who are joint heirs, shall inherit the earth. The place in the Old Testament whence the words are taken, leads to a true interpretation of them. Psal. 37:11, "The meek shall inherit the earth, and shall delight themselves in the abundance of peace." That there is reference in these latter words, "the abundance of peace," to the peace and blessedness of the latter days. We may be satisfied by comparing these words with Psal. 72:7, "In his days shall be abundance of peace so long as the moon endureth," and Jer. 33:6, "I will reveal to them the abundance of peace and truth." Also Isai. 2:4, Micah 4:3, Isai. 11:6–9, and many other parallel places.

The saints in heaven will be as much with Christ in reigning over the nations, and in the glory of his dominion at that time, as they will be with him in the honor of judging the world at the last day. That promise of Christ to his disciples, Matt. 19:28, 29, seems to have a special respect to the former of these. In verse 28, Christ promises to the disciples, that hereafter, "when the Son of Man shall sit on the throne of his glory, they shall sit on twelve thrones, judging the twelve tribes of Israel." The saints in heaven reigning on earth in the glorious latter day, are described in language accommodated to this promise of Christ, Rev. 20:4: "And I saw thrones, and they sat upon them; and judgment was given them. And they reigned with Christ." And the promise in the next verse, in that 19th [chapter] of Matthew, seems to have its fulfillment at the same time:

> And every one that hath forsaken houses, or brethren, or sisters, or fathers, or wife, or children, or lands, for my name's sake shall receive a hundred fold, and shall inherit everlasting life;

i.e., in the time when the saints shall inherit the earth and reign on earth, the earth, with all its blessings and good things, shall be given in great abundance to the church, to be possessed by the saints. This shall they receive in this present world, and in the time to come everlasting life.

The saints in heaven shall partake with Christ in the triumph and glory of those victories that he shall obtain in that future glorious time, over the kings and nations of the world, that are sometimes represented by his ruling them with a rod of iron, and dashing them in pieces as a potter's vessel. Which doubtless there is respect to in Rev. 2:26, 27:

> He that overcometh, and keepeth my words unto the end, to him will I give power over the nations: (and he shall rule them with a rod of iron; as the vessel of a potter shall they be broken to shivers:) even as I received of my Father.

And Psal. 149:5, to the end:

> Let the saints be joyful in glory; let them sing aloud upon their beds;"

(i.e., in their separate state after death; compare Isai. 57:1, 2.)

> Let the high praises of God be in their mouth, and a two-edged sword in their hand: to execute vengeance upon the heathen, and punishments upon the people; to bind their kings with chains, and their nobles with fetters of iron, to execute upon them the judgment written: this honor have all the saints.

Accordingly, when Christ appears riding forth to his victory over Antichrist, (Rev. 19), the hosts of heaven appear going forth with him in robes of triumph, verse 14. And when Antichrist is destroyed, the inhabitants of heaven, and the holy apostles and prophets, are called upon to rejoice, (Rev. 18:20). And accordingly the whole multitude of the inhabitants of heaven, on that occasion, do appear to exult and praise God with exceeding joy, chap. 19:1–8, and chap. 11:15; and are also represented as greatly rejoicing on occasion of the ruin of the heathen empire, in the days of Constantine, chap 12:10.

And it is observable all along in the visions of that book, the hosts of heaven appear as much concerned and interested in the events appertaining to the kingdom of Christ here below, as the saints on earth. The day of the commencement of the church's latter day glory is eminently

> the day of Christ's espousals; the day of the gladness of his heart, when as the bridegroom rejoiceth over the bride, so he will rejoice over his church.

And then will all heaven exceedingly rejoice with him. And therefore they say at that time, Rev. 19:7, "Let us be glad, and rejoice, and give glory to him; for the marriage of the Lamb is come."

Thus Abraham enjoys these things when they come to pass, that were of old promised to him, and that he saw beforehand, and rejoiced in. He will enjoy the fulfillment of the promise of all the families of the earth being blessed in his seed, when it shall be accomplished. And all the ancient patriarchs, who died in faith of promises of glorious things that should be accomplished in this world, "who had not received the promises, but saw them afar off, and were persuaded of them, and embraced them," [Heb. 11:13] do actually enjoy them when fulfilled. David actually saw and enjoyed the fulfillment of that promise, in its due time, which was made to him many hundred years before, and was all his salvation and all his desire. Thus Daniel shall stand in his lot at the end of the days pointed out by his own prophecy. Thus the saints of old that died in faith, not having received the promises, are made perfect, and have their faith crowned by the better things accomplished in these latter days of the gospel, Heb. 11:39, 40, which they see and enjoy in their time.

3. The departed souls of saints have fellowship with Christ, in his blessed and eternal employment of glorifying the Father. The happiness of heaven consists not only in contemplation, and a mere passive enjoyment, but consists very much in action. And particularly in actively serving and glorifying God. This is expressly mentioned as a great part of the blessedness of the saints in their most perfect state, Rev. 22:3: "And there shall be no more curse; but the throne of God and of the Lamb shall be in it; and his servants shall serve him." The angels are as a flame of fire in their ardor and activity in God's service: the four animals in Rev. 4 (which are generally supposed to signify the angels), are represented as continually giving praise and glory to God, and are said not to rest day nor night, verse 8. The souls of departed saints are, doubtless, become as the angels of God in heaven in this respect. And Jesus Christ is the head of the whole glorious assembly; as in other things appertaining to their blessed state, so in this, of their praising and glorifying the Father.

When Christ, the night before he was crucified, prayed for his exaltation to glory, it was that he might glorify the Father: John 17:1, "These words spake Jesus, and lift up his eyes to heaven, and said, 'Father, the hour is come, glorify thy Son, that thy Son also may glorify thee.' " And this he doubtless does, now he is in heaven; not only in fulfilling the Father's will, in what he does as head of the church and ruler of the universe, but also in leading the heavenly assembly in their praises.

When Christ instituted the Supper, and ate and drank with his disciples at his table (giving them therein a representation and pledge of their future feasting with him, and drinking new wine in his heavenly Father's kingdom), he at that time led them in their praises to God, in that hymn that they sang. And so doubtless he leads his glorified disciples in heaven. David was the sweet psalmist of Israel, and he led the great congregation of God's people in their songs of praise. Herein, as well as in innumerable other things, he was a type of Christ, who is often spoken of in Scripture by the name of David. And many of the psalms that David penned, were songs of praise, that he, by the spirit of prophecy, uttered in the name of Christ, as Head of the church, and leading the saints in their praises. Christ in heaven leads the glorious assembly in their praises to God, as Moses did the congregation of Israel at the Red Sea; which is implied in its being said, that "they sing the song of Moses and the Lamb," Rev. 15:2, 3.

In Rev. 14:5, John tells us, that "he heard a voice come out of the throne, saying, 'Praise our God, all ye his servants, and ye that fear him, both small and great.' " Who can it be that utters this voice out of the throne, but the Lamb that is in the midst of the throne, calling on the glorious assembly of saints to praise his Father and their Father, his God and their God? And what the consequence of this voice is, we have an account in the next words:

> And I heard as it were the voice of a great multitude, and as the voice of many waters, and as the voice of mighty thunderings, saying, "Alleluia; for the Lord God omnipotent reigneth."

Application

The use that I would make of what has been said on this subject is of *exhortation*. Let us all be exhorted hence earnestly to seek after that great privilege that has been spoken of, that when "we are absent from the body, we may be present with the Lord." We cannot continue always in these earthly tabernacles: they are very frail, and will soon decay and fall; and are continually liable to be overthrown by innumerable means: our souls must soon leave them, and go into the eternal world.

O, how infinitely great will the privilege and happiness of such be, who at that time shall go to be with Christ in his glory, in the manner that has been represented! The privilege of the twelve disciples was great, in being so constantly with Christ as his family, in his state of humiliation. The privilege of those three disciples was great, who were with him in the mount of his transfiguration; where was exhibited to them some little semblance of his future glory in heaven, such as they might behold in the present frail, feeble, and sinful state: they were greatly entertained and delighted with what they saw; and were for making tabernacles to dwell there, and return no more down the mount. And great was the privilege of Moses when he was with Christ in Mount Sinai, and besought him to show him his glory, and he saw his back parts as he passed by, and proclaimed his name.

But is not that privilege infinitely greater, that has now been spoken of, the privilege of being with Christ in heaven, where he sits on the right hand of God, in the glory of the King and God of angels, and of the whole universe, shining forth as the great light, the bright sun of that world of glory; there to dwell in the full, constant and everlasting view of his beauty and brightness; there most freely and intimately to converse with him, and fully to enjoy his love, as his friends and spouse; there to have fellowship with him in the infinite pleasure and joy he has in the enjoyment of his Father; there to sit with him on his throne, and reign with him in the possession of all things, and partake with him in the joy and glory of his victory over his enemies, and the advancement of his kingdom in the world, and to join with him in joyful songs of praise to his Father and their Father, to his God and their God, forever and ever? Is not such a privilege worth the seeking after?

But here, as a special enforcement of this exhortation, I would improve that dispensation of God's holy providence, that is the sorrowful occasion of our coming together at this time, viz., the death of that eminent servant of Jesus Christ, in the work of the gospel ministry, whose funeral is this day to be attended; together with what was observable in him, living and dying.

In this dispensation of Providence, God puts us in mind of our mortality, and forewarns us that the time is approaching when we must be absent from the body, and "must all appear" (as the apostle observes in the next verse but one to my text)

> before the judgment seat of Christ, that every one of us may receive the things done in the body, according to what we have done, whether it be good or bad.

And in him, whose death we are now called to consider and improve, we have not only an instance of mortality, but an instance of one that, being absent from the body, is present with the Lord; as we have all imaginable reason to conclude. And that, whether we consider the nature of the operations he was under, or about the time whence he dates his conversion, or the nature and course of his inward exercises from that time forward, or his outward conversation and long space wherein he looked death in the face.

His convictions of sin, preceding his first consolations in Christ (as appears by a written account he has left of his inward exercises and experiences), were exceeding deep and thorough: his trouble and exercise of mind, through a sense of guilt and misery, very great and long continued, but yet sound and solid; consisting in no unsteady, violent and unaccountable hurries and frights, and strange perturbations of mind; but arising from the most serious consideration, and proper illumination of the conscience to discern and consider the true state of things. And the light let into his mind at conversion, and the influences and exercises that his mind was subject to at that time, appear very agreeable to reason and the gospel of Jesus Christ; the change very great and remarkable, without any appearance of strong impressions on the imagination, sudden flights and pangs of the affections, and vehement emotions in animal nature; but attended with proper intellectual views of the supreme glory of the divine Being, consisting in the infinite dignity and beauty of the perfections of his nature, and of the transcendent excellency of the way of salvation by Christ. This was about eight years ago, when he was about twenty-one years of age.

Thus God sanctified and made meet for his use, that vessel that he intended to make eminently a vessel of honor in his house, and which he had made of large capacity, having endowed him with very uncommon abilities and gifts of nature. He was a singular instance of a ready invention, natural eloquence, easy flowing expression, sprightly apprehension, quick discerning, and a very strong memory; and yet of a very penetrating genius, close and clear thought, and piercing judgment. He had an exact taste: his understanding was (if I may so express it) of a quick, strong and distinguishing scent.

His learning was very considerable: he had a great taste for learning; and applied himself to his studies in so close a manner when he was at college, that he much injured his health; and was obliged on that account for a while to leave the college, throw by his studies and return home. He was esteemed one that excelled in learning in that society.

He had an extraordinary knowledge of men, as well as things. [He] had a great insight into human nature, and excelled most that ever I knew in a communicative faculty: he had a peculiar talent at accommodating himself to the capacities, tempers and circumstances, of those that he would instruct or counsel.

He had extraordinary gifts for the pulpit: I never had opportunity to hear him preach, but have often heard him pray: and I think his manner of addressing himself to God, and expressing himself before him, in that duty, almost inimitable; such (so far as I may judge) as I have very rarely known equaled. He expressed himself with that exact propriety and pertinency, in such significant, weighty, pungent expressions; with that decent appearance of sincerity, reverence, and solemnity, and great distance from all affectation, as forgetting the presence of men, and as being in the immediate presence of a great and holy God, that I have scarcely ever known paralleled. And his manner of preaching, by what I have often heard of it from good judges, was no less excellent; being clear and instructive, natural, nervous, forcible, and moving, and very searching and convincing. He [was] nauseated [by] an affected noisiness, and violent boisterousness in the pulpit; and yet much disrelished a flat, cold delivery, when the subject of discourse, and matter delivered, required affection and earnestness.

Not only had he excellent talents for the study and the pulpit, but also for conversation. He was of a sociable disposition; and was remarkably free, entertaining, and profitable in ordinary discourse; and had much of a faculty of disputing, defending truth and confuting error.

As he excelled in his judgment and knowledge of things in general, so especially in divinity. He was truly, for one of his standing, an extraordinary divine. But above all, in matters relating to [discernment regards to] experimental religion. In this, I know I have the concurring opinion of some that have had a name for persons of the best judgment. And according to what ability I have to judge things of this nature, and according to my opportunities, which of late have been very great, I never knew his equal, of his age and standing, for clear, accurate notions of the nature and essence of true religion, and its distinctions from its various false appearances; which I suppose to be owing to these three things meeting together in him;—the strength of his natural genius, the great opportunities he had of observation of others, in various parts, both white people and Indians, and his own great experience.

His experiences of the holy influences of God's Spirit were not only great at his first conversion, but they were so, in a continued course, from that time forward; as appears by a record, or private journal, he kept of his daily inward exercises, from the time of his conversion, until he was disabled by the failing of his strength, a few days before his death. The change which he looked upon as his conversion, was not only a great change of the present views, affections, and frame of his mind; but was evidently the beginning of that work of God on his heart, which God carried on, in a very wonderful manner, from that time to his dying day.* He greatly abhorred the way of such [persons] as live on their first work, as though they had now got through their work, and are thence forward, by degrees, settled in a cold, lifeless, negligent, worldly frame; he had an ill opinion of such persons' religion.

His experiences were very diverse from many things that have lately obtained the reputation, with multitudes, of the very height of Christian experience. About the time that the false religion, which arises chiefly from impressions on the imagination, began first to make a very great appearance in the land, he was for a little while deceived with it, so as to think highly of it. And though he knew he never had such experiences as others told of, he thought it was because others' attainments were beyond his; and so coveted them. He told me, that he never had what is called an impulse, or a strong impression on his imagination, in things of religion, in his life.

*See Note 1 in Edwards' post-sermon comments (at the end of this chapter).

But [he] owned, that during the short time that he thought well of these things, he was tinged with that spirit of false zeal that is wont to attend them. But [he] said that then he was not in his element, but as a fish out of water. And when, after a little while, he came clearly to see the vanity and perniciousness of such things, it cost him abundance of sorrow and distress of mind, and to my knowledge he afterwards freely and openly confessed the errors in conduct that he had run into, and laid himself low before them whom he had offended.

And since his conviction of his error in those respects, he has ever had a peculiar abhorrence of that kind of bitter zeal, and those delusive experiences that have been the principal source of it. He detested enthusiasm [religious fanaticism] in all its forms and operations; and abhorred whatever in opinion or experience seemed to verge towards antinomianism*; as, the experiences of those whose first faith consists in believing that Christ died for them in particular; and their first love, in loving God, because they supposed they were the objects of his love; and their assurance of their good estate from some immediate testimony, or suggestion, either with or without texts of Scripture, that their sins are forgiven, that God loves them, etc., and the joys of such as rejoiced more in their own supposed distinction from others, in honor, and privileges, and high experiences, than in God's excellency and Christ's beauty; and the spiritual pride of such laymen, that are for setting up themselves as public teachers, and cry down human learning, and a learned ministry.

He greatly disliked a disposition in persons to much noise and show in religion, and affecting to be abundant in publishing and proclaiming their own experience; though he did not condemn, but approved of Christians speaking of their experiences, on some occasions, and to some persons, with modesty, discretion, and reserve. He abominated the spirit and practice of the generality of the Separatists† in this land. I heard him say, once and again, that he had been much with this kind of people, and was acquainted with many of them, in various parts; and that by this acquaintance, he knew that what was chiefly and most generally in repute amongst them, as the power of godliness, was entirely a different thing from that vital piety recommended in the Scripture, and had nothing in it of that

*Anti-nomianism: the doctrine or belief that the Gospel frees Christians from required obedience to any law, whether scriptural, civil, or moral, and that salvation is attained solely through faith and the gift of divine grace. *(American Heritage Dictionary.)*

†The Separatists of Edwards' time were a Christian religious sub-group who insisted on direct God-to-man ties and challenged connections to older, traditional churches.

nature. He never was more full in condemning these things than in his last illness, and after he ceased to have any expectation of life: and particularly when he had the greatest and nearest views of approaching eternity; and several times, when he thought himself actually dying, and expected in a few minutes to be in the eternal world, as he himself told me.*

As his inward experiences appear to have been of the right kind, and were very remarkable as to their degree, so was his outward behavior and practice agreeable. He in his whole course acted as one who had indeed sold all for Christ, and had entirely devoted himself to God, and made his glory his highest end, and was fully determined to spend his whole time and strength in his service. He was lively in religion, in the right way; lively, not only, nor chiefly, with his tongue, in professing and talking; but lively in the work and business of religion. He was not one of those who are for contriving ways to shun the cross, and get to heaven with ease and sloth; but was such an instance of one living a life of labor and self-denial, and spending his strength and substance in pursuing that great end, and the glory of his Redeemer, that perhaps is scarcely to be paralleled in this age in these parts of the world. Much of this may be perceived by anyone that reads his printed Journal; but much more has been learned by long intimate acquaintance with him, and by looking into his Diary since his death, which he purposely concealed in what he published.

And as his desires and labors for the advancement of Christ's kingdom were great, so was his success. God was pleased to make him the instrument of bringing to pass the most remarkable things among the poor savages—in enlightening, awakening, reforming, and changing their disposition and manners, and wonderfully transforming them—that perhaps can be produced in these latter ages of the world. An account of this has been given the public in his Journals, drawn up by order of the Honorable Society in Scotland, that employed him; which I would recommend to the perusal of all such as take pleasure in the wonderful works of God's grace, and would read that which will peculiarly tend both to entertain and profit a Christian mind.†

No less extraordinary than the things already mentioned of him in life, was his constant calmness, peace, assurance, and joy in God, during the long time he looked death in the face, without the least hope of recovery; continuing without interruption to the last; while his distemper very sensibly [with physical sensation] preyed upon his vitals, from day to day, and

*See Note 2 in Edwards' post-sermon comments.

†See "Mr. Brainerd's Journal," *Works of Jonathan Edwards* (Hendrickson, 1998).

oft brought him to that state in which he looked upon himself, and was thought by others, to be dying. The thoughts of approaching death never seemed in the least to damp[en], but rather to encourage him, and exhilarate his mind. And the nearer death approached, the more desirous he seemed to be of it. He said, not long before his death, that "the consideration of the day of death, and the day of judgment, had a long time been peculiarly sweet to him." And at another time, that "he could not but think of the meetness [appropriateness] there was in throwing such a rotten carcass as his into the grave: it seemed to him to be the right way of disposing of it." He often used the epithet "glorious," when speaking of the day of his death, calling it "that glorious day." On a Sabbath-day morning, September 27, feeling an unusual appetite to food, and looking on it as a sign of approaching death, he said, "he should look on it as a favor, if this might be his dying day, and that he longed for the time."

He had before expressed himself desirous of seeing his brother again, whose return had been expected from the Jerseys; but then (speaking of him) he said, "I am willing to go, and never see him again: I care not what I part with, to be forever with the Lord." Being asked, that morning, how he did, he answered, "I am almost in eternity: God knows, I long to be there. My work is done; I have done with all my friends: all the world is nothing to me." On the evening of the next day, when he thought himself dying, and was apprehended to be so by others, and he could utter himself only by broken whispers, he often repeated the word "eternity"; and said, "I shall soon be with the holy angels. He will come; he will not tarry." He told me one night, as he went to bed, that "he expected to die that night." And added, "I am not at all afraid, I am willing to go this night, if it be the will of God. Death is what I long for." He sometimes expressed himself as [having] "nothing to do but to die: and being willing to go that minute, if it was the will of God." He sometimes used that expression, "Oh, why is his chariot so long in coming?"

He seemed to have remarkable exercises of resignation to the will of God. He once told me, that

> he had longed for the outpouring of the Holy Spirit of God, and the glorious times of the church, and hoped they were coming; and should have been willing to have lived to promote religion at that time, if that had been the will of God. But, (says he) I am willing it should be as it is: I would not have the choice to make myself for ten thousand worlds.*

*See Note 3 in Edwards' post-sermon comments.

He several times spake of the different kinds of willingness to die: and spoke of it as an ignoble mean kind [of willingness], to be willing, only to get rid of pain, or to go to heaven only to get honor and advancement there. His own longings for death seemed to be quite of a different kind, and for nobler ends. When he was first taken with something like a diarrhea, which is looked upon as one of the last and most fatal symptoms in a consumption, he said, "Oh, now the glorious time is coming? I have longed to serve God perfectly; and God will gratify these desires." And at one time or another, in the latter part of his illness, he uttered these expressions:

> My heaven is to please God, and glorify him, and give all to him, and to be wholly devoted to his glory. That is the heaven I long for; that is my religion; and that is my happiness; and always was, ever since I supposed I had any true religion: and all those that are of that religion, shall meet me in heaven. I do not go to heaven to be advanced, but to give honor to God. It is no matter where I shall be stationed in heaven, whether I have a high or low seat there, but to love, and please, and glorify God. If I had a thousand souls, if they were worth any thing, I would give them all to God: but I have nothing to give, when all is done.
>
> It is impossible for any rational creature to be happy without acting all for God. God himself could not make me happy any other way.—I long to be in heaven, praising and glorifying God with the holy angels; all my desire is to glorify God.—My heart goes out to the burying-place, it seems to me a desirable place: But oh to glorify God! That is it! That is above all!—It is a great comfort to me to think that I have done a little for God in the world. It is but a very small matter; yet I have done a little; and I lament it, that I have not done more for him.—There is nothing in the world worth living for, but doing good, and finishing God's work, doing the work that Christ did. I see nothing else in the world that can yield any satisfaction, besides living to God, pleasing him, and doing his whole will. My greatest joy and comfort has been to do something for promoting the interest of religion, and the souls of particular persons.*

After he came to be in so low a state that he ceased to have the least expectation of recovery, his mind was peculiarly carried forth with earnest concern for the prosperity of the church of God on earth; which seemed very manifestly to arise from a pure disinterested love to Christ, and desire of his glory. The prosperity of Zion was a theme he dwelt much upon, and

*See Note 4 in Edwards' post-sermon comments.

of which he spake much; and more and more, the nearer death approached. He told me when near his end, that

> he never, in all his life, had his mind so led forth in desires and earnest prayers for the flourishing of Christ's kingdom on earth, as since he was brought so exceeding low at Boston.

He seemed much to wonder, that there appeared no more disposition in ministers and people, to pray for the flourishing of religion through the world. And particularly, he several times expressed his wonder, that there appeared no more forwardness to comply with the proposal lately made from Scotland, for united extraordinary prayer among God's people, for the coming of Christ's kingdom, and sent it as his dying advice to his own congregation, that they should practice agreeably to that proposal.*

A little before his death, he said to me, as I came into the room,

> My thoughts have been employed on the old dear theme, the prosperity of God's church on earth. As I waked out of sleep, (said he) I was led to cry for the pouring out of God's Spirit, and the advancement of Christ's kingdom, which the dear Redeemer did and suffered so much for: it is that especially [that] makes me long for it.

But a few days before his death, he desired us to sing a psalm concerning the prosperity of Zion; which he signified his mind was engaged in above all things; and at his desire we sang a part of the 102nd Psalm. And when we had done, though he was then so low that he could scarcely speak, he so exerted himself, that he made a prayer, very audibly, wherein, besides praying for those present, and for his own congregation, he earnestly prayed for the reviving and flourishing of religion in the world. His own congregation especially lay much on his heart. He often spake of them; and commonly when he did so, it was with extraordinary tenderness; so that his speech was interrupted and drowned with weeping.

Thus I have endeavored to represent something of the character and behavior of that excellent servant of Christ, whose funeral is now to be attended. Though I have done it very imperfectly; yet I have endeavored to do it faithfully, and as in the presence and fear of God, without flattery; which surely is to be abhorred in ministers of the gospel, when speaking as messengers of the Lord of hosts. Such reason have we to be satisfied that the person spoken of, now he is absent from the body, is present with the Lord; and now wearing a crown of glory, of distinguished brightness.

---

§See "A Call to United Extraordinary Prayer," *Works of Jonathan Edwards* (Hendrickson, 1998).

And how much is there in the consideration of such an example, and so blessed an end, to excite us, who are yet alive, with the greatest diligence and earnestness, to improve the time of life, that we also may go to be with Christ, when we forsake the body! The time is coming, and will soon come, we know not how soon, when we must take leave of all things here below, to enter on a fixed unalterable state in the eternal world. Oh, how well is it worth the while to labor and suffer, and deny ourselves, to lay up in store a good foundation of support and supply, against that time! How much is such a peace as we have heard of, worth at such a time!

And how dismal would it be, to be in such circumstances, under the outward distresses of a consuming, dissolving frame, and looking death in the face from day to day, with hearts uncleansed, and sin unpardoned, under a dreadful load of guilt and divine wrath, having much sorrow and wrath in our sickness, and nothing to comfort and support our minds; nothing before us but a speedy appearance before the judgment seat of an almighty, infinitely holy, and angry God, and an endless eternity in suffering his wrath without mercy! The person we have been speaking of, had a great sense of this. He said, not long before his death,

> It is sweet to me to think of eternity: the endlessness of it makes it sweet. But, oh, what shall I say to the eternity of the wicked! I cannot mention it, nor think of it!—The thought is too dreadful!

At another time, speaking of a heart devoted to God and his glory, he said,

> Oh, of what importance is it to have such a frame of mind, such a heart as this, when we come to die! It is this now that gives me peace.

How much is there, in particular, in the things that have been observed of this eminent minister of Christ, to excite us, who are called to the same great work of the gospel-ministry, to earnest care and endeavors, that we may be in like manner faithful in our work; that we may be filled with the same spirit, animated with the like pure and fervent flame of love to God, and the like earnest concern to advance the kingdom and glory of our Lord and Master, and the prosperity of Zion! How amiable did these principles render this servant of Christ in his life, and how blessed in his end! The time will soon come, when we also must leave our earthly tabernacles, and go to our Lord that sent us to labor in his harvest, to render an account of ourselves to him. Oh how does it concern us so to run as not uncertainly; so to fight, not as those that beat the air! And should not what we have heard excite us to depend on God for his help and assistance in our great work, and to be much in seeking the influences of his Spirit, an success in our labors, by fasting and prayer; in which the person spoken of was abundant? This practice he earnestly recommended on his death-bed, from his own experience of its great benefits, to some candidates for the ministry that stood by his bedside. He was often speaking of the great need ministers have of much of the Spirit of Christ in their work, and how little good they are like to do without it; and how,

> when ministers were under the special influences of the Spirit of God, it assisted them to come at the consciences of men, and (as he expressed it) as it were to handle them with hands: whereas, without the Spirit of God, said he, whatever reason and oratory we make use of, we do but make use of stumps, instead of hands.

Oh that the things that were seen and heard in this extraordinary person, his holiness, heavenliness, labor and self-denial in life, his so remarkably devoting himself and his all, in heart and practice, to the glory of God, and the wonderful frame of mind manifested, in so steadfast a manner, under the expectation of death, and the pains and agonies that brought it on, may excite in us all, both ministers and people, a due sense of the greatness of the work we have to do in the world, the excellency and amiableness of thorough religion in experience and practice, and the blessedness of the end of such, whose death finishes such a life, and the infinite value of their eternal reward, when absent from the body and present with the Lord; and effectually stir us up to endeavors, that in the way of such a holy life, we may at last come to so blessed an end. *Amen.*

Edwards' Post-Sermon Comments

As published in the 1834 edition of Works of Jonathan Edwards.

Note 1: This more abundantly appears by further opportunity of acquaintance with his [Brainerd's] Diary, since this sermon was delivered. Grace to him seems to have been almost continually, with scarcely the intermission of a day, in very sensible, and indeed vigorous and powerful, *exercise*, in one respect or other.

His heart appears to have been exercised, in a continued course, in such things as these, viz. the most ardent and pure love to God; great weariness from the world, and sense of its vanity; great humiliation; a most abasing sense of his own vileness; a deep sense of in-dwelling sin, which indeed was most evidently by far the greatest burden of his life, and more than all other afflictions that he met with, put together; great brokenness of heart before God, for his small attainments in grace, that he loved God so little, etc., mourning that he was so unprofitable; longings and earnest reachings of soul after holiness; earnest desires that God might be glorified, and the Christ's kingdom might be advanced in the world; wrestlings with God in prayer for these things; delight in the gospel of Jesus Christ, and the way of salvation by him; sweet complacence in those whose conversation savored of true holiness; compassion to the souls of men, and earnest intercessions in secret for them; great resignation to the will of God; a very frequent, most sensible renewed renunciation of all things for Christ, and giving up himself wholly to God, in soul and body; great distrust of his own heart, and universal dependence on God; longings after full deliverance from the body of sin and death, and perfect conformity to God, and perfectly glorifying him in heaven; clear views of eternity, almost as though he were actually out of the body, and had his eyes open in another world; a constant watchfulness over his own heart, and continual earnestness in his inward warfare with sin; together with great care, to the utmost, to improve time for God, in his service, and to his glory.

Note 2: Since this sermon was preached, I find what follows in his Diary for the last summer.

"Thursday, June 18. I was this day taken exceeding ill, and brought to the gates of death.—In this extreme weak state I continued for several weeks; and was frequently reduced so low as to be utterly speechless, and not able so much as to whisper a word. And even after I had so far revived as to walk about the house, and to step out of doors, I was exercised every day with a faint turn, which continued usually four or five hours. At which times, though I was not so utterly speechless, but that I could say "yes" or "no"; yet I could not converse at all, nor speak one sentence without making stops for breath. And diverse times, in this season, my friends gathered round my bed, to see me breathe my last; which they looked for every moment, as I myself also did.

"How I was the first day or two of my illness, with regard to the exercise of reason, I scarcely know; but I believe I was something [somewhat] shattered, with the violence of the fever, at times. But the third day of my illness, and constantly afterwards, for four or five weeks together, I enjoyed as much serenity of mind, and clearness of thought, as perhaps I ever did in my life. And I think my mind never penetrated with so much ease and freedom into divine things as at this time; and I never felt so capable of demonstrating the truth of many important doctrines of the gospel as now.

"And as I saw clearly the truth of those great doctrines, which are justly styled the doctrines of grace; so I saw with no less clearness, that the essence of true religion consisted in the soul's conformity to God, and acting above all selfish views, for his glory, longing to be for him, to live to him, and please and honor him in all things; and that, from a clear view of his infinite excellency and worthiness in himself, to be beloved, adored, worshiped, and served, by all intelligent creatures. Thus I saw, that when a soul loves God with a supreme love, he therein acts like the blessed God himself, who most justly loves himself in that manner; so when God's interest and his are become one, and he longs that God should be glorified, and rejoices to think that he is unchangeably possessed of the highest glory and blessedness, herein also he acts in conformity to God. In like manner, when the soul is fully resigned to, and rests satisfied and contented with, the divine will, here he is also conformed to God.

"I saw further, that as this divine temper, whereby the soul exalts God, and treads itself in the dust, is wrought in the soul by God's discovering his own glorious perfections, in the face of Jesus Christ, to it, by the special influences of his Holy Spirit; so he could not but have regard to it, as his own work; and as it is his image in the soul, he could not but take delight in it. Then I saw again that if God should slight and reject his own moral image, he must needs deny himself; which he cannot do. And thus I saw the stability and infallibility of this religion; and that those who were truly possessed of it, had the most complete and satisfying evidence of their being interested in all the benefits of Christ's redemption, having their hearts conformed to him; and that these, and these only, were qualified for the employments and entertainments of God's kingdom of glory; as not but these would have any relish of the business of heaven, which is to ascribe glory to God, and not to themselves; and that God (though I would speak it with great reverence of his name and perfections) could not, without denying himself, finally cast such away.

"The next thing I had then to do, was to inquire whether this was my religion. And here God was pleased to help me to the most easy remembrance and critical review of what had passed in course, of a religious nature, through several of the latter years of my life. And although I could discover much corruption attending my best duties, many selfish views and carnal ends, much spiritual pride, and self-exaltation, and innumerable other evils which compassed me about; I say, although I now discerned the sins of my holy things, as well as other actions; yet God was pleased, as I was reviewing, quickly to put this question out of doubt by showing me that I had, from time to time, acted above the utmost influence of mere self-love, that I had longed to please and glorify him, as my highest happiness, etc. And this review was through grace attended with a present feeling of the same divine temper of mind.

"I felt now pleased to think of the glory of God; and longed for heaven, as a state wherein I might glorify God perfectly, rather than a place of happiness for myself. And this feeling of the love of God in my heart, which I trust the Spirit of God excited in me afresh, was sufficient to give me full satisfaction, and make me long, as I had many times before done, to be with Christ. I did not now want any of the sudden suggestions that many are so pleased with—that Christ and his benefits are mine, that God loves me—in order to give me satisfaction about my state. No, my soul now abhorred those delusions of Satan; which are thought to be the immediate witness of the Spirit, while there is nothing but an empty suggestion of a certain fact, without any gracious discovery of the divine glory, or of the Spirit's work in their own hearts. I saw the awful delusion of this kind of confidence; as well as of the whole of that religion, which they usually spring from, or at least are the attendants of, the false religion of the late day, though a day of wondrous grace; the imaginations and impressions made only on the animal affections; together with the sudden suggestions made to the mind by Satan, transformed into an angel of light, of certain facts not revealed in Scripture; these, I say, and many like things, I fear have made up the greater part of the religious appearances in many places.

"These things I saw with great clearness, when I was thought to be dying, and God gave me great concern for his church and interest in the world at this time; not so much because the late remarkable influence upon the minds of people was abated, and almost wholly gone, as because of the false religion, the heats of imagination, and wild and selfish commotions of the animal affections, which attended the work of grace, had prevailed so far. This was that which my mind dwelt upon, almost day and night; and this to me was the darkest appearance respecting religion in the land. For it was this chiefly that had prejudiced the world against inward religion. And this I saw was the great misery of all, that so few saw any manner of difference between those exercises that were spiritual and holy, and those which have self-love only, for their beginning, center, and end."

Note 3: He writes thus in his Diary:

"August 23, 1747. In the week past, I had diverse turns of inward refreshing. Though my body was inexpressibly weak, followed continually with agues and fevers, sometimes my soul centered in God as my only portion; and I felt I should be forever unhappy if he did not reign. I saw the sweetness and happiness of being his subject, at his disposal. This made all my difficulties quickly vanish."

Note 4: In his diary he writes thus:

"September 7, 1747. When I was in great distress of body, my soul desired that God should be glorified. I saw there was no heaven but this. I could not but speak to the by-standers then of the only happiness, viz., pleasing God. Oh that I could forever live to God! The day, I trust, is at hand, the perfect day! Oh, the day of deliverance from all sin!"

"September 19. Near night, while I attempted to walk a little, my thoughts turned thus: How infinitely sweet it is to love God, and be all for him! Upon which it was suggested to me, 'You are not an angel, not lively and active.' To which my whole soul immediately replied, 'I as sincerely desire to love and glorify God as any angel in heaven.' Upon which it was suggested again, 'But you are filthy, not fit for heaven.' Hereupon instantly appeared the blessed robe of Christ's righteousness, which I could not but exult and triumph in.

"I viewed the infinite excellency of God: and my soul even broke with longings, that God should be glorified. I thought of dignity in heaven; but instantly the thought returned, 'I do not go to heaven to get honor, but to give all possible glory and praise.' Oh, how I longed that God should be glorified on earth also! Oh, I was made for eternity, if God might be glorified! Bodily pains I cared not for; though I was then in extremity, I never felt easier; I felt willing to glorify God in that state of bodily distress, as long as he pleased I should continue so. The grave appeared really sweet, and I longed to lodge my weary bones in it: but oh, that God might be glorified! This was the burden of all my cry. Oh, I knew I should be active as an angel in heaven, and that I should be stripped of my filthy garments! So that there was no objection. But oh, to love and praise God more, to please him forever! This my soul panted after, and even now pants for, while I write. Oh, that God may be glorified in the whole earth! Lord, let thy kingdom come.

"I longed for a spirit of preaching to descend and rest on ministers, that they might address the consciences of men with closeness and power. I saw God had the residue of the Spirit; and my soul longed it should be poured out from on high. I could not but plead with God for my dear congregation, that he would preserve it, and not suffer his great name to lose its glory in that work; my soul still longing, that God might be glorified."

Christ, the Example of Ministers

Preached at Portsmouth, at the ordination of the Rev. Mr. Job Strong, June 28, 1749.

"For I have given you an example, that he should do as I have done to you. Verily, verily, I say unto you, 'The servant is not greater than his lord, neither he that is sent greater than he that sent him.' "—John 13:15–16

We have in the context [of this verse] an account of one of the many very remarkable things that passed that night wherein Christ was betrayed (which was on many accounts the most remarkable night that ever was), viz. Christ's washing his disciples' feet. This action, as it was exceeding wonderful in itself, so it manifestly was symbolical, and represented something else far more important and more wonderful, even that greatest and most wonderful of all things that ever came to pass, which was accomplished the next day in his last sufferings. There were three symbolical representations given of that great event this evening; one in the passover, which Christ now partook of with his disciples; another in this remarkable action of his washing his disciples' feet. Washing the feet of guests was the office of servants, and one of their meanest offices. And therefore [it] was fitly chosen by our Savior to represent that great abasement which he was to be the subject of in the form of a servant, in becoming obedient unto death, even that ignominious and accursed death of the cross, that he might cleanse the souls of his disciples from their guilt and spiritual pollution.

This spiritual washing and cleansing of believers was the end for which Christ so abased himself for them. Tit. 2:14: "Who gave himself for us, that he might redeem us from all iniquity, and purify unto himself a peculiar people." Eph. 5:25, 26: "Christ loved the church, and gave himself for it, that he might sanctify and cleanse it with the washing of water." That Christ's washing his disciples' feet signified this spiritual washing of the soul, is manifest by his own words in the 8th verse of the context, "Peter saith unto him, 'Thou shalt never wash my feet.' Jesus answered him. 'If I wash thee not, thou has no part with me.' " Christ, in being obedient unto death, even the death of the cross, not only did the part of a servant unto God, but in some respects also of a servant unto us. And this is not the only place where his so abasing himself for our sakes is compared to the doing of the part of a servant to guests. We have the like representation made in Luke 22:27: "For whether is greater, he that sitteth at meat, or he that serveth? Is not he that sitteth at meat? But I am among you as he that serveth." And wherein Christ was among the disciples as he that did serve, is explained in Mat. 20:28. Namely, in *his giving his life a ransom for them.*

When Christ had finished washing his disciples' feet, he solemnly requires their attention to what he had done, and commands them to follow his example therein. Verses 12–17:

> So after he had washed their feet, and had taken his garments, and was set down again, he said unto them, Know ye what I have done unto you? Ye call me Master and Lord, and ye say well, for so I am. If I then, your Lord and Master, have washed your feet, ye also ought to wash one another's feet: for I have given you an example, that ye should do as I have done to you. Verily, verily, I say unto you, The servant is not greater than his Lord, neither he that is sent greater than he that sent him. If ye know these things, happy are ye if ye do them.

When our Savior calls on his disciples to imitate the example he had given them in what he had done, we are to understand him, not merely by the example he gave in the emblematical action, in washing his disciples' feet, in itself considered, but more especially, of that much greater act of his that was signified by it, in abasing himself so low, and suffering so much, for the spiritual cleansing and salvation of his people.

This is what is chiefly insisted on as the great example Christ has given us to follow. So it is once and again afterward, in the discourse Christ had with his disciples, this same night, verse 34 of the chapter wherein is the text, "A new commandment I give unto you, that ye love one another; as I have loved you, that ye also love one another." John 15:12, 13,

> This is my commandment, that ye love one another, as I have loved you. Greater love hath no man than this, that a man lay down his life for his friends.

And so in 1 John 3:16, "Hereby perceive we the love of God, because he laid down his life for us; and we ought to lay down our lives for the brethren."

Christ, in the words of the text, does not only intend to recommend this example of his to the disciples as Christians, or some of his professing people, but especially as his ministers. This is evident by those words he uses to enforce this counsel. "Neither he that is sent, is greater than he that sent him." In which words he manifestly has respect to that great errand on which he had sent them, when he bid them *go and preach the gospel to the lost sheep of the house of Israel;* Mat. 10:5, 6. And on which they were to be sent after his resurrection, when he said to them, "Go ye into all the world, and preach the gospel to every creature." The same errand that Christ has respect to John 20:21, "As my Father hath sent me, even so send I you."

And what confirms this is, that Christ elsewhere recommends to officers in his church, that are in that respect chief among his followers, the example which he set in his abasing himself to be as a servant that minister, to guests at a table, in his giving for us; Mat. 20:27, 28, "Whosoever will be chief among you, let him be your servant: even as the Son of man came not to be ministered unto, but to minister, and to give his life a ransom for many." Compare Luke 22:25–28 [referred to earlier in this sermon].

The work and business of ministers of the gospel is as it were that of servants, to wash and cleanse the souls of men. For this is done by the preaching of the word, which is their main business. Eph. 5:26, "That he might sanctify and cleanse it with the washing of water by the word."

The words of the text thus considered, do undoubtedly lead us to this conclusion, and teach us this doctrine, viz. that it is the duty of ministers of the gospel, in the work of their ministry, to follow the example of their great Lord and Master. And this is what I would by divine assistance make the subject of my present discourse.

And I propose to handle this subject in the following method:

I. I would observe wherein ministers of the gospel ought to follow the example of Christ.

II. Give some reasons why they should follow his example.

III. I would endeavor to make a proper application of those things to myself, and others that are called to this work of the ministry.

IV. I would show what improvement should be made of them by the people of this church and congregation.

I. Then, I would show wherein ministers of the gospel ought, in the work of their ministry, to follow the example of their great Lord and Master, Jesus Christ.

1. *And here, in general, ministers should follow their Lord and Master in all those excellent virtues, and in that universal and eminent holiness of life, which he set an example of in this human nature.*

The ministers of Christ should be persons of the same spirit that their Lord was of: the same spirit of humility and lowliness of heart; for the servant is not greater than his Lord. They should be of the same spirit of heavenly-mindedness, and contempt of the glory, wealth, and pleasures of this world. They should be of the same spirit of devotion and fervent love to God. They should follow the example of his prayerfulness; of whom we read from time to time of his retiring from the world, away from the noise and applause of the multitudes, into mountains and solitary places, for secret prayer, and holy converse with his Father; and once of his rising up in the morning a great while before day, and going and departing into a solitary place to pray, Mark 1:35. And another time, of his going out into a mountain to pray, and continuing all night in prayer to God, Luke 6:12. Ministers should follow Christ's example, in his strict, constant, and inflexible observance of the commands which God has given him, touching what he should do and what he should say; he spake nothing of himself, but those things which the Father had commanded him, those he spake, and always did those things that pleased him, and continued in thorough obedience in the greatest trials, and through the greatest opposition that ever there was any instance of. Ministers should be persons of the same quiet, lamb-like spirit that Christ was of, the same spirit of submission to God's will, and patience under afflictions, and meekness towards men; of the same calmness and composure of spirit under reproaches and sufferings from the malignity of evil men; of the same spirit of forgiveness of injuries; of the same spirit of charity, of fervent love and extensive benevolence; the same disposition to pity the miserable, to weep with those that weep, to help men under their calamities of both soul and body, to hear and grant the requests of the needy, and relieve afflicted; the same spirit of condescension to the poor and mean, tenderness and gentleness toward the weak, and great and effectual love to enemies. They should also be of the same spirit of zeal, diligence, and self-denial for the glory of God, and advancement for his kingdom, and for the good of mankind; for which things' sake Christ went though the greatest labors, and endured the most extreme sufferings.

2. *More particularly should ministers of the gospel follow the example of their great Master, in the manner in which they seek the salvation and happiness of the souls of men.* They should follow his example of love to souls. Though it be impossible that they should love them to so great a degree, yet they should have the same spirit of love to them, and concern for their salvation, according to their capacity. Love to men's souls in Christ was far above any regard he had to his temporal interest, his ease, his honor, his meat and drink. And so it should be with his ministers. They should have the same spirit of compassion to men under their spiritual calamities and miseries that he had, of whom we read, Mark 6:34,

> That when he came out an d saw much people, he was moved with compassion towards them, because they were as sheep not having a shepherd; and he began to teach them many things.

The word translated "moved with compassion," signifies, that he was most sensibly affected, and his inmost bowels moved with pity. And again we read, Luke 19, that when Christ was riding to Jerusalem, that wicked city, but a few days before his crucifixion, and was come to the descent of the mount of Olives, where he had a fair view of the city, when he beheld it, he wept over it, on account of the misery and ruin they brought themselves into danger of by their sin. Although the sin by which especially they had made themselves thus miserable, was their vile treatment of him (for Jerusalem was a city that had been peculiarly injurious to him). And though Christ knew how cruelly he should be treated in that city before that week was past, how he there should be set at nought, and with great malignity bound, falsely accused and condemned, reviled, spit upon, scourged, and crucified; yet all does not prevent his most affectionate tears of compassion towards them.

> When he was come near, he beheld the city, and wept over it, saying, "If thou hadst know, even thou (thou, as wicked as thou art, and as vile as thou hast been in thy treatment of me; even thou), the things which belong unto thy peace! But now they are hid from thine eyes."

(Compare Mat. 23:37, and Luke 13:34). One would have thought he would have been more concerned for himself than Jerusalem, who had such a dreadful cup to drink, and was to suffer such extreme things by the cruelty of Jerusalem that week. But he, as it were, forgets his own sorrow and death, and weeps over the misery of his cruel enemies.

Ministers should imitate their great Master in his fervent prayers for the good of the souls of men. We find it to be Christ's manner, whenever he undertook anything of special importance in the work of his ministry, first to retire and pour out his soul in extraordinary prayer to this Father. Thus when he was about to enter on a journey, and go a circuit throughout all Galilee, to preach in their synagogues, "he rose up a great while before day, and went out, and departed into a solitary place, and there prayed." (Mark 1:35–39.) And when he was about to choose his twelve apostles, and send them out to preach the gospel, he first "went out into a mountain to pray, and continued all night in prayer to God" (Luke 6:12, etc.) And the night before his crucifixion, wherein he offered up himself a sacrifice for the souls of men, he pours out his soul in extraordinary prayer for those he was about to die for, as we have an account in John 17. That wonderful and most affecting prayer of his, was not so much for himself as for his people. Although he knew what amazing sufferings he was to undergo the next day, yet he seems as it were to be unmindful of himself, and to have his heart all taken up with concern about his disciples; which he manifests in his spending so much time in comforting and counseling them, and praying for them with great affection, compassion, earnest care, and fatherly tenderness.

And the prayers that he made in the garden of Gethsemane, under the amazing view of the cup he was to drink the next day, seem to be intercessory; especially the last of the three prayers which he there made, "when being in an agony, he prayed more earnestly; and his sweat was as it were great drops of blood falling down to the ground:" when he did not pray that the cup might pass from him, as he had done before, but that "God's will might be done." (Compare Luke 22:44 with Mat. 26:42). That prayer, as the apostle teaches us, Heb. 5:6, 7, was a prayer that he put up as our High Priest; and therefore must be a prayer of intercession for us, a prayer offered up with his blood which he sweat in his agony; as prayers were wont to be offered up with the blood of the sacrifices in the temple. His prayer at that time, "Thy will be done," was not only an expression of submission, but had the form of a petition, as it is in the Lord's prayer. He prayed that God's will might be done in *his* being enabled *to do the will of God*, persevering in obedience unto death; and in the success of his sufferings;

which might in an eminent manner be called the will of God, as it is in Psa. 40:7, 8, "Then said I, 'Lo, I come, I delight to do thy will, O my God.' "

Ministers should follow the example of Christ in his diligence and laboriousness in his work. "He went about doing good, and healing all that were oppressed of the devil." (Acts 10:38.) So abundant was he in labors, that oftentimes he scarcely allowed himself time to eat or drink; insomuch that his friends sometimes went out to lay hold of him, saying, "He is beside himself."(Mark 3:20, 21.) That three years and a half of his public ministry was so filled with action and labor, that one of his disciples, who constantly attended him, and was an eyewitness of his activity, tells us that if "all that he did should be written, the world would not contain the books."

Ministers should follow the example of Christ, in his readiness not only to labor, but suffer, for the salvation of souls, to spend and be spent for them. In this respect the apostle Paul imitated his Lord and Master. Phil. 2:17, "Yea, and if I be offered upon the sacrifice and service of your faith, I joy and rejoice with you all." Col. 1:24, "Who now rejoice in my sufferings for you, and fill up that which is behind of the afflictions of Christ in my flesh, for his body's sake, which is the church." 2 Cor. 12:15, "And I will very gladly spend and be spent for you." Christ, in his prayers, labors, and sufferings for the souls of men, is represented as travailing in birth with them. Isa. 53:11, "He shall see of the travail of his soul."

In like manner should ministers travail for the conversion and salvation of their hearers. They should imitate the faithfulness of Christ in his ministry, in speaking whatsoever God had commanded him, and declaring the whole counsel of God. They should imitate him the manner of his preaching; who taught not as the scribes, but with authority, boldly, zealously, and fervently; insisting chiefly on the most important things in religion, being much in warning men of the danger of damnation, setting forth the greatness of the future misery of the ungodly; insisting not only on the outward, but also the inward and spiritual, duties of religion. [He was b]eing much in declaring the great provocation and danger of spiritual pride, and a self-righteous disposition; yet much insisting on the necessity and importance of inherent holiness, and the practice of piety. [He was b]ehaving himself with admirable wisdom in all that he said and did in his ministry, amidst the many difficulties, enemies, and temptations he was surrounded with, wonderfully adapting his discourses to persons, seasons, and occasions. Isa. 50:4, "The Lord hath given me the tongue of the learned, that I should know how to speak a word in season to him that is weary."

Ministers should follow their Master in his zeal, so wonderfully mixed and tempered with gentleness and condescension in his dealing with souls, preaching the gospel to the poor, and taking a gracious notice from time to time of little children. And they should imitate their Lord in his following the work of ministry, not from mercenary views, or for the sake of worldly advantages, but for God's glory, and men's salvation. And in having his heart engaged in his work; it being his great delight, and his meat, to do the will of his Father, and finish his work, John 4:34, and having his heart set on the success of his great undertaking in the salvation of souls; this being the joy that was set before him, for which he run his race, endured the cross, and despised the shame. His delight in the prospect of the eternal salvation of souls more than countervailing the dread he had of his extreme sufferings. Many waters could not quench his love, neither could the floods drown it, for his love was stronger than death; yea, than the mighty pains and torments of such a death.

II. I now proceed to the second thing proposed in the handling of this subject, which was to give some reasons why ministers of the gospel should follow the example of their great Lord and Master, Jesus Christ.

1. They should follow his example, because he is their Lord and Master. Christ, as he is a divine person, is the Lord of heaven and earth, and so one of infinite dignity, to whom our supreme respect is due. And on that account he is infinitely worthy that we should regard, not only his precepts but example. The infinite honorableness of his person recommends his virtues, and a conformity to them as our greatest dignity and honor.

Christ is more especially the Lord of Christians; who are therefore under special obligations to follow him. He is their shepherd; and surely the flock should follow their shepherd. He is the captain of their salvation; and it becomes soldiers to follow their captain and leader. He is their head, not only their head of rule and authority, but their head of influence and communication, their vital head. And Christians are members of his body; but members, as partakers of the life and spirit of the head, are conformed to the head.

But Christ is still in a more peculiar manner the Lord and Master of ministers of the gospel, as they are not only members of his church, but the officers of his kingdom, and the dignified servants of his family. It is the manner of a people to imitate their prince, but especially the ministers of his kingdom, and officers of his household. It is the duty of the whole army to follow their general, but especially of those officers that have a commission under him.

2. *Ministers of the gospel are in some respects called and devoted to the same work and business that Christ himself was appointed to.* Ministers are not men's mediators; for there is but one Mediator between God and man, the man Christ Jesus. They are not our priests to make atonement and work out righteousness for us. For Christ by one offering has perfected forever them that are sanctified. They are not lords over God's heritage; for one is their Master, even Christ. But yet, ministers of the gospel, as Christ's servants and officers under him, are appointed to promote the designs of that great work of Christ, the work of salvation. It is the work that ministers are devoted to; and therefore they are represented as co-workers with Christ. 2 Cor. 6:1, "We then as workers together with him, beseech you also that ye receive not the grace of God in vain." Christ is the Savior of the souls of men. Ministers, also, are spoken of in Scripture as saving men's souls. 1 Tim. 4:16, "In doing this, thou shalt both save thyself and them that hear thee." Rom. 11:14, "If by any means I may provoke to emulation them which are my flesh, and might save some of them." 1 Cor. 9:22, "That I might by all means save some." And whereas it is said, Oba. 21, "Saviors shall come upon mount Zion;" ministers of the gospel are supposed to be there intended.

The work of ministers is in many respects like the work that Christ himself was appointed to, as the Savior of men; and especially the same with the work which Christ does in his prophetical office; only with this difference, that ministers are to speak and act wholly under Christ, as taught of him, as holding forth his word, and by light and strength communicated from him. Christ himself, after his baptism, followed the work of the ministry. He was a minister of the true sanctuary (Heb. 8:2), he spake and acted as his Father's minister; was a minister of the gospel, and as such preached and administered sacraments.

Pastors of churches are ministers of the same gospel. But in their ministry, they act as the ministers of Christ. Jesus Christ is the great Bishop of souls. Ministers are also bishops under him. Christ came into the world "that he might be the light of the world." Ministers are set to be lights unto the churches, and are also set to be "the light of the world," Mat. 5:14. Christ is the "bright and morning star." Ministers are "stars in the Christ's hand." Christ is "the messenger of the covenant." Ministers are called "messengers of the Lord of hosts." Christ is his people's "shepherd, the good shepherd, the great shepherd of his sheep." Ministers are also frequently called shepherds and are directed to feed the flock of Christ, which he purchased with his own blood.

Seeing therefore it is thus, that the work that ministers are called and devoted to, is no other than the work of Christ, or the work that Christ does, certainly they ought to do his work; which they do not do unless they imitate him, and do as he does, or as he hath set them an example.

3. The example of Christ is most worthy of ministers' imitation. His example was perfect, without error, blemish, or defect; and therefore worthy to be made our rule, and to be regarded and followed without exception, limitation, or reserve; unless in those things which he did that were proper to his peculiar office. Christ's virtue was not only perfect, but was exercised in those circumstances, and under those trials, that rendered his virtuous acts vastly the most amiable of any that ever appeared in any creature whether man or angel. If we consider the perfection of the virtue that Christ exercised, his virtue did exceed that of the most eminent saints, more than the purest gold exceeds the meanest and foulest ore. And if we consider the manner of its exercise, and the trials under which it was exercised, and the blessed fruits it has brought forth, so his virtue exceeds that of all other perfectly innocent creatures, and even of the brightest angel, as the sun in its glory exceeds the stars.

And this example was set us in our own nature, and so is especially fitted for our imitation. There was in the man Christ Jesus, who was one of us, and dwelt among us, such exercises of virtue as became our state and circumstances in the world, as those who dwell in frail flesh and blood, and as members of human society, and dwellers in such a world of sorrow and death.

And then these amiable exercises of virtue in Christ were exhibited chiefly in the things which he did in that work wherein ministers are called to act as coworkers with him. The bright and glorious example of Christ that is set before us is chiefly in what he did during the three years and a half of his public ministry; and in the devotion, heavenly-mindedness, humility patience, meekness, forgiveness, self-denial, and charity, which he exercised in the labors and sufferings he went through for the good of the souls of men. And therefore is especially set for the imitation of those who are set apart that they may make it the whole business of their lives to seek the same good of souls.

4. Ministers should follow that example of Christ which has been spoken of, because if they are fit for ministers, and are such as have any right to take that work upon themselves, Christ has set them this example in what he has done for their souls. "I have given you an example" (says Christ in the text) "that you should do as I have done to you." Ministers should be animated in this work by a great love to the souls of men, and should be ready to spend and be spent for them; for Christ loved them, and gave himself for them. He loved them with a love stronger than death. They should have compassion to men under their spiritual miseries, as Christ had pity on them. They should be much in prayer for the people of their flock, considering how Christ prayed and agonized for them, in tears of blood. They should travail in birth with the souls that are committed to their care, seeing their own salvation is the fruit of the travail of Christ's soul. They should exercise a meek and condescending spirit to the mean and weak and poor, and should as it were wash the feet of Christ's disciples; considering how Christ condescended to them, when they were wretched, and miserable, and poor, and blind, and naked, and abased himself to wash their feet.

The chief trials of Christ's virtue, and so their most bright and eminent exercises, were in the abasement, labor, and suffering that he was the subject of for our salvation. Which certainly may well endear those virtues to us, and greatly engage us to imitate that example. So the things whereof this example consists, were things by which we have infinite benefit, without which we should have been unspeakably miserable forever and ever, and by virtue of which we have the glorious privilege of the children of God, and have a full title to the crown of exceeding glory, and pleasures for evermore, at God's right hand.

III. I now proceed, as was proposed, in the third place, to apply what has been said to myself, and others that are employed in this sacred work of the gospel ministry, and to such as are about to undertake it, or are candidates for it; and particularly to him that is now to be solemnly set apart to this work in this place.

We are those to whom these things especially belong. We may hear Christ saying to us this day, "I have given you an example, that ye should do as I have done." For the words of Christ in the text were not only spoken to the twelve, but are also spoken unto us. We have now had represented to us, though in a very imperfect manner, the example that Christ has set, and what reasons there are that we, above all others, should imitate it.

It is not only our great duty, but will be our greatest honor, to imitate Christ, and do the work that he has done, and so act as coworkers with him.

There are two kinds of persons that are given to Christ, and appointed and devoted of God to be his servants, to be employed with Christ, and under him, in his great work of the salvation of the souls of men; and they are angels and ministers. The angels are all of them, even the most exalted of them, subjected of God the Father to our Redeemer, and given to him as his servants, to be subservient to the great designs of his saving and glorifying his elect. Heb. 1:14, "Are they not all ministering spirits, sent forth to minister for them who shall be heirs of salvation?" And doubtless they were created for this very end; God made them for his Son, to be subservient to him in this great work; which seems to be the chief design of all God's works. And the employment of ministers of the gospel in this respect, is like that of the glorious angels. The principalities and powers in heavenly places, esteem it not any debasement, but their great honor, to be employed as Christ's ministers in this work. For therein they are employed as the ministers of God, in the greatest and most honorable of all God's works; that work of God wherein his glory is chiefly displayed, and which his heart was chiefly upon from eternity.

It is the honor of the Son of God himself, that he is appointed to this work. It was because God the Father infinitely loved his Son, and delighted to put honor upon him, that he appointed him to be the author of that glorious work of the salvation of men. And when we consider the greatness, importance, and excellency of it, we have reason to be astonished at the condescension of God, that he would ever improve mere creatures as coworkers and ministers of Christ in this affair; *for who is sufficient for these things?* 2 Cor. 2:6, "Which is fit, or worthy? Who is equal to a work of such dignity, and vast importance?" Especially have we reason to wonder that God will employ, not only holy and glorious angels, but feeble, frail, sinful worms of the dust in this work, who need redemption themselves. And yet the honor that is put upon faithful ministers is, in some respects, greater than that of the angels. They seem to be that kind of servants that are the most dignified of the two. For Christ makes his angels to be ministering spirits unto them, unto the faithful ministers. And the angels are their angels: as faithful ministers of the gospel are not only ministers to the church, but dignified members of the church, that spouse of the King of glory, on whom the most glorious angels, the highest ministers in the court of heaven, are appointed to attend. And then Christ seems especially to delight to carry on his work of the salvation of souls, through the ministrations of men, who have that nature that Christ is united to, and that are of those sons of men with whom he had his delight before the world was made. So it is by the ministration of men, that the Scriptures are given. They were the penmen of the Holy Bible; and by them the gospel is preached to the world. By them ordinances are administered, and, through their ministrations, especially, souls are converted. When Christ himself was employed in the work of the ministry, in the time of his humiliation, but few, comparatively, were brought home to him, immediately by his ministrations. It pleased Christ to reserve this honor for his disciples and ministers, after his ascension, to whom he promised that they should, in this respect, do greater works than he, John 14:12. And accordingly it was by their preaching that the Gentile world was converted, and Satan's kingdom overthrown. Thus God delights "to perfect praise out of the mouths of babes and suckling, that he may still the enemy and the avenger."

It will be our great honor that we are called to this work of Christ, if therein we follow him. For therein we shall be like the Son of God. But if we are unfaithful in this office, and do not imitate our Master, our offense will be heinous in proportion to the dignity of our office, and our final and everlasting disgrace and ignominy proportionably great. And we, who in honor are exalted up to heaven, shall be cast down proportionably low in Hell.

Let us further consider, that our following the example of Christ in the work of the ministry, is the way to enjoy the sensible joyful presence of Christ with us. The disciples had the comfort of Christ's presence and conversation by following him, and going where he went. When we cease to follow him, he will go from us, and we shall soon lose sight of him.

Our being conformed to Christ's example, will also be the way for us to be conformed to him, and partake with him in his privileges. It is the way for us to have his joy fulfilled in us. Christ, in doing the work to which the Father appointed him, obtained a glorious victory over his enemies, and having spoiled principalities and powers, triumphed over them. If we imitate his example, it will be the way for us in like manner to conquer the principalities and powers, yea, to be much more than conquerors. It will be the way for us always to triumph in Jesus Christ. It will be the way for us to obtain success in our ministry, and actually to be made the happy instruments of the eternal salvation of souls. Christ has not only *told* us, but *shown* us, the way to success in our business, and the way to victory over all that oppose us in it. And our imitating Christ in our ministry, will be the way for us to be partakers with him in his glory; the way for us in like manner to be approved, and openly honored and rewarded by God; the way to be brought to sit with Christ on his throne, as he is set down with the Father on his throne. And as Christ is now exalted to shine as the bright luminary and glory of heaven, so our following his example will be the way for us to be exalted, to *shine* with him, "as the stars forever and ever," Dan. 12:3. And as Christ in heaven rejoices in his success, and will receive his church, presented to him without spot, as his everlasting crown; so our imitating Christ in our work, will be the way to partake with Christ in this joy, and have the souls whose salvation we are the instruments of, to be our crown of rejoicing for ever. Thus Christ and we shall rejoice together in that world of glory and joy where there is no more labor or sorrow. And we must enter into that joy and glory, in the way of following Christ in our work. There is no other way for ministers to enter there.

And that we may thus follow Christ's example, and be partakers with him in his glory, we had need to be much in prayer for his Spirit. Christ himself, though the eternal Son of God, obtained the Holy Spirit for himself in a way of prayer. Luke 3:21, 22, "Jesus being baptized, and praying, the heaven was opened, and the Holy Ghost descended like a dove upon him." If we have the Spirit of Christ dwelling in us, we shall have Christ himself thereby living in us, and then we shall undoubtedly live like him. If that fountain of light dwells richly in us, we shall shine like him, and so shall be burning and shining lights.

That we may *be* and *behave* like Christ, we should earnestly seek much acquaintance with him, and much love to him, and be much in secret converse with him. It is natural, and as it were necessary, for us to imitate those whom we are much acquainted and conversant with, and have a strong affection for.

And in order to our imitating Christ in the work of the ministry, in any tolerable degree, we had need not to have our hearts overcharged, and time filled up with worldly affections, cares, and pursuits. The duties of a minister that have been recommended, are absolutely inconsistent with a mind much taken up with worldly profit, glory, amusements, and entertainments.

And another thing that is of very great importance, in order to our doing the work that Christ did, is that we take heed that the religion we promote, be that same religion that Christ taught and promoted, and not any of its counterfeits and delusive appearances, or anything substituted by the subtle devices of Satan, or vain imaginations of men, in lieu of it. If we are zealous and very diligent to promote religion, but do not take good care to distinguish true from false religion, we shall be in danger of doing much more hurt than good with all our zeal and activity.

IV. I come now to the fifth and last thing at first proposed, viz. to show what improvement should be made of what has been said, by the people of this church and congregation, who are now about solemnly to commit their souls to the charge of him whom they have chosen to be their pastor, and who is now about to be set apart to that office.

And *you, my brethren,* as all of you have immortal souls to save, if you have considered the things that have been spoken, cannot but be sensible, that it not only greatly concerns your elect pastor to take heed how he behaves himself in his great work, wherein he is to act as a coworker with Christ for your salvation; but that it infinitely concerns you how you receive him, and behave towards him. Seeing that it is for *your* eternal salvation that he is appointed to watch and labor; and seeing his business is to do the work of Christ for you, it is natural and easy to infer, that your reception and entertainment of him should in some respect imitate the church's reception of Jesus Christ. Gal. 4:14, "My temptation which was in my flesh, ye despised not, nor rejected; but received me as an angel of God, even as Christ Jesus." Christ, in the text, commands those whom he sends to follow his example, and then in the 20th verse following, he directs those to whom he sends them, how to treat them. "Verily, verily, I say unto you, 'He that receiveth whomsoever I send, receiveth me; and he that receiveth me, receiveth him that sent me.' " Seeing the work of your minister is in some respects the same with the work of Christ, and he is to be appointed and devoted to do this work for your souls in particular, surely you should esteem him very highly in love for his work's sake and do all that is in your power to help him, and put him under the best advantages to imitate his great Master *in* this work, to give himself wholly *to* his work, as Christ did during the time of his ministry, and to be successful *in* his work. And as it was observed before, that it is impossible that ministers should in any tolerable degree imitate the example of Christ in their work, if their minds are overcharged with worldly cares and concerns, you ought so to provide for him and support him, that he shall have no need to entangle himself with these things; otherwise you will not only bring a great temptation upon him, which will vastly tend to hinder him in the work of Christ among you, but will, for the sake of sparing a little of your worldly substance to yourselves, foolishly and miserably starve your own souls and the souls of your children, and will but cheat yourselves. For you will not be in the way to prosper either in your spiritual or temporal concerns. The way to have your houses filled with plenty, is to "honor the Lord with your substance, and with the first-fruits of all your increase." Pro. 3:9.

And as it is your duty and interest well to support your minister, so it concerns you to pray earnestly for him, and each one to do what in him lies in all respects to encourage and help him, and strengthen his hands, by attending diligently to his ministry, receiving the truth in love, treating him with the honor due to a messenger of Christ, carefully avoiding all contention with him, and one with another. And take heed in particular, that you do not forsake him to follow those, who under pretense of extraordinary purity, are doubtless doing the devil's work, in separating themselves, and endeavoring to draw off others from the ministers and churches in the land in general.

If you think I have spoken something freely to you, I hope it will be considered, that this is probably the last time you will ever hear me speak from the pulpit, and that I shall never see you again, till we see one another in the invisible and eternal world, where these things will open to us all in their just importance.

And now nothing is left but to express my sincerest wishes and prayers, that the God of all grace would be with you and your elect pastor, and that he would give you in him a great and long-lasting blessing, that you may enjoy much of the presence of Christ with you in him. That in him may be made up the great loss you sustained by the death of your former faithful and eminent pastor, whose praise was in all the churches. And that you may receive him as you ought to receive a faithful minister of Jesus Christ, and may be a great comfort to him, and may receive great spiritual and eternal benefit by his means And that you may be each other's crown of rejoicing in the day of the Lord Jesus.

Christ's Agony

Preached in October 1739, and re-preached in the winter and spring of 1757.

"And being in an agony, he prayed more earnestly, and his sweat was, as it were, great drops of blood falling down to the ground."—Luke 22:44

Our Lord Jesus Christ, in his original nature, was infinitely above all suffering, for he was "God over all, blessed for evermore;" but, when he became man, he was not only capable of suffering, but partook of that nature that is remarkably feeble and exposed to suffering.

The human nature, on account of its weakness, is in Scripture compared to the grass of the field, which easily withers and decays. So it is compared to a leaf; and to the dry stubble; and to a blast of wind: and the nature of feeble man is said to be but dust and ashes, to have its foundation in the dust, and to be crushed before the moth.

It was this nature, with all its weakness and exposedness to sufferings, which Christ, who is the Lord God omnipotent, took upon him. He did not take the human nature on him in its first, most perfect and vigorous state, but in that feeble forlorn state which it is in since the fall; and therefore Christ is called "a tender plant," and "a root out of a dry ground." Isa. 53:2:

> For he shall grow up before him as a tender plant, and as a root out of a dry ground: he hath no form nor comeliness; and when we shall see him, there is no beauty that we should desire him.

Thus, as Christ's principal errand into the world was suffering; so, agreeably to that errand, he came with such a nature and in such circumstances, as most made way for his suffering; so his whole life was filled up with suffering, he began to suffer in his infancy, but his suffering increased the more he drew near to the close of his life. His suffering after his public ministry began was probably much greater than before; and the latter part of the time of his public ministry seems to have been distinguished by suffering. The longer Christ lived in the world, the more men saw and heard of him, the more they hated him. His enemies were more and more enraged by the continuance of the opposition that he made to their lusts; and the devil having been often baffled by him, grew more and more enraged, and strengthened the battle more and more against him: so that the cloud over Christ's head grew darker and darker, as long as he lived in the world, till it was in its greatest blackness when he hung upon the cross and cried out, "My God, my God, why hast thou forsaken me!" Before this, it was exceedingly dark, in the time of his agony in the garden; of which we have an account in the words now read; and which I propose to make the subject of my present discourse.

The word "agony" properly signifies *an earnest strife*, such as is witnessed in wrestling, running, or fighting. And therefore in Luke 13:24: "Strive to enter in at the strait gate: for many, I say unto you, will seek to enter in, and shall not be able;" the word in the original, translated *strive*, is αγωνιζεσθε. "*Agonize*, to enter in at the strait gate." The word is especially used for that sort of strife, which in those days was exhibited in the Olympic games, in which men strove for the mastery in running, wrestling, and other such kinds of exercises; and a prize was set up that was bestowed on the conqueror. Those, who thus contended, were, in the language then in use, said to *agonize*.

Thus the apostle in his epistle to the Christians of Corinth, a city of Greece, where such games were annually exhibited, says in allusion to the strivings of the combatants, "And every man that *striveth for the mastery*," in the original, every one that *agonizeth*, "is temperate in all things." The place where those games were held was called Αγων, or *the place of agony*; and the word is particularly used in Scripture for that striving in earnest prayer wherein persons wrestle with God: they are said *to agonize*, or to *be in agony*, in prayer. So the word is used Rom. 15:30: "Now I beseech you, brethren, for the Lord Jesus Christ's sake, and for the love of the Spirit, that ye *strive* together with me in your prayers to God for me:" in the original συναγωνιζεσθαι μοι, that ye *agonize together* with me. So Col. 4:12: "Always *laboring* fervently for you in prayer, that ye may stand perfect and complete in all the will of God:" in the original αγωνιζων *agonizing* for you.

So that when it is said in the text that Christ was *in an agony*, the meaning is, that his soul was *in a great and earnest strife and conflict*. It was so in two respects:

- As his soul was in a great and sore conflict with those terrible and amazing views and apprehensions which he then had.
- As he was at the same time in great labor and earnest strife with God in prayer.

I propose therefore, in discoursing on the subject of Christ's agony, distinctly to unfold it, under these two propositions,

I. That the soul of Christ in his agony in the garden had a sore conflict with those terrible and amazing views and apprehensions, of which he was then the subject.

II. That the soul of Christ in his agony in the garden had a great and earnest labor and struggle with God in prayer.

Part I

The soul of Christ in his agony in the garden had a sore conflict with those terrible amazing views and apprehensions, of which he was then the subject.

In illustrating this proposition I shall endeavor to show,

- What those views and apprehensions were.
- That the conflict or agony of Christ's soul was occasioned by those views and apprehensions.
- That this conflict was peculiarly great and distressing; and,
- What we may suppose to be the special design of God in giving Christ those terrible views and apprehensions, and causing him to suffer that dreadful conflict, before he was crucified.

I. I proposed to show, what were those terrible views and amazing apprehensions which Christ had in his agony.

This may be explained by considering,

- The cause of those views and apprehensions; and,
- The manner in which they were then experienced.

1. *The cause of those views and apprehensions, which Christ had in his agony in the garden, was the bitter cup which he was soon after to drink on the cross.* The sufferings which Christ underwent in his agony in the garden, were not his greatest sufferings; though they were so very great. But his last sufferings upon the cross were his principal sufferings; and therefore they are called "the cup that he had to drink." The sufferings of the cross, under which he was slain, are always in the Scriptures represented as the main sufferings of Christ; those in which especially "he bare our sins in his own body," and made atonement for sin. His enduring the cross, his humbling himself, and becoming obedient unto death, even the death of the cross, is spoken of as the main thing wherein his sufferings appeared. This is the cup that Christ had set before him in his agony. It is manifest that Christ had this in view at this time, from the prayers which he then offered.

According to Matthew, Christ made three prayers that evening while in the garden of Gethsemane, and all on this one subject, the bitter cup that he was to drink. Of the first, we have an account in Matt. 26:39.

> And he went a little farther, and fell on his face and prayed, saying, "O my Father, if it be possible, let this cup pass from me; nevertheless, not as I will but as thou wilt";

of the second, in the forty-second verse,

> He went away again the second time and prayed, saying, "O my Father, if this cup may not pass from me, except I drink it, thy will be done";

and of the third, in the forty-fourth verse,

> And he left them, and went away again, and prayed the third time, saying the same words.

From this it plainly appears *what it was* of which Christ had such terrible views and apprehensions at that time. What he thus insists on in his prayers, shows on what his mind was so deeply intent. It was his sufferings on the cross, which were to be endured the next day, when there should be darkness over all the earth, and at the same time a deeper darkness over the soul of Christ, of which he had now such lively views and distressing apprehensions.

2. The manner in which this bitter cup was now set in Christ's view.

First, he had a lively apprehension of it impressed at that time on his mind. He had an apprehension of the cup that he was to drink before. His principal errand into the world was to drink that cup, and he therefore was never unthoughtful of it, but always bore it in his mind, and often spoke of it to his disciples. Thus Matt. 16:21:

> From that time forth began Jesus to show unto his disciples how that he must go unto Jerusalem, and suffer many things of the elders, and chief priests, and scribes, and be killed, and be raised again the third day.

Again ch. 20:17–19:

> And Jesus going up to Jerusalem, took the twelve disciples apart in the way, and said unto them, "Behold, we go up to Jerusalem; and the Son of man shall be betrayed unto the chief priests, and unto the scribes, and they shall condemn him to death. And shall deliver him to the Gentiles to mock, and to scourge, and to crucify him: and the third day he shall rise again."

The same thing was the subject of conversation on the mount with Moses and Elias when he was transfigured. So he speaks of his bloody baptism, Luke 12:50:

> "But I have a baptism to be baptized with; and how am I straitened till it be accomplished!"

He speaks of it again to Zebedee's children, Matt. 20:22:

> "Are ye able to drink of the cup that I shall drink of, and to be baptized with the baptism that I am baptized with?" They say unto him, "We are able."

He spake of his being lifted up. John 8:28:

> Then said Jesus unto them, "When ye have lifted up the Son of man, then shall ye know that I am he, and that I do nothing of myself; but as my Father hath taught me, I speak these things."

John 12:34:

> The people answered him, "We have heard out of the law that Christ abideth for ever: and how sayest thou, 'The Son of man must be lifted up?' Who is this Son of man?"

So he spake of destroying the temple of his body, John 2:19:

> Jesus answered and said unto them, "Destroy this temple, and in three days I will raise it up."

And he was very much in speaking of it a little before his agony, in his dying counsels to his disciples in the 12th and 13th chapter of John.

Thus this was not the first time that Christ had this bitter cup in his view. On the contrary, he seems always to have had it in view. But it seems that at this time God gave him an extraordinary view of it. A sense of that wrath that was to be poured out upon him, and of those amazing sufferings that he was to undergo, was strongly impressed on his mind by the immediate power of God; so that he had far more full and lively apprehensions of the bitterness of the cup which he was to drink than he ever had before, and these apprehensions were so terrible, that his feeble human nature shrunk at the sight, and was ready to sink.

Secondly, the cup of bitterness was now represented as just at hand. He had not only a more clear and lively view of it than before; but it was now set directly before him, that he might without delay take it up and drink it; for then, within that same hour, Judas was to come with his band of men, and he was then to deliver up himself into their hands to the end that he might drink this cup the next day; unless indeed he refused to take it, and so made his escape from that place where Judas would come; which he had opportunity enough to do if he had been so minded.

Having thus shown what those terrible views and apprehensions were which Christ had in the time of his agony; I shall endeavor to show,

II. That the conflict which the soul of Christ then endured was occasioned by those views and apprehensions.

The sorrow and distress which his soul then suffered, arose from that lively, and full, and immediate view which he had then given him of that cup of wrath; by which God the Father did as it were set the cup down before him, for him to take it and drink it. Some have inquired, what was the occasion of that distress and agony, and many speculations there have been about it, but the account which the Scripture itself gives us is sufficiently full in this matter, and does not leave room for speculation or doubt. The thing that Christ's mind was so full of at that time was, without doubt, the same with that which his mouth was so full of: it was the dread which his feeble human nature had of that dreadful cup, which was vastly more terrible than Nebuchadnezzar's fiery furnace. He had then a near view of that furnace of wrath, into which he was to be cast; he was brought to the mouth of the furnace that he might look into it, and stand and view its raging flames, and see the glowings of its heat, that he might know where he was going and what he was about to suffer. This was the thing that filled his soul with sorrow and darkness, this terrible sight as it were overwhelmed him. For what was that human nature of Christ to such mighty wrath as this? it was in itself, without the supports of God, but a feeble worm of the dust, a thing that was crushed before the moth, none of God's children ever had such a cup set before them, as this first being of every creature had. But not to dwell any longer on this, I hasten to show,

III. That the conflict in Christ's soul, in this view of his last sufferings, was dreadful, beyond all expression or conception.

This will appear,

1. *From what is said of its dreadfulness in the history.* By one evangelist we are told, (Matt. 26:37.) "He began to be sorrowful and very heavy;" and by another, (Mark 14:33.) "And he taketh with him Peter, and James, and John, and began to be sore amazed, and to be very heavy." These expressions hold forth the intense and overwhelming distress that his soul was in. Luke's expression in the text of his being in an agony, according to the signification of that word in the original, implies no common degree of sorrow, but such extreme distress that his nature had a most violent conflict with it, as a man that wrestles with all his might with a strong man, who labors and exerts his utmost strength to gain a conquest over him.

2. *From what Christ himself says of it, who was not wont to magnify things beyond the truth.* He says, "My soul is exceeding sorrowful even unto death." Matt. 26:38. What language can more strongly express the most extreme degree of sorrow? His soul was not only "sorrowful," but "exceeding sorrowful;" and not only so, but because that did not fully express the degree of his sorrow, he adds, "even unto death;" which seems to intimate that the very pains and sorrows of Hell, of eternal death, had got hold upon him. The Hebrews were wont to express the utmost degree of sorrow that any creature could be liable to by the phrase, *the shadow of death.* Christ had now, as it were, the shadow of death brought over his soul by the near view which he had of that bitter cup that was now set before him.

3. *From the effect which it had on his body, in causing that bloody sweat that we read of in the text.* In our translation [KJV] it is said, that "his sweat was, as it were, great drops of blood, falling down to the ground." The word rendered *great drops,* is in the original θρομβοι, which properly signifies lumps or clots; for we may suppose that the blood that was pressed out through the pores of his skin by the violence of that inward struggle and conflict that

there was, when it came to be exposed to the cool air of the night, congealed and stiffened, as is the nature of blood, and so fell off from him not in drops, but in clots. If the suffering of Christ had occasioned merely a violent sweat, it would have shown that he was in great agony; for it must be an extraordinary grief and exercise of mind that causes the body to be all of a sweat abroad in the open air, in a cold night as that was, as is evident from John 18:18.

> And the servants and officers stood there, who had made a fire of coals, (for it was cold,) and they warmed themselves; and Peter stood with them, and warmed himself.

This was the same night in which Christ had his agony in the garden. But Christ's inward distress and grief was not merely such as caused him to be in a violent and universal sweat, but such as caused him to *sweat blood*. The distress and anguish of his mind was so unspeakably extreme as to force his blood through the pores of his skin, and that so plentifully as to fall in great clots or drops from his body to the ground.

I come now to show,

IV. What may be supposed to be the special end of God's giving Christ beforehand these terrible views of his last sufferings?

In other words, *why* it was needful that he should have a more full and extraordinary view of the cup that he was to drink, a little before he drank it, than ever he had before; or why he must have such a foretaste of the wrath of God to be endured on the cross, before the time came that he was actually to endure it.

Answer. It was needful, in order that he might take the cup and drink it, as *knowing what he did*. Unless the human nature of Christ had had an extraordinary view given him beforehand of what he was to suffer, he could not, as man, fully know beforehand what he was going to suffer, and therefore could not, as man, know what he did when he took the cup to drink it, because he would not fully have known what the cup was, it being a cup that he [had] never drunk before.

If Christ had plunged himself into those dreadful sufferings without being fully sensible beforehand of their bitterness and dreadfulness, he must have done [something] he knew not what. As man, he would have plunged himself into sufferings of the amount of which he was ignorant, and so have acted blindfold[ed]; and of course his taking upon him these sufferings could not have been so fully his own act. Christ, as God, perfectly knew what these sufferings were; but it was more needful also that he should know as man; for he was to suffer as man, and the act of Christ in taking that cup was the act of Christ as God-man. But the man Christ Jesus hitherto never had had experience of any such sufferings as he was now to endure on the cross; and therefore he could not fully know what they were beforehand, but by having an extraordinary view of them set before him, and an extraordinary sense of them impressed on his mind.

We have heard of tortures that others have undergone, but we do not fully know what they were, because we never experienced them; and it is impossible that we should fully know what they were but in one of these two ways, either by experiencing them, or by having a view given of them, or a sense of them impressed in an extraordinary way. Such a sense was impressed on the mind of the man Christ Jesus, in the garden of Gethsemane, of his last sufferings, and *that* caused his agony. When he had a full sight given him what that wrath of God was, that he was to suffer, the sight was overwhelming to him; it made his soul exceeding sorrowful, even unto death.

Christ was going to be cast into a dreadful furnace of wrath, and it was not proper that he should plunge himself into it blindfold, as not knowing how dreadful the furnace was. Therefore, that he might not do so, God first brought him and set him at the mouth of the furnace, that he might look in, and stand and view its fierce and raging flames, and might see where he was going, and might voluntarily enter into it and bear it for sinners, as knowing what it was. This view Christ had in his agony. Then God brought the cup that he was to drink, and set it down before him, that he might have a full view of it, and see what it was before he took it and drank it.

If Christ had not fully known what the dreadfulness of these sufferings was, before he took them upon him, his taking them upon him could not have been fully his own act as man; there could have been no explicit act of his will about that which he was ignorant of; there could have been no proper trial, whether he would be willing to undergo such dreadful sufferings or not, unless he had known beforehand how dreadful they were; but when he had seen what they were, by having an extraordinary view given him of them, and then undertaken to endure them afterwards; then he acted as knowing what he did; then his taking that cup, and bearing such dreadful sufferings, was properly his own act by an explicit choice; and so his love to sinners, in that choice of his, was the more wonderful, as also his obedience to God in it.

And it was necessary that this extraordinary view that Christ had of the cup he was to drink should be given at that time, just before he was apprehended. This was the most proper season for it, just before he took the cup, and while he yet had opportunity to refuse the cup; for before he was apprehended by the company led by Judas, he had opportunity to make his escape at pleasure. For the place where he was, was without the city, where he was not at all confined, and was a lonesome, solitary place; and it was the night season; so that he might have gone from that place where he would, and his enemies not have known where to have found him. This view that he had of the bitter cup was given him while he was yet fully at liberty, before he was given into the hands of his enemies.

Christ's delivering himself up into the hands of his enemies, as he did when Judas came, which was just after his agony, was properly his act of taking the cup in order to drink; for Christ knew that the issue [result] of that would be his crucifixion the next day. These things may show us the end of Christ's agony, and the necessity there was of such an agony before his last sufferings.

Application

I. Hence we may learn how dreadful Christ's last sufferings were.

We learn it from the dreadful effect which the bare foresight of them had upon him in his agony. His last sufferings were so dreadful, that the view which Christ had of them before overwhelmed him and amazed him, as it is said, he began to be sore amazed.

The very sight of these last sufferings was so very dreadful as to sink his soul down into the dark shadow of death; yea, so dreadful was it, that in the sore conflict which his nature had with it, he was all in a sweat of blood, his body all over was covered with clotted blood, and not only his body, but the very ground under him with the blood that fell from him, which had been forced through his pores through the violence of his agony.

And if only the foresight of the cup was so dreadful, how dreadful was the cup itself, how far beyond all that can be uttered or conceived! Many of the martyrs have endured extreme tortures, but from what has been said, there is all reason to think those all were a mere nothing to the last sufferings of Christ on the cross. And what has been said affords a convincing argument that the sufferings which Christ endured in his body on the cross, though they were very dreadful, were yet the least part of his last sufferings; and that beside those, he endured sufferings in his soul which were vastly greater. For if it had been only the sufferings which he endured in his body, though they were very dreadful, we cannot conceive that the mere anticipation of them would have such an effect on Christ. Many of the martyrs, for aught we know, have endured as severe tortures in their bodies as Christ did. Many of the martyrs have been crucified, as Christ was; and yet their souls have not been so overwhelmed. There has been no appearance of such amazing sorrow and distress of mind either at the anticipation of their sufferings, or in the actual enduring of them.

II. From what has been said, we may see the wonderful strength of the love of Christ to sinners.

What has been said shows the strength of Christ's love two ways.

1. *That it was so strong as to carry him through that agony that he was then in.* The suffering that he then was actually subject to, was dreadful and amazing, as has been shown; and how wonderful was his love that lasted and was upheld still! The love of any mere man or angel would doubtless have sunk under such a weight, and never would have endured such a conflict in such a bloody sweat as that of Jesus Christ. The anguish of Christ's soul at that time was so strong as to cause that wonderful effect on his body. But his love to his enemies, poor and unworthy as they were, was stronger still. The heart of Christ at that time was full of distress, but it was fuller of love to vile worms: his sorrows abounded, but his love did much more abound. Christ's soul was overwhelmed with a deluge of grief, but this was from a deluge of love to sinners in his heart sufficient to overflow the world, and overwhelm the highest mountains of its sins. Those great drops of blood that fell down to the ground were a manifestation of an ocean of love in Christ's heart.

2. *The strength of Christ's love more especially appears in this, that when he had such a full view of the dreadfulness of the cup that he was to drink, that so amazed him, he would, notwithstanding, even then take it up, and drink it.* Then seems to have been the greatest and most peculiar trial of the strength of the love of Christ, when God set down the bitter portion before him, and let him see what he had to drink, if he persisted in his love to sinners; and brought him to the mouth of the furnace that he might see its fierceness, and have a full view of it, and have time then to consider whether he would go in and suffer the flames of this furnace for such unworthy creatures, or

not. This was, as it were, proposing it to Christ's last consideration what he would do; as much as if it had then been said to him,

> Here is the cup that you are to drink, unless you will give up your undertaking for sinners, and even leave them to perish as they deserve. Will you take this cup, and drink it for them, or not? There is the furnace into which you are to be cast, if they are to be saved; either they must perish, or you must endure this for them. There you see how terrible the heat of the furnace is; you see what pain and anguish you must endure on the morrow, unless you give up the cause of sinners. What will you do? Is your love such that you will go on? Will you cast yourself into this dreadful furnace of wrath?

Christ's soul was overwhelmed with the thought; his feeble human nature shrunk at the dismal sight. It put him into this dreadful agony which you have heard described; but his love to sinners held out.

Christ would not undergo these sufferings needlessly, if sinners could be saved without. If there was not an absolute necessity of his suffering them in order to their salvation, he desired that the cup might pass from him. But if sinners, on whom he had set his love, could not, agreeably to the will of God, be saved without his drinking it, he chose that the will of God should be done. He chose to go on and endure the suffering, awful as it appeared to him.

And this was his final conclusion, after the dismal conflict of his poor feeble human nature, after he had had the cup in view, and for at least the space of one hour, had seen how amazing it was. Still he finally resolved that he would bear it, rather than those poor sinners whom he had loved from all eternity should perish. When the dreadful cup was before him, he did not say within himself,

> Why should I, who am so great and glorious a person, infinitely more honorable than all the angels of heaven, why should I go to plunge myself into such dreadful, amazing torments for worthless wretched worms that cannot be profitable to God, or me, and that deserve to be hated by me, and not to be loved? Why should I, who have been living from all eternity in the enjoyment of the Father's love, go to cast myself into such a furnace for them that never can requite me for it? Why should I yield myself to be thus crushed by the weight of divine wrath, for them who have no love to me, and are my enemies? they do not deserve any union with me, and never did, and never will do, anything to recommend themselves to me. What shall I be the richer for having saved a number of miserable haters of God and me, who deserve to have divine justice glorified in their destruction?

Such, however, was not the language of Christ's heart, in these circumstances; but on the contrary, his love held out, and he resolved even then, in the midst of his agony, to yield himself up to the will of God, and to take the cup and drink it.

He would not flee to get out of the way of Judas and those that were with him, though he knew they were coming, but that same hour delivered himself voluntarily into their hands. When they came with swords and staves to apprehend him, and he could have called upon his Father, who would immediately have sent many legions of angels to repel his enemies, and have delivered him, he would not do it; and when his disciples would have made resistance, he would not suffer them, as you may see in Matt. 26:51, and onward:

> And, behold, one of them which were with Jesus stretched out his hand, and drew his sword, and struck a servant of the high priest's, and smote off his ear. Then said Jesus unto him, "Put up again thy sword into its place: for all they that take the sword shall perish with the sword. Thinkest thou that I cannot now pray to my Father, and he will presently give me more than twelve legions of angels? But how then shall the scriptures be fulfilled, that thus it must be?" In that same hour said Jesus to the multitudes, "Are ye come out as against a thief, with swords and staves for to take me? I sat daily with you teaching in the temple, and ye laid no hold on me. But all this was done that the scriptures of the prophets might be fulfilled."

And Christ, instead of hiding himself from Judas and the soldiers, told them, when they seemed to be at a loss whether he was the person whom they sought. And when they seemed still somewhat to hesitate, being seized with some terror in their minds, he told them so again, and so yielded himself up into their hands, to be bound by them, after he had shown them that he could easily resist them if he pleased, when a single word spoken by him, threw them backwards to the ground, as you may see in John 18:3, etc.

> Judas then, having received a band of men and officers from the chief priests and Pharisees, cometh thither with lanterns, and torches, and weapons. Jesus therefore, knowing all things that should come upon him, went forth, and said unto them, "Whom seek ye?" They answered him, "Jesus of Nazareth." Jesus said unto them, "I am he." As soon then as he had said unto them, "I am he," they went backward and fell to the ground.

Thus powerful, constant, and violent was the love of Christ; and the special trial of his love above all others in his whole life seems to have been in the time of his agony. For though his sufferings were greater afterwards, when he was on the cross, yet he saw clearly what those sufferings were to be, in the time of his agony; and that seems to have been the first time that ever Christ Jesus had a clear view what these sufferings were; and after this the trial was not so great, because the conflict was over. His human nature had been in a struggle with his love to sinners, but his love had got the victory. The thing, upon a full view of his sufferings, had been resolved on and concluded; and accordingly, when the moment arrived, he actually went through with those sufferings.

3. But there are two circumstances of Christ's agony that do still make the strength and constancy of his love to sinners the more conspicuous.

- At the same time that he had such a view of the dreadfulness of his sufferings,
- he had also an extraordinary view of the hatefulness of the wickedness of those for whom those sufferings were to make atonement.

There are two things that render Christ's love wonderful: that he should be willing to endure sufferings that were so great; and that he should be willing to endure them to make atonement for wickedness that was so great. But in order to its being properly said, [that] Christ of his own act and choice endured sufferings that were so great, to make atonement for wickedness that was so great, two things were necessary. First, that he should have an extraordinary sense how great these sufferings were to be, before he endured them. (This was given in his agony.) And second, that he should also at the same time have an extraordinary sense how great and hateful was the wickedness of men for which he suffered to make atonement; or how unworthy those were for whom he died. And both these were given at the same time.

When Christ had such an extraordinary sense how bitter his cup was to be, he [also] had much to make him sensible how unworthy and hateful that wickedness of mankind was, for which he suffered; because the hateful and malignant nature of that corruption never appeared more fully than in the spite and cruelty of men in these sufferings; and yet his love was such that he went on, notwithstanding, to suffer for them who were full of such hateful corruption.

It was the corruption and wickedness of men that contrived and effected his death; it was the wickedness of men that agreed with Judas, it was the wickedness of men that betrayed him, and that apprehended him, and bound him, and led him away like a malefactor; it was by men's corruption and wickedness that he was arraigned, and falsely accused, and unjustly judged. It was by men's wickedness that he was reproached, mocked, buffeted, and spit upon. It was by men's wickedness that Barabbas was preferred before him. It was men's wickedness that laid the cross upon him to bear, and that nailed him to it, and put him to so cruel and ignominious a death.

This tended to give Christ an extraordinary sense of the greatness and hatefulness of the depravity of mankind.

- *Because hereby in the time of his sufferings he had that depravity set before him as it is, without disguise.* When it killed Christ, it appeared in its proper colors. Here Christ saw it in its true nature, which is the utmost hatred and contempt of God; in its ultimate tendency and desire, which is to kill God; and in its greatest aggravation and highest act, which is killing a person that was God.
- *Because in these sufferings he felt the fruits of that wickedness.* It was then directly leveled against himself, and exerted itself against him to work his reproach and torment, which tended to impress a stronger sense of its hatefulness on the human nature of Christ.

But yet at the same time, so wonderful was the love of Christ to those who exhibited this hateful corruption, that he endured those very sufferings to deliver them from the punishment of that very corruption. The wonderfulness of Christ's dying love appears partly in that he died for those that were so unworthy in themselves, as all mankind have the same kind of corruptions in their hearts, and partly in that he died for those who were not only so wicked, but whose wickedness consists in being enemies to him. So that he did not only die for the wicked, but for his own enemies; and partly in that he was willing to die for his enemies at the same time that he was feeling the fruits of their enmity, while he felt the utmost effects and exertions of their spite against him in the greatest possible contempt and cruelty towards him in his own greatest ignominy, torments, and death; and partly in that he was willing to atone for their being his enemies in these very sufferings, and by that very ignominy, torment, and death that was the fruit of it.

The sin and wickedness of men, for which Christ suffered to make atonement, was, as it were, set before Christ in his view.

- *In that this wickedness was but a sample of the wickedness of mankind; for the corruption of all mankind is of the same nature, and the wickedness that is in one man's heart is of the same nature and tendency as in another's.* As in water, face answereth to face, so the heart of man to man.

- *It is probable that Christ died to make atonement for that individual actual wickedness that wrought his sufferings, that reproached, mocked, buffeted, and crucified him.* Some of his crucifiers, for whom he prayed that they might be forgiven, while they were in the very act of crucifying him, were afterwards, in answer to his prayer, converted, by the preaching of Peter; as we have an account of in the second chapter of Acts.

4. *Another circumstance of Christ's agony that shows the strength of his love, is the ungrateful carriage of his disciples at that time.* Christ's disciples were among those for whom he endured this agony, and among those for whom he was going to endure those last sufferings, of which he now had such dreadful apprehensions.

Yet Christ had already given them an interest in the benefits of those sufferings. Their sins had already been forgiven them through that blood that he was going to shed, and they had been infinite gainers already by that dying pity and love which he had to them, and had through his sufferings been distinguished from all the world besides. Christ had put greater honor upon them than any other, by making them his disciples in a more honorable sense than he had done any other.

And yet now, when he had that dreadful cup set before him which he was going to drink for them, and was in such an agony at the sight of it, he saw no return on their part but indifference and ingratitude. When he only desired them to watch with him, that he might be comforted in their company, now at this sorrowful moment they fell asleep; and showed that they had not concern enough about it to induce them to keep awake with him even for one hour, though he desired it of them once and again.

But yet this ungrateful treatment of theirs, for whom he was to drink the cup of wrath which God had set before him, did not discourage him from taking it, and drinking it for them. His love held out to them; having loved his own, he loved them to the end. He did not say within himself when this cup of trembling was before him,

> Why should I endure so much for those that are so ungrateful; why should I here wrestle with the expectation of the terrible wrath of God to be borne by me tomorrow, for them that in the meantime have not so much concern for me as to keep awake with me when I desire it of them even for one hour?

But on the contrary, with tender and fatherly compassions, he excuses this ingratitude of his disciples, and says, Matt. 26:41. "Watch and pray, that ye enter not into temptation; the spirit indeed is willing, but the flesh is weak;" and went and was apprehended, and mocked, and scourged, and crucified, and poured out his soul unto death, under the heavy weight of God's dreadful wrath on the cross—for them.

III. From what has been said, we may learn the wonderfulness of Christ's submission to the will of God.

Christ, as he was a divine person, was the absolute sovereign of heaven and earth, but yet he was the most wonderful instance of submission to God's sovereignty that ever was. When he had such a view of the terribleness of his last sufferings, and prayed if it were possible that that cup might pass from him, i.e. if there was not an absolute necessity of it in order to the salvation of sinners—yet it was with a perfect submission to the will of God. He adds, "Nevertheless, not my will, but thine be done."

He chose rather that the inclination of his human nature, which so much dreaded such exquisite torments, should be crossed, than that God's will should not take place. He delighted in the thought of God's will being done; and when he went and prayed the second time, he had nothing else to say but, "O my Father, if this cup may not pass from me except I drink it, thy will be done;" and so the third time.

What are such trials of submission as any of us sometimes have in the afflictions that we suffer in comparison of this? If God does but in his providence signify it to be his will that we should part with a child, how hardly are we brought to yield to it, how ready to be unsubmissive and froward [obstinate]! Or if God lays his hand upon us in some acute pain of body, how ready are we to be discontented and impatient; when the innocent Son of God, who deserved no suffering, could quietly submit to sufferings inconceivably great, and say it over and over, "God's will be done!" When he was brought and set before that dreadful furnace of wrath into which he was to be cast, in order that he might look into it and have a full view of its fierceness, when his flesh shrunk at it, and his nature was in such a conflict, that his body was all covered with a sweat of blood falling in great drops to the ground, yet his soul quietly yielded that the will of God should be done, rather than the will or inclination of his human nature.

IV. What has been said on this subject also shows us the glory of Christ's obedience.

Christ was subject to the moral law as Adam was, and he was also subject to the ceremonial and judicial laws of Moses; but the principal command that he had received of the Father was, that he should lay down his life, that he should voluntarily yield up himself to those terrible sufferings on the cross. To do this was his principal errand into the world; and doubtless the principal command that he received, was about that which was the principal errand on which he was sent.

The Father, when he sent him into the world, sent him with commands concerning what he should do in the world; and his chief command of all was about that, which was the errand he was chiefly sent upon, which was to lay down his life. And therefore this command was the principal trial of his obedience. It was the greatest trial of his obedience, because it was by far the most difficult command: all the rest were easy in comparison of this.

And the main trial that Christ had, whether he would obey this command, was in the time of his agony; for that was within an hour before he was apprehended in order to his sufferings, when he must either yield himself up to them, or fly from them. And then it was the first time that Christ had a full view of the difficulty of this command; which appeared so great as to cause that bloody sweat. Then was the conflict of weak human nature with the difficulty, then was the sore struggles and wrestling with the heavy trial he had, and then Christ got the victory over the temptation, from the dread of his human nature. His obedience held out through the conflict.

Then we may suppose that Satan was especially let loose to set in with the natural dread that the human nature had of such torments, and to strive to his utmost to dissuade Christ from going on to drink the bitter cup; for about that time, towards the close of Christ's life, was he especially delivered up into the hands of Satan to be tempted of him, more than he was immediately after his baptism; for Christ says, speaking of that time, (Luke 22:53): "When I was daily with you in the temple, ye stretched forth no hands against me; but this is your hour, and the power of darkness."

So that Christ, in the time of his agony, was wrestling not only with overwhelming views of his last sufferings, but he also wrestled, in that bloody sweat, with principalities and powers—he contended at that time with the great leviathan that labored to his utmost to tempt him to disobedience. So that then Christ had temptations every way to draw him off from obedience to God. He had temptations from his feeble human nature, that exceedingly dreaded such torments; and he had temptations from men, who were his enemies; and he had temptations from the ungrateful carriage of his own disciples; and he had temptations from the devil. He had also an overwhelming trial from the manifestation of God's own wrath; when, in the words of Isaiah, it pleased the Lord to bruise him and put him to grief.

But yet he failed not, but got the victory over all, and performed that great act of obedience at that time to that same God that hid himself from him, and was showing his wrath to him for men's sins, which he must presently suffer. Nothing could move him away from his steadfast obedience to God, but he persisted in saying, "Thy will be done:" expressing not only his submission, but his obedience; not only his compliance with the disposing will of God, but also with his preceptive [principle-driven] will. God had given him this cup to drink, and had commanded him to drink it, and that was reason enough with him to drink it; hence he says, at the conclusion of his agony, when Judas came with his band, "The cup which my Father giveth me to drink, shall I not drink it?"(John 18:11.)

Christ, at the time of his agony, had an inconceivably greater trial of obedience than any man or any angel ever had. How much was this trial of the obedience of the second Adam beyond the trial of the obedience of the first Adam! How light was our first father's temptation in comparison of this! And yet our first surety failed, and our second failed not, but obtained a glorious victory, and went and became obedient unto death, even the death of the cross. Thus wonderful and glorious was the obedience of Christ, by which he wrought out righteousness for believers, and which obedience is imputed to them. No wonder that it is a sweet penalty sown, and that God stands ready to bestow heaven as its reward on all that believe on him.

V. What has been said shows us the sottishness [stupefaction, as from drink] of secure sinners in being so fearless of the wrath of God.

If the wrath of God was so dreadful that, when Christ only *expected* it, his human nature was nearly overwhelmed with the fear of it, and his soul was amazed, and his body all over in a bloody sweat; then how sottish are sinners, who are under the threatening of the same wrath of God, and are condemned to it, and are every moment exposed to it; and yet, instead of manifesting intense apprehension, are quiet and easy, and unconcerned? Instead of being sorrowful and very heavy, [they] go about with a light and careless heart; instead of crying out in bitter agony, are often gay and cheerful, and eat and drink, and sleep quietly, and go on in sin, provoking the wrath of God more and more, without any great matter of concern! How stupid and sottish are such persons!

Let such senseless sinners consider, that that misery, of which they are in danger from the wrath of God, is infinitely more terrible than that [misery], the fear of which, occasioned in Christ his agony and bloody sweat. It is more terrible, both as it differs both in its nature and degree, and also as it differs in its duration. It is more terrible in its nature and degree.

Christ suffered that which, as it upheld the honor of the divine law, was fully equivalent to the misery of the damned; and in some respect it was the same suffering; for it was the wrath of the same God; but yet in other respects it vastly differed. The difference does not arise from the difference in the wrath poured out on one and the other, for it is the same wrath, but from the difference of the subject, which may be best illustrated from Christ's own comparison in Luke 23:31: "For if they do these things in a green tree, what shall be done in the dry?" Here he calls himself the green tree, and wicked men the dry, intimating that the misery that will come on wicked men will be far more dreadful than those sufferings which came on him, and the difference arises from the different nature of the subject. The green tree and the dry are both cast into the fire; but the flames seize and kindle on the dry tree much more fiercely than on the green.

The sufferings that Christ endured differ from the misery of the wicked in Hell in nature and degree in the following respects.

1. *Christ felt not the gnawings of a guilty, condemning conscience.*

2. *He felt no torment from the reigning of inward corruptions and lusts, as the damned do.* The wicked in Hell are their own tormentors, their lusts are their tormentors, and being without restraint, (for there is no restraining grace in Hell,) their lusts will rage like raging flames in their hearts. They shall be tormented with the unrestrained violence of a spirit of envy and malice against God, and against the angels and saints in heaven, and against one another. Now Christ suffered nothing of this.

3. *Christ had not to consider that God hated him.* The wicked in Hell have this to make their misery perfect, they know that God perfectly hates them without the least pity or regard to them, which will fill their souls with inexpressible misery. But it was not so with Christ. God withdrew his comfortable presence from Christ, and hid his face from him, and so poured out his wrath upon him, as made him feel its terrible effects in his soul; but yet he knew at the same time that God did not hate him, but infinitely loved him. He cried out of God's forsaking him, but yet at the same time calls him "My God, my God!" knowing that he was his God still, though he had forsaken him. But the wicked in Hell will know that he is not their God, but their judge and irreconcilable enemy.

4. Christ did not suffer despair, as the wicked do in Hell. He knew that there would be an end to his sufferings in a few hours; and that after that he should enter into eternal glory. But it will be far otherwise with you that are impenitent; if you die in your present condition, you will be in perfect despair. On these accounts, the misery of the wicked in Hell will be immensely more dreadful in nature and degree, than those sufferings with the fears of which Christ's soul was so much overwhelmed.

5. It [this misery] will infinitely differ in duration. Christ's sufferings lasted but a few hours, and there was an eternal end to them, and eternal glory succeeded. But you that are a secure, senseless sinner, are every day exposed to be cast into everlasting misery, a fire that never shall be quenched.

If then the Son of God was in such amazement, in the expectation of what he was to suffer for a few hours, how sottish are you who are continually exposed to sufferings, immensely more dreadful in nature and degree, and that are to be without any end, but which must be endured without any rest, day or night, forever and ever!

If you had a full sense of the greatness of that misery to which you are exposed, and how dreadful your present condition is on that account, it would this moment put you into as dreadful an agony as that which Christ underwent; yea, if your nature could endure it, one much more dreadful. We should now see you fall down in a bloody sweat, wallowing in your gore, and crying out in terrible amazement.

Part II

Having thus endeavored to explain and illustrate the former of the two propositions mentioned in the commencement of this discourse, I shall now proceed to show,

That the soul of Christ in his agony in the garden was in a great and earnest strife and conflict in his prayer to God.

The labor and striving of Christ's soul in prayer was a part of his agony, and was without doubt a part of what is intended in the text, when it is said that Christ was in an agony; for, as we have shown, the word is especially used in Scripture in other places for striving or wrestling with God in prayer. From this fact, and from the evangelist mentioning his being in agony, and his praying earnestly in the same sentence, we may well understand him as mentioning his striving in prayer as part of his agony. The words of the text seem to hold forth as much as that Christ was in an agony in prayer: "Being in an agony, he prayed more earnestly; and his sweat was, as it were, great drops of blood falling to the ground." This language seems to imply thus much, that the labor and earnestness of Christ's soul was so great in his wrestling with God in prayer, that he was in a mere agony, and all over in a sweat of blood.

What I propose now, in this second proposition, is by the help of God to explain this part of Christ's agony which consisted in the agonizing and wrestling of his soul in prayer; which is the more worthy of a particular inquiry, being that which probably is but little understood; though, as may appear in the sequel, the right understanding of it is of great use and consequence in divinity.

It is not as I conceive ordinarily well understood what is meant when it is said in the text that Christ prayed more earnestly; or what was the thing that he wrestled with God for, or what was the subject matter of this earnest prayer, or what was the reason of his being so very earnest in prayer at this time. And therefore, to set this whole matter in a clear light, I would particularly inquire,

- Of what nature this prayer was;
- What was the subject matter of this earnest prayer of Christ to the Father;
- In what capacity Christ offered up this prayer to God;
- Why he was so earnest in his prayer;
- What was the success of this his earnest wrestling with God in prayer;
- And then make some improvement.

I. Of what nature [was] this prayer of Christ?

Addresses that are made to God may be of various kinds. Some are confessions on the part of the individual, or expressions of his sense of his own unworthiness before God, and are thus penitential addresses to God. Others are doxologies or prayers intended to express the sense which the person has of God's greatness and glory. Such are many of the psalms of David. Others are [con-]gratulatory addresses, or expressions of thanksgiving and praise for mercies received. Others are submissive addresses, or expressions of submission and resignation to the will of God, whereby he that addresses the Majesty of heaven, expresses the compliance of his will with the sovereign will of God; saying, "Thy will, O Lord, be done!" as David, in 2 Sam. 15:26. "But if he thus say, I have no delight in thee; behold, here am I; let him do to me as seemeth good unto him." Others are petitory or supplicatory; whereby the person that prays, begs of God and cries to him for some favor desired of him.

Hence the inquiry is, of which of these kinds was the prayer of Christ, that we read of in the text.

Answer. It was chiefly supplicatory. It was not penitential or confessional; for Christ had no sin or unworthiness to confess. Nor was it a doxology or a thanksgiving or merely an expression of submission; for none of these agree with what is said in the text, viz. that he prayed more earnestly.

When anyone is said to pray earnestly, it implies an earnest request for some benefit, or favor desired; and not merely a confession, or submission, or gratulation. So what the apostle says of this prayer, in Heb. 5:7.

> Who in the days of his flesh, when he had offered up prayers and supplications, with strong crying and tears, unto him that was able to save him from death, and was heard, in that he feared. . .

shows that it was petitory, or an earnest supplication for some desired benefit. They are not confessions, or doxologies, or thanksgivings, or resignations, that are called "supplications" and "strong cryings," but petitions for some benefit earnestly desired. And having thus resolved the first inquiry, and shown that this earnest prayer of Christ was of the nature of a supplication for some benefit or favor which Christ earnestly desired, I come to inquire,

II. What was the subject matter of this supplication; or what favor and benefit that was for which Christ so earnestly supplicated in this prayer, of which we have an account in the text?

Now the words of the text are not express on this matter. It is said that Christ, "being in an agony, prayed more earnestly;" but yet it is not said what he prayed so earnestly for. And here is the greatest difficulty attending this account: even what that was which Christ so earnestly desired, for which he so wrestled with God at that time. And though we are not expressly told in the text, yet the Scriptures have not left us without sufficient light in this matter. And the more effectually to avoid mistakes, I would answer,

1. *Negatively, the thing that Christ so earnestly prayed for at this time, was* not *that the bitter cup which he had to drink might pass from him.* Christ had before prayed for this, as in the next verse but one before the text, saying:

> Father, if thou be willing, remove this cup from me! nevertheless, not my will, but thine be done!

It is *after* this that we have an account that Christ being in an agony, prayed more earnestly; but we are not to understand that he prayed more earnestly than he had done before, that the cup might pass from him.

That this was not the thing that he so earnestly prayed for in this second prayer, the following things seem to prove:

First, this second prayer was after the angel had appeared to him from heaven, strengthening him, the more cheerfully to take the cup and drink it. The evangelists inform us that when Christ came into the garden, he began to be sorrowful, and very heavy, and that he said his soul was exceeding sorrowful, even unto death, and that then he went and prayed to God, that if it were possible the cup might pass from him. Luke says in the forty-first and forty-second verses,

> that being withdrawn from his disciples about a stone's cast, he kneeled down and prayed, saying, "Father, if thou be willing, remove this cup from me; nevertheless, not my will, but thine be done!"

And then, after this, it is said in the next verse, that there appeared an angel from heaven unto him strengthening him.

Now this can be understood no otherwise than that the angel appeared to him, strengthening him and encouraging him to go through his great and difficult work, to take the cup and drink it. Accordingly we must suppose, that now Christ was more strengthened and encouraged to go through with his sufferings: and therefore we cannot suppose that after this he would pray more earnestly than before to be delivered from his sufferings; and of course that it was something else that Christ more earnestly prayed for, after that strengthening of the angel, and not that the cup might pass from him. Though Christ seems to have a greater sight of his sufferings given him after this strengthening of the angel than before, that caused such an agony, yet he was more strengthened to fit him for a greater sight of them, he had greater strength and courage to grapple with these awful apprehensions, than before. His strength to bear sufferings is increased with the sense of his sufferings.

Secondly, Christ, before his second prayer, had had an intimation from the Father, that it was not his will that the cup should pass from him. The angel's coming from heaven to strengthen him must be so understood.

Christ first prays, that if it may be the will of the Father, the cup might pass; but not, if it was not his will; and then God immediately upon this sends an angel to strengthen, and encourage him to take the cup, which was a plain intimation to Christ that it was the Father's will that he should take it, and that it should not pass from him. And so Christ received it; as appears from the account which Matthew gives of this second prayer, Matt. 26:42:

> He went away again the second time and prayed, saying, "O my Father, if this cup may not pass away from me except I drink it, thy will be done."

He speaks as one that now had had an intimation, since he prayed before, that it was not the will of God. And Luke tells us how, viz. by God's sending an angel. Matthew informs us, as Luke does, that in his first prayer, he prayed that if it were possible the cup might pass from him; but then God sends an angel to signify that it was not his will, and to encourage him to take it. And then Christ, having received this plain intimation that it was not the will of God that the cup should pass from him, yields to the message he had received, and says, "O my Father, if it be so as thou hast now signified, thy will be done."

Therefore we may surely conclude that what Christ prayed more earnestly for after this, was not that the cup might pass from him, but something else; for he would not go to pray more earnestly that the cup might pass from him, after God had signified that it was not his will that it should pass from him, than he did before; that would be blasphemous to suppose. And then,

Thirdly, the language of the second prayer, as recited by Matthew, "O my Father, if this cup may not pass from me except I drink it, thy will be done," shows that Christ did not then pray that the cup might pass from him. This certainly is not praying more earnestly that the cup might pass: it is rather a yielding that point, and ceasing any more to urge it, and submitting to it as a thing now determined by the will of God, made known by the angel. And,

Fourth, from the apostle's account of this prayer in the fifth chapter of Hebrews. The words of the apostle are these,

> Who in the days of his flesh, when he had offered up his prayers and supplications, with strong crying and tears, unto him that was able to save him from death, and was heard in that he feared.

The strong crying and tears of which the apostle speaks, are doubtless the same that Luke speaks of in the text, when he says, "he, being in an agony, prayed more earnestly;" for this was the sharpest and most earnest crying of Christ, of which we have anywhere any account.

But according to the apostle's account, that which Christ feared, and that for which he so strongly cried to God in this prayer, was something that he was heard in, something that God granted him his request in, and therefore it was not that the cup might pass from him. Having thus shown what it was *not* that Christ prayed for in this earnest prayer, I proceed to show,

2. *What* was *it that Christ so earnestly sought of God in this prayer?*

I answer in one word. It was, *that God's will might be done, in what related to his sufferings.* Matthew gives this express account of it, in the very language of the prayer which has been recited several times already, "O my Father, if this cup may not pass from me, except I drink it, thy will be done!" This is a yielding, and an expression of submission; but it is not merely that.

Such words, "The will of the Lord be done," as they are most commonly used, are not understood as a supplication or request, but only as an expression of submission. But the words are not always to be understood in that sense in Scripture, but sometimes are to be understood as a request. So they are to be understood in the third petition of the Lord's prayer, "Thy will be done, in earth as in heaven." There, the words are to be understood both as an expression of submission, and also a request, as they are explained in the Assembly's Catechism—and so the words are to be understood here.

The evangelist Mark says that Christ went away again and spake the same words that he had done in his first prayer. (Mark 14:39.) But then we must understand it as of the same words with the latter part of his first prayer, "nevertheless not my will, but thine be done," as Matthew's more full and particular account shows. So that the thing mentioned in the text, for which Christ was wrestling with God in this prayer, was, that God's will might be done in what related to his sufferings.

3. *But then here another inquiry may arise, viz., what is implied in Christ's praying that God's will might be done in what related to his sufferings?* To this I answer,

First, this implies a request that he might be strengthened and supported, and enabled to do God's will, by going through with these sufferings. The same as when he says, "Lo, I come, in the volume of the book it is written of me, to do thy will, O God." It was the preceptive will of God that he should take that cup and drink it: it was the Father's command to him. The Father had given him the cup, and, as it were, set it down before him with the command that he should drink it.

This was the greatest act of obedience that Christ was to perform. He prays for strength and help, that his poor feeble human nature might be supported, that he might not fail in this great trial, that he might not sink and be swallowed up, and his strength so overcome that he should not hold out, and finish the appointed obedience. This was the thing that he feared, of which the apostle speaks in the fifth chapter of Hebrews, when he says, "he was heard in that he feared." When he had such an extraordinary sense of the dreadfulness of his sufferings impressed on his mind, the fearfulness of it amazed him. He was afraid lest his poor feeble strength should be overcome, and that he should fail in so great a trial, that he should be swallowed up by that death that he was to die, and so should not be saved from death; and therefore he offered up strong crying and tears unto him that was able to strengthen him, and support, and save him from death, that the death he was to suffer might not overcome his love and obedience, but that he might overcome death, and so be saved from it.

If Christ's courage had failed in the trial, and he had not held out under his dying sufferings, he never would have been saved from death, but he would have sunk in the deep mire; he never would have risen from the dead, for his rising from the dead was a reward of his victory. If his courage had failed, and he had given up, he would have remained from under the power of death, and so we should all have perished, we should have remained yet in our sins. If he had failed, all would have failed. If he had not overcome in that sore conflict, neither he nor we could have been freed from death, we all must have perished together.

Therefore this was the saving from death that the apostle speaks of, that Christ feared and prayed for with strong crying and tears. His being overcome of death was the thing that he feared, and so he was heard in that he feared. This Christ prayed, that the will of God might be done in his sufferings, even that he might not fail of obeying God's will in his sufferings; and therefore it follows in the next verse in that passage of Hebrews, "Though he were a Son, yet learned he obedience by the things which he suffered."

That it was in this respect that Christ in his agony so earnestly prayed that the will of God might be done, viz. that he might have strength to do his will, and might not sink and fail in such great sufferings; is confirmed from the scriptures of the Old Testament, as particularly from the 69th Psalm. The psalmist represents Christ in that psalm, as is evident from the fact that the words of that psalm are represented as Christ's words in many places of the New Testament. That psalm is represented as Christ's prayer to God when his soul was overwhelmed with sorrow and amazement, as it was in his agony; as you may see in the first and second verses,

> Save me, O God, for the waters are come in unto my soul: I sink in deep mire, where there is no standing: I am come into deep waters, where the floods overflow me.

But then the thing that is represented as being the thing that he feared, was failing, and being overwhelmed, in this great trial: verses 14 and 15.

> Deliver me out of the mire, and let me not sink: let me be delivered from them that hate me, and out of the deep waters. Let not the water-flood overflow me, neither let the deep swallow me up, and let not the pit shut her mouth upon me.

So again in the twenty-second Psalm, which is also represented as the prayer of Christ under his dreadful sorrow and sufferings, verses 19–21.

> But be not thou far from me, O Lord; O my Strength, haste thee to help me. Deliver my soul from the sword; my darling from the power of the dog. Save me from the lion's mouth.

It was meet and suitable that Christ, when about to engage in that terrible conflict, should thus earnestly seek help from God to enable him to do his will; for he needed God's help the strength of his human nature, without divine help, was not sufficient to carry him through. This was, without doubt, that in which the first Adam failed in his first trial, that when the trial came he was not sensible of his own weakness and dependence. If he had been, and had leaned on God, and cried to him for his assistance and strength against the temptation, in all likelihood we should have remained innocent and happy creatures to this day.

Second, it implies a request that God's will and purpose might be obtained in the effects and fruits of his sufferings, in the glory to his name, that was his design in them; and particularly in the glory of his grace, in the eternal salvation and happiness of his elect. This is confirmed by John 12:27,28.

> "Now is my soul troubled; and what shall I say? Father, save me from this hour: but for this cause came I unto this hour. Father, glorify thy name." Then came there a voice from heaven, saying, "I have both glorified, and will glorify it again."

There, the first request is the same with the first request of Christ here, in like trouble: "Now is my soul troubled; and what shall I say? Father, save me from this hour." He first prays, as he does here, that he might be saved from his last sufferings. Then, after he was determined within himself that the will of God must be otherwise, that he should not be saved from that hour, "but for this cause," says he, "came I to this hour;" and then his second request after this is, "Father, glorify thy name!"

So this is doubtless the purport of the second request in his agony, when he prayed that God's will might be done. It is that God's will might be done in that glory to his own name that he intended in the effects and fruits of his sufferings, that seeing that it was his will that he should suffer, he earnestly prays that the end of his suffering, in the glory of God and the salvation of the elect, may not fail.

And these things are what Christ so earnestly wrestled with God for in his prayer, of which we have an account in the text, and we have no reason to think that they were not expressed in prayer as well as implied. It is not reasonable to suppose that the evangelist in his other account of things mentions all the words of Christ's prayer. He only mentions the substance.

III. In what capacity did Christ offer up those earnest prayers to God in his agony?

In answer to this inquiry, I observe that he offered them up not as a private person, but as high priest. The apostle speaks of the strong crying and tears, as what Christ offered up as high priest. Heb. 5:6–7:

> As he says also in another place, "Thou art a priest for ever, after the order of Melchisedek: who in the days of his flesh, when he had offered up prayers and supplications with strong crying and tears," etc.

The things that Christ prayed for in those strong cryings, were things not of a private nature, but of common concern to the whole church of which he was the high priest. That the will of God should be done in his obedience unto death, that his strength and courage should not fail, but that he should hold out, was of common concern; for, if he had failed, all would have failed and perished for ever. And of course, that God's name should be glorified in the effects and fruits of his sufferings, and in the salvation and glory of all his elect, was a thing of common concern.

Christ offered up these strong cries with his flesh in the same manner as the priests of old were wont to offer up prayers with their sacrifices. Christ mixed strong crying and tears with his blood, and so offered up his blood and his prayers together, that the effect and success of his blood might be obtained. Such earnest agonizing prayers were offered with his blood, and his infinitely precious and meritorious blood was offered with his prayers.

IV. Why was Christ so earnest in those supplications?

Luke speaks of them as very earnest; the apostle speaks of them as strong crying; and his agony partly consisted in this earnestness: and the account that Luke gives us, seems to imply that his bloody sweat was partly at least with the great labor and earnest sense of his soul in wrestling with God in prayer. There were three things that concurred at that time, especially to cause Christ to be thus earnest and engaged.

1. *He had then an extraordinary sense how dreadful the consequence would be, if God's will should fail of being done.* He had then an extraordinary sense of his own last suffering under the wrath of God, and if he had failed in those sufferings, he knew the consequence must be dreadful. He having now such an extraordinary view of the terribleness of the wrath of God, his love to the elect tended to make him more than ordinarily earnest that they might be delivered from suffering that wrath to all eternity, which could not have been if he had failed of doing God's will, or if the will of God in the effect of his suffering had failed.

2. *No wonder that that extraordinary sense that Christ then had of the costliness of the means of sinners' salvation, made him very earnest for the success of those means, as you have already heard.*

3. *Christ had an extraordinary sense of his dependence on God, and his need of his help to enable him to do God's will in this great trial.* Though he was innocent, yet he needed divine help. He was dependent on God, as man, and therefore we read that he trusted in God. Matt. 27:43. "He trusted in God; let him deliver him now, if he will have him: for he said, I am the Son of God." And when he had such an extraordinary sight of the dreadfulness of that wrath he was to suffer, he saw how much it was beyond the strength of his human nature alone.

V. What was the success of this prayer of Christ?

To this I answer, he obtained all his requests. The apostle says, "He was heard in that he feared;" in *all* that he feared. He obtained strength and help from God, all that he needed, and was carried through. He was enabled to do and to suffer the whole will of God; and he obtained the whole of the end of his sufferings a full atonement for the sins of the whole world, and the full salvation of every one of those who were given him in the covenant of redemption, and all that glory to the name of God, which his mediation was designed to accomplish, not one jot or tittle hath failed.

Herein Christ in his agony was above all others Jacob's antitype, in his wrestling with God for a blessing; which Jacob did, not as a private person, but as the head of his posterity, the nation of Israel, and by which he obtained that commendation of God, "As a prince thou hast power with God;" and therein was a type of him who was the Prince of princes.

Application

Great improvement may be made of the consideration of the strong crying and tears of Christ in the days of his flesh, many ways for our benefit.

I. This may teach us after what manner we should pray to God.

Not in a cold and careless manner, but with great earnestness and engagedness of spirit, and especially when we are praying to God for those things that are of infinite importance, such as spiritual and eternal blessings. Such were the benefits that Christ prayed for with such strong crying and tears, that he might be enabled to do God's will in that great and difficult work that God had appointed him, that he might not sink and fail, but might get the victory, and so finally be delivered from death, and that God's will and end might be obtained as the fruit of his sufferings, in the glory of God, and the salvation of the elect.

When we go before God in prayer with a cold, dull heart, and in a lifeless and listless manner pray to him for eternal blessings, and those of infinite import to our souls, we should think of Christ's earnest prayers that he poured out to God, with tears and a bloody sweat. The consideration of it may well make us ashamed of our dull, lifeless prayers to God, wherein, indeed, we rather ask a denial than ask to be heard; for the language of such a manner of praying to God, is, that we do not look upon the benefit that we pray for as of any great importance, that we are indifferent whether God answers us or not. The example of Jacob in wrestling with God for the blessing, should teach us earnestness in our prayers, but more especially the example of Jesus Christ, who wrestled with God in a bloody sweat. If we were sensible as Christ was of the great importance of those benefits that are of eternal consequence, our prayers to God for such benefits would be after another manner than now they are. Our souls also would with earnest labor and strife be engaged in this duty.

There are many benefits that we ask of God in our prayers, which are every whit of as great importance to us as those benefits which Christ asked of God in his agony were to him. It is of as great importance to us that we should be enabled to do the will of God, and perform a sincere, universal, and persevering obedience to his commands, as it was to Christ that he should not fail of doing God's will in his great work. It is of as great importance to us to be saved from death, as it was to Christ that he should get the victory over death, and so be saved from it. It is of as great, and infinitely greater, importance to us, that Christ's redemption should be successful in us, as it was to him that God's will should be done, in the fruits and success of his redemption.

Christ recommended earnest watchfulness and prayerfulness to his disciples, by prayer and example, both at the same time. When Christ was in his agony, and came and found his disciples asleep, he bid them watch and pray, Matt. 26:41. "Watch and pray, that ye enter not into temptation: the spirit indeed is willing, but the flesh is weak." At the same time he set them an example of that which he commanded them, for though they slept, he watched, and poured out his soul in those earnest prayers that you have heard of; and Christ has elsewhere taught us to ask those blessings of God that are of infinite importance, as those that will take no denial.

We have another example of the great conflicts and engagedness of Christ's spirit in this duty. Luke 6:12: "And it came to pass in those days, that he went out into a mountain to pray, and continued all night in prayer to God." And he was often recommending earnestness in crying to God in prayers. In the parable of the unjust judge (Luke 18 at the beginning):

> And he spake a parable unto them to this end, that men ought always to pray, and not to faint; saying "There was in a city a judge, which feared not God, neither regarded man; and there was a widow in that city; and she came unto him, saying, 'Avenge me of mine adversary.' And he would not for awhile: but afterwards he saith within himself, 'Though I fear not God nor regard man, yet because this widow troubleth me, I will avenge her, lest by her continual coming she weary me.' " And the Lord said, "Hear what the unjust judge saith."

Luke 6:5, etc.:

> And he said unto them, "Which of you shall have a friend, and shall go unto him at midnight, and say unto him, 'Friend, lend me three loaves; for a friend of mine in his journey is come to me, and I have nothing to set before him?' And he from within shall answer and say, 'Trouble me not: the door is now shut, and my children are with me in bed; I cannot rise and give thee.' I say unto you, though he will not rise and give him because he is his friend, yet because of his importunity, he will rise and give him as many as he needeth."

He taught it in his own way of answering prayer, as in answering the woman of Canaan, Matt. 15:22, etc.:

> And behold a woman of Canaan came out of the coasts, and cried unto him, saying, "Have mercy on me, O Lord, thou Son of David; my daughter is grievously vexed with a devil." But he answered her not a word. And his disciples came and besought him, saying, "Send her away; for she crieth after us." But he answered and said, "I am not sent but unto the lost sheep of the house of Israel." Then came she and worshiped him, saying, "Lord, help me." But he answered and said, "It is not meet to take the children's bread and cast it to dogs." And she said, "Truth, Lord; yet the dogs eat of the crumbs which fall from their master's table." Then Jesus answered and said unto her, "O woman, great is thy faith; be it unto thee even as thou wilt." And her daughter was made whole from that very hour.

And as Christ prayed in his agony, so I have already mentioned several texts of Scripture wherein we are directed to agonize in our prayers to God.

II. These earnest prayers and strong cries of Christ to the Father in his agony, show the greatness of his love to sinners.

For, as has been shown, these strong cries of Jesus Christ were what he offered up to God as a public person, in the capacity of high priest, and in the behalf of those whose priest he was. When he offered up his sacrifice for sinners whom he had loved from eternity, he withal offered up earnest prayers. His strong cries, his tears, and his blood, were all offered up together to God, and they were all offered up for the same end, for the glory of God in the salvation of the elect. They were all offered up for the same persons, viz. for his people. For them he shed his blood, and that bloody sweat, when it fell down in clotted lumps to the ground; and for them he so earnestly cried to God at the same time. It was that the will of God might be done in the success of his sufferings, in the success of that blood, in the salvation of those for whom that blood was shed, and therefore this strong crying shows his strong love; it shows how greatly he desired the salvation of sinners.

He cried to God that he might not sink and fail in that great undertaking, because if he did so, sinners could not be saved, but all must perish. He prayed that he might get the victory over death, because if he did not get the victory, his people could never obtain that victory, and they can conquer no otherwise than by his conquest. If the Captain of our salvation had not conquered in this sore conflict, none of us could have conquered, but we must have all sunk with him. He cried to God that he might be saved from death, and if he had not been saved from death in his resurrection, none of us could ever have been saved from death.

It was a great sight to see Christ in that great conflict that he was in his agony, but everything in it was from love, that strong love that was in his heart. His tears that flowed from his eyes were from love; his great sweat was from love; his blood, his prostrating himself on the ground before the Father, was from love; his earnest crying to God was from the strength and ardency of his love. It is looked upon as one principal way wherein true love and good will is shown in Christian friends one towards another, heartily to pray one for another; and it is one way wherein Christ directs us to show our love to our enemies, even praying for them. Matt. 5:44: "But I say unto you, Love your enemies, bless them that curse you, and pray for them which despitefully use you, and persecute you."

But was there ever any prayer that manifested love to enemies to such a degree, as those strong cries and tears of the Son of God for the success of his blood in the salvation of his enemies; the strife and conflict of whose soul in prayer was such as to produce his agony and his bloody sweat?

III. If Christ was thus earnest in prayer to God, that the end of his sufferings might be obtained in the salvation of sinners, then how much ought those sinners to be reproved that do not earnestly seek their own salvation!

If Christ offered up such strong cries for sinners as their high priest, that bought their salvation, who stood in no need of sinners, who had been happy from all eternity without them, and could not be made happier by them; then how great is the sottishness of those sinners that seek their own salvation in a dull and lifeless manner; that content themselves with a formal attendance on the duties of religion, with their hearts in the meantime much more earnestly set after other things!

They—after a sort—attend on the duty of social prayer, wherein they pray to God that he would have mercy on them and save them; but after what a poor dull way is it that they do it! They do not apply their heart unto wisdom, nor incline their ear to understanding; they do not cry after wisdom, nor lift up their voice for understanding; they do not seek it as silver, nor search for it as for hidden treasures. Christ's earnest cries in his agony may convince us that it was not without reason that he insisted upon it, in Luke 13:24, that we should strive to enter in at the strait gate, which, as I have already observed to you, is, in the original, Αγωνιζεσθε, "*Agonize* to enter in at the strait gate."

If sinners would be in a hopeful way to obtain their salvation, they should agonize in that great concern as men that are taking a city by violence, as Matt. 11:12. "And from the days of John the Baptist until now the kingdom of heaven suffereth violence, and the violent take it by force." When a body of resolute soldiers are attempting to take a strong city in which they meet with great opposition, what violent conflicts are there before the city is taken! How do the soldiers press on against the very mouths of the enemies' cannon, and upon the points of their swords! When the soldiers are scaling the walls, and making their first entrance into the city, what a violent struggle is there between them and their enemies that strive to keep them out! How do they, as it were, agonize with all their strength! So ought we to seek our salvation, if we would be in a likely way to obtain it. How great is the folly then of those who content themselves with seeking with a cold and lifeless frame of spirit, and so continue from month to month, and from year to year, and yet flatter themselves that they shall be successful!

How much more still are they to be reproved, who are not in a way of seeking their salvation at all, but wholly neglect their precious souls, and attend the duties of religion no further than is just necessary to keep up their credit among men; and instead of pressing into the kingdom of God, are rather violently pressing on towards their own destruction and ruin, being hurried on by their many headstrong lusts, as the herd of swine were hurried on by the legion of devils, and ran violently down a steep place into the sea, and perished in the waters! (Matt. 8:32.)

IV. From what has been said under this proposition, we may learn after what manner Christians ought to go through the work that is before them.

Christ had a great work before him when that took place, of which we have an account in the text. Though it was very near the close of his life, yet he then, when his agony began, had the chief part of the work before him that he came into the world to do; which was to offer up that sacrifice which he offered in his last sufferings, and therein to perform the greatest act of his obedience to God. And so the Christians have a great work to do, a service they are to perform to God, that is attended with great difficulty. They have a race set before them that they have to run, a warfare that is appointed them. Christ was the subject of a very great trial in the time of his agony; so God is wont to exercise his people with great trials. Christ met with great opposition in that work that he had to do; so believers are like to meet with great opposition in running the race that is set before them. Christ, as man, had a feeble nature, that was in itself very insufficient to sustain such a conflict, or to support such a load as was coming upon him. So the saints have the same weak human nature, and beside that, great sinful infirmities that Christ had not, which lay them under great disadvantages, and greatly enhance the difficulty of their work. Those great tribulations and difficulties that were before Christ, were the way in which he was to enter into the kingdom of heaven; so his followers must expect, "through much tribulation to enter into the kingdom of heaven." The cross was to Christ the way to the crown of glory, and so it is to his disciples.

The circumstances of Christ and of his followers in those things are alike—their case, therefore, is the same; and therefore Christ's behavior under those circumstances, was a fit example for them to follow. They should look to their Captain, and observe after what manner he went through his great work, and the great tribulations which he endured. They should observe after what manner he entered into the kingdom of heaven, and obtained the crown of glory, and so they also should run the race that is set before them.

> Wherefore, seeing we also are compassed about with so great a cloud of witnesses, let us lay aside every weight, and the sin which doth so easily beset us, and let us run with patience the race that is set before us. Looking unto Jesus, the author and finisher of our faith; who for the joy that was set before him, endured the cross, despising the shame, and is set down at the right hand of the throne of God."

Particularly,

1. *When others are asleep, they should be awake, as it was with Christ.* The time of Christ's agony was the night season, the time wherein persons were wont to be asleep: it was the time wherein the disciples that were about Christ were asleep; but Christ then had something else to do than to sleep; he had a great work to do; he kept awake, with his heart engaged in this work. So should it be with the believers of Christ; when the souls of their neighbors are asleep in their sins, and under the power of a lethargic insensibility and sloth, they should watch and pray, and maintain a lively sense of the infinite importance of their spiritual concerns. 1 Thess. 5:6. "Therefore let us not sleep, as do others, but let us watch and be sober."

2. They should go through their work with earnest labor, as Christ did. The time when others were asleep was a time when Christ was about his great work, and was engaged in it with all his might, agonizing in it; conflicting and wrestling, in tears, and in blood. So should Christians with the utmost earnestness improve their time with souls engaged in this work, pushing through the opposition they meet within it, pushing through all difficulties and sufferings there are in the way, running with patience the race set before them, conflicting with the enemies of their souls with all their might; as those that wrestle not with flesh and blood, but with principalities and powers, and the rulers of the darkness of this world, and spiritual wickedness in high places.

3. This labor and strife should be, that God may be glorified, and their own eternal happiness obtained in a way of doing God's will. Thus it was with Christ: what he so earnestly strove for was, that he might do the will of God, that he might keep his command, his difficult command, without failing in it, and that in this way God's will might be done, in that glory to his ever great name, and that salvation to his elect that he intended by his sufferings. Here is an example for the saints to follow in that holy strife, and race, and warfare, which God has appointed them; they should strive to do the will of their heavenly Father, that they may, as the apostle expresses it, (Rom. 12:2), "Prove what is that good, and acceptable, and perfect will of God," and that in this way they may glorify God, and may come at last to be happy forever in the enjoyment of God.

4. In all the great work they have to do, their eye should be to God for his help to enable them to overcome. Thus did the man Christ Jesus: he strove in his work even to such an agony and bloody sweat. But how did he strive? It was not in his own strength, but his eyes were to God, he cries unto him for his help and strength to uphold him, that he might not fail; he watched and prayed, as he desired his disciples to do; he wrestled with his enemies and with his great sufferings, but at the same time wrestled with God to obtain his help, to enable him to get the victory. Thus the saints should use their strength in their Christian course to the utmost, but not as depending on their own strength, but crying mightily to God for his strength to make them conquerors.

5. In this way they should hold out to the end as Christ did. Christ in this way was successful, and obtained the victory, and won the prize; he overcame, and is set down with the Father in his throne. So Christians should persevere and hold out in their great work to the end; they should continue to run their race till they have come to the end of it; they should be faithful unto the death as Christ was; and then, when they have overcome, they shall sit down with him in his throne. Rev. 3:21. "To him that overcometh will I grant to sit with me in my throne, even as I also overcame, and am set down with my Father in his throne."

V. Hence burdened and distressed sinners, if any such are here present, may have abundant ground of encouragement to come to Christ for salvation.

Here is great encouragement to sinners to come to this high priest that offered up such strong crying and tears with his blood, for the success of his sufferings in the salvation of sinners. For,

1. *Here is great ground of assurance that Christ stands ready to accept of sinners, and bestow salvation upon them; for those strong cries of his that he offered up in the capacity of our high priest, show how earnestly desirous he was of it.* If he was not willing that sinners should be saved, be they ever so unworthy of it, then why would he so wrestle with God for it in such a bloody sweat? Would anyone so earnestly cry to God with such costly cries, in such great labor and travail of soul, for that, that he did not desire that God should bestow? No, surely! but this shows how greatly his heart was set on the success of his redemption; and therefore since he has by such earnest prayers, and by such a bloody sweat, obtained salvation of the Father to bestow on sinners, he will surely be ready to bestow it upon them, if they come to him for it; otherwise he will frustrate his own design; and he, who so earnestly cried to God that his design might not be frustrated, will not, after all, frustrate it himself.

2. *Here is the strongest ground of assurance that God stands ready to accept of all those that come to him for mercy through Christ.* For this is what Christ prayed for in those earnest prayers, whose prayers were always heard, as Christ says, John 11:42. "And I knew that thou hearest me always." And especially may they conclude, that heard their high priest in those strong cries that he offered up with his blood, and that especially on the following account.

First, they were the most earnest prayers that ever were made. Jacob was very earnest when he wrestled with God; and many others have wrestled with God with many tears; yea, doubtless, many of the saints have wrestled with God with such inward labor and strife as to produce powerful effects on the body. But so earnest was Christ, so strong was the labor and fervency of his heart, that he cried to God in a sweat of blood; so that if any earnestness and importunity in prayer ever prevailed with God, we may conclude that *that* prevailed.

Secondly, he who then prayed was the most worthy person that ever put up a prayer. He had more worthiness than ever men or angels had in the sight of God, according as by inheritance he has obtained a more excellent name than they; for he was the only-begotten Son of God, infinitely lovely in his sight, the Son in whom he declared once and again he was well-pleased. He was infinitely near and dear to God, and had more worthiness in his eyes ten thousand times than all men and angels put together. And can we suppose any other than that such a person was heard when he cried to God with such earnestness? Did Jacob, a poor sinful man, when he had wrestled with God, obtain of God the name of ISRAEL, and that encomium [tribute], that as a prince he had power with God, and prevailed? And did Elijah, who was a man of like passions, and of like corruptions with us, when he prayed, earnestly prevail on God to work such great wonders? And shall not the only-begotten Son of God, when wrestling with God in tears and blood, prevail, and have his request granted him?

Surely there is no room to suppose any such thing; and therefore, there is no room to doubt whether God will bestow salvation on those that believe in him, at his request.

Third, Christ offered up these earnest prayers with the best plea for an answer that ever was offered to God, viz. his own blood; which was an equivalent for the thing that he asked. He not only offered up strong cries, but he offered them up with a price fully sufficient to purchase the benefit he asked.

Fourth, Christ offered this price and those strong cries both together; for at the same time that he was pouring out these earnest requests for the success of his redemption in the salvation of sinners, he also shed his blood. His blood fell down to the ground at the same instant that his cries went up to heaven. Let burdened and distressed sinners, that are ready to doubt of the efficacy of Christ's intercession for such unworthy creatures as they, and to call in question God's readiness to accept them for Christ's sake, consider these things. Go to the garden where the Son of God was in an agony, and where he cried to God so earnestly, and where his sweat was, as it were, great drops of blood, and then see what a conclusion you will draw up from such a wonderful sight.

VI. The godly may take great comfort in this, that Christ has as their high priest offered up such strong cries to God.

You that have good evidence of your being believers in Christ, and his true followers and servants, may comfort yourselves in this, that Christ

Jesus is your high priest, that that blood, which Christ shed in his agony, fell down to the ground for you, and that those earnest cries were sent up to God for you, for the success of his labors and sufferings in all that good you stood in need of in this world, and in your everlasting happiness in the world to come. This may be a comfort to you in all losses, and under all difficulties, that you may encourage your faith, and strengthen your hope, and cause you greatly to rejoice. If you were under any remarkable difficulties, it would be a great comfort to you to have the prayers of some man that you looked upon to be a man of eminent piety, and one that had a great interest at the throne of grace, and especially if you knew that he was very earnest and greatly engaged in prayer for you. But how much more may you be comforted in it, that you have an interest in the prayers and cries of the only-begotten and infinitely worthy Son of God, and that he was so earnest in his prayers for you, as you have heard!

VII. Hence we may learn how earnest Christians ought to be in their prayers and endeavors for the salvation of others.

Christians are the followers of Christ, and they should follow him in this. We see from what we have heard, how great the labor and travail of Christ's soul was for others' salvation, and what earnest and strong cries to God accompanied his labors. Here he hath set us an example.

Herein he hath set an example for ministers, who should as co-workers with Christ travail in birth with them till Christ be found in them. Gal. 4:19, "My little children, of whom I travail in birth again, until Christ be formed in you." They should be willing to spend and be spent for them. They should not only labor for them, and pray earnestly for them, but should, if occasion required, be ready to suffer for them, and to spend not only their strength, but their blood for them. 2 Cor. 12:15, "And I will very gladly spend and be spent for you, though the more abundantly I love you, the less I be loved."

Here is an example for parents, showing how they ought to labor and cry to God for the spiritual good of their children. You see how Christ labored and strove and cried to God for the salvation of his spiritual children; and will not you earnestly seek and cry to God for your natural children?

Here is an example for neighbors one towards another, how they should seek and cry for the good of one another's souls, for this is the command of Christ, that they should love one another as Christ loved them. (John 15:12).

Here is an example for us, showing how we should earnestly seek and pray for the spiritual and eternal good of our enemies, for Christ did all this for his enemies, and when some of those enemies were at that very instant plotting his death, and busily contriving to satiate their malice and cruelty, in his most extreme torments, and most ignominious destruction.